Edzard Höfig

Interpretation of Behaviour Models at Runtime

Edzard Höfig

Interpretation of Behaviour Models at Runtime

Performance Benchmark and Case Studies

Südwestdeutscher Verlag für Hochschulschriften

Impressum/Imprint (nur für Deutschland/only for Germany)
Bibliografische Information der Deutschen Nationalbibliothek: Die Deutsche Nationalbibliothek verzeichnet diese Publikation in der Deutschen Nationalbibliografie; detaillierte bibliografische Daten sind im Internet über http://dnb.d-nb.de abrufbar.

Coverbild: www.ingimage.com

Verlag: Südwestdeutscher Verlag für Hochschulschriften GmbH & Co. KG
Heinrich-Böcking-Str. 6-8, 66121 Saarbrücken, Deutschland
Telefon +49 681 37 20 271-1, Telefax +49 681 37 20 271-0
Email: info@svh-verlag.de

Approved by: Berlin, TU, Diss., 2011

Herstellung in Deutschland:
Schaltungsdienst Lange o.H.G., Berlin
Books on Demand GmbH, Norderstedt
Reha GmbH, Saarbrücken
Amazon Distribution GmbH, Leipzig
ISBN: 978-3-8381-3017-0

Imprint (only for USA, GB)
Bibliographic information published by the Deutsche Nationalbibliothek: The Deutsche Nationalbibliothek lists this publication in the Deutsche Nationalbibliografie; detailed bibliographic data are available in the Internet at http://dnb.d-nb.de.

Cover image: www.ingimage.com

Publisher: Südwestdeutscher Verlag für Hochschulschriften GmbH & Co. KG
Heinrich-Böcking-Str. 6-8, 66121 Saarbrücken, Germany
Phone +49 681 37 20 271-1, Fax +49 681 37 20 271-0
Email: info@svh-verlag.de

Printed in the U.S.A.
Printed in the U.K. by (see last page)
ISBN: 978-3-8381-3017-0

Abstract

Modelling system behaviour by means of statechart-based formalisms, such as the state machine formalism defined in the Unified Modeling Language, is an established practice in software engineering. As part of a model-driven workflow, engineers usually employ a code generation approach to create software components that implement an intended runtime behaviour. Although this approach yields software components with a good runtime performance, the resulting system behaviour is static. Changes to the behaviour model necessarily provoke an iteration in the code generation workflow and a re-deployment of the generated artefacts.

In the area of autonomic systems engineering, it is assumed that systems are able to adapt their runtime behaviour in response to a changing context. Thus, the constraints imposed by a code generation approach make runtime adaptation difficult, if not impossible. We investigate a solution to this problem by employing interpretation techniques for the runtime execution of behaviour models, enabling the adaptability of a system's runtime behaviour on the level of single model elements. This is done by devising concepts for behaviour model interpretation, which are then used in proof-of-concept implementations to demonstrate the feasibility of the approach. It is insufficient to show only the general feasibility of behaviour model interpretation, as the usefulness of this approach depends on the context the model is used in, which is determined by a specific application domain. Therefore, an assessment of the approach is carried out, using quantitative as well as qualitative methods. For the quantitative evaluation, a novel benchmark is introduced, that enables a performance comparison between the proof-of-concept implementations and generated code. The qualitative assessment is based on use case studies conducted in the area of network and systems management.

Behaviour model interpretation has a performance overhead when compared to code generation. In the context of the network and systems management domain, the performance of the approach is found to be adequate for the vast majority of situations, except when dealing with high-throughput or delay-sensitive data.

This book is dedicated to my parents.

Acknowledgements

I would like to acknowledge Prof. Ina Schieferdecker for her friendly advice and constructive criticism. Over the course of the last six years she provided an environment that allowed me to work on theoretical research questions as well as practical engineering tasks. I am certain that this combination improved both the quality of my day-to-day work as well as the quality of this text and I am grateful for having been given this opportunity. I would also like to acknowledge Prof. John Strassner for providing fair, timely and thorough criticism on my ideas and course of action. I admire his impressive knowledge, diligent work attitude and true personality.

The work on this text has been a long process and I am thankful that many of my colleagues have contributed by offering comments. First and foremost Dr. Peter H. Deussen did offer advice and guidance that helped me to structure my thoughts in a way that eventually led to a sequential text. I am also thankful to Dr. Mikhail Smirnow, who is the reason why I am at Fraunhofer FOKUS and who I find to always be a source of inspiration. I am also grateful to Ranganai Chaparadza for his support. Due to his deep understanding of networking technology, Hakan Coşkun's comments were very helpful for creation of the network management use case studies. As we are sharing an office, he was the person that heard all of my ideas and thoughts first and I am especially grateful that he always had an open ear to listen and comment on every one of them. Dr. Sven van der Meer provided much appreciated advice during the final stages of the work and generally pushed me in the right direction. I would also like to acknowledge Andreas Hinnerichs for his contributions to the TMPL runtime optimisation concepts and Carsten Jaekel for his support during implementation of the MPU concepts and recording of the benchmarking results.

I would like to thank Joseph Bauer, Matthias Veit and Timmo Gierke, the aquanauten, for being awesome. I profoundly enjoy our friendship and draw inspiration from each of our technical discussions and tossing around of ideas. I am also deeply grateful to Yvonne Rathmann, who offered her knowledge, skills and time to review the final version of the text.

Finally, I would like to thank my wife Julia. Without her love and support this endeavour would have been a much harder and far less joyful experience.

Thank you!

Edzard Höfig
Berlin, May 2011

Contents

1 Introduction

If it ain't from the heart then it can't be art
If you ain't got proof then it can't be truth
If it ain't got legs then it cannot run
If it ain't never started then it can't be done
Everlast

Autonomic Systems Engineering research is concerned with the creation, assessment and maintenance of Autonomic Systems (AS). Such systems are regarded as technical entities that are able to execute management decisions without direct human control.

Our work in this field was mainly inspired by the idea of Autonomic Communication, as outlined in [180]; Autonomic Communication aims at applying a set of computing principles, originally developed by IBM [112], to the management of communication networks and services. The idea is to delegate the execution management processes from human administrators to devices operating in the network with the goal of reducing the administration complexity and consequently the operational expenditures, as well as to enable the evolvability of systems.

Designing a system for evolvability implies that it does not only scale in terms of resource utilisation, but also in terms of functionality. For achieving such functional scalability, it is necessary to design a system in such a way that it is able to continue to operate, without human intervention, in the face of changes in its environment. We denote such an ability with the term *homeostasis*, in reference to the concept introduced by cyberneticist W.R. Ashby [8, chapter 5/3]. The major challenge of functional scalability is to enable AS to adapt to environmental changes that are unknown at the design time of a system.

1.1 Subject of Research

Homeostasis requires that a system is able to modify its own behaviour by extending or re-shaping its functionality to suit a changing operational environment. From a software engineering perspective, this requires employing a suitable format for behaviour representation (corresponds to a program) and an adequate mechanism that executes the behaviour, while allowing for a modification of the underlying representation (corresponds to a runtime system). For the former we propose to use models. Thus, such a behaviour representation format is called a Behaviour Model (BM). For the latter we propose to use interpretation mechanisms, which are referred to as *BM interpreters*, or just as *interpreters*. By *interpretation* we refer to the direct evaluation of a BM at runtime, which also includes the ability to dynamically modify the BM.

Depending on the formalism that is used to express the runtime behaviour of a system, an adaptation of the BM can be easy or more difficult. We restrict ourselves to the study of BMs that are defined by state-transition systems, which are also known as automata. Automata can be used as models to describe the behaviour of a system in the simple language of states and transitions. They have already been employed in this function at least since the doctoral thesis of D. Huffman [111]. In this thesis, we will not use the original formalism, but investigate models using a modern formalism, more precisely the statechart formalism invented by D. Harel [88, 90]. For this approach to work, we require that changes in the environment of a system are communicated to the system using discrete messages (referred to as *input events*). This is a standard engineering approach for reactive systems and we will not discuss it in more detail.

One of the most valuable properties of state-transition systems is that they are reactive. On receiving an input event, a BM will be interpreted until all consequential actions, in reaction to the input event, have been processed (this is called a processing *step*). The BM is inactive after this, which allows us to safely modify the BM without needing to worry about consistency problems.

It is noteworthy to point out that our use of statecharts for representation of BMs is substantially different to current software engineering practice. In a conventional Model Driven Architecture (MDA) workflow [256], an automata-based BM (such as a set of state machines) would typically be executed for simulation or model checking purposes at pre-deployment time. Once system design comes to an end, engineers would utilise code generation to create appropriate runtime execution systems based on the specified BMs. This approach is able to produce system components with a decent execution performance, but which also rely on the generation of static executable artefacts that determine the system's runtime behaviour (e. g. source code and application binaries). An approach that is based on code-generation cannot be used for engineering AS, as it would prevent modification of the BM at runtime. The problem is that, although there are techniques that enable a dynamic modification of already deployed functionality (i. e. Just In Time (JIT) compilation or dynamic binding), the traceability between the model and the generated binary code artefacts is not given. Therefore, after the code generation step has concluded, it is not possible to identify which parts of the generated code corresponded to a certain element in the original model. When using interpretation, it is much easier to trace the connections between the BM and a given execution representation (referred to as a *BM instance*).

Within the thesis, we study the practical applicability of interpretation of BMs, restricted to the network and systems management domains. The general feasibility of the approach in other domains remains interesting; however, the focus is on exploring how BM interpretation can be beneficial to these specific application areas, which allows us to conduct an assessment of our work in regard to their specific requirements. Network and systems management are well established fields, concerned with the monitoring and administration of networked computer systems [40, 93]. While network management concentrates on the management of the devices that make up a network (e. g. routers, gateways, etc.), systems management also takes into account the computer systems that are connected by the network (e. g. servers, end-user devices, etc.). We are considering BM interpretation as applicable in both areas of management.

1.1.1 Problem Statement

Utilising models for representation of system behaviour is a good approach for implementing self-regulating systems. This has been shown for cases where the system behaviour can be modelled numerically and where only a small number of variables need to be considered, e. g. in hardware systems that regulate mechanical processes based on control theory, like a brake assistance system in a car. We think that the general idea of using BMs for the formalisation of runtime behaviour is also applicable to AS, although there are a number of considerable differences.

For example, a numerical modelling of self-regulating systems based on control theory uses a closed-world assumption: the complete parameter space of a system behaviour is supposed to be known at design time. Therefore, a BM using this approach has to be considered static at runtime, it cannot be modified to react to hitherto unknown input events. In AS, due to the homeostatic property, an open-world assumption has to be made: systems are part of a changing environment and need to be able to change themselves to react to previously unknown events. This requires the ability to dynamically modify the BM at runtime, which is something that has not been thoroughly investigated before.

Another important difference regarding AS lies in the large number of input events that they need to react to. BMs for this type of software-intensive systems are far too complex to be representable with only a small number of variables. Dealing with such a complexity is a problem that is very well known in software engineering. Therefore, formalisms used for modelling system behaviour in established software design methodologies, e. g. statecharts, are more appropriate.

Runtime modification of behaviour that is modelled using statecharts is not a well researched topic. There is little research done on the feasibility and properties of mechanisms that enable the modification of autonomic systems that rely on models for the specification of behaviour. Such mechanisms are a prerequisite for implementing any form of runtime behaviour optimisation for systems, which are designed with an open-world assumption in mind.

1.1.2 Research Hypothesis

We assume that it is viable to execute statechart-based BMs by interpretation at runtime instead of using a BM to generate code in a programming language, which would then be compiled and executed. It has only been shown very recently that BM interpretation is practicable at all [16] and there is no substantial information on the performance or implementation of such mechanisms.

Experience dictates that it is computationally more expensive to employ an interpretation mechanism than to rely on compilation techniques; thus, we believe that a performance penalty is incurred by following the interpretation approach. We suppose that an interpretation mechanism's performance can be measured using its runtime execution speed and memory consumption characteristics; by comparing these values to the execution characteristics of a mechanism based on compilation, we will be able to accurately determine the performance differences between the two approaches. Such a comparison is only possible when based on a common platform and we will use a standardised performance benchmark to achieve this.

Furthermore, we hypothesise that the performance penalty incurred by such an approach is small enough to allow a utilisation of this technique in the system and network management domains. We also believe that the innovative benefits, offered by an approach that relies on the interpretation of BMs, clearly outweighs its performance disadvantages. To support this argument, a number of use case studies are employed.

1.2 Methodology

Our goal is to to assess the practical usefulness of the approach. As it is generally possible to interpret statechart-based BMs, we are interested in the implementation details of mechanisms that supports a modification of the BM at runtime, with the resulting behaviour changes immediately observable. As a tool for experimenting with different facets of such mechanisms we are constructing a proof-of-concept implementation of a BM Interpreter that supports the complete feature set of Unified Modeling Language (UML) Behavioral State Machines [255, Section 15]. This interpreter is from now on referred to as the UML interpreter. The UML has been chosen because of its widespread use and the feature richness of the UML State Machines formalism. We found little published work on the subject of BM interpretation in general and even less on the interpretation of statechart-based BMs. Therefore, for creating a working implementation, we will need to create algorithms and discover solutions to key aspects arising when designing and implementing such a kind of interpretation mechanism. As the UML interpreter is mainly an academic tool for demonstrating the runtime interpretation of the widest range of possible BM features, it is not the best solution for a practical application. We therefore create a number of additional prototypes that each have a more restricted set of BM features, but that fit better to the requirements for a certain platform and purpose.

After we created suitable implementations of the concepts, we carry out an assessment of the usefulness of the approach by following two methods. The first method is a qualitative assessment that employs four use case studies from the domains of network and systems management. The second method is a quantitative assessment of the approach's performance that is conducted by comparing the speed and consumed memory of two proof-of-concept implementations with generated code. To ensure the comparability between the different platforms and technologies, we will need to define a novel performance benchmark suite. The reason for this is the lack of existing instruments for performance comparison of statechart execution mechanisms. By using the results from the quantitative and qualitative assessment steps, we can discuss their impact on the practical usefulness of the approach and can come to a conclusion on the tradeoffs between performance and the provided benefits of BM interpretation at runtime.

1.3 Scientific Contributions

The following four items are considered the main scientific contributions of this thesis.

A performance benchmark suite Comprising ten measurement scenarios that collect an overall of 100 performance indicators, we introduce a comprehensive performance benchmarking suite for assessment of statechart-based BM execution mechanisms. The benchmark is validated by application to three different implementations. As it is designed in a platform-independent way, there is only a minimal effort necessary to adapt the benchmark suite to a new technology. This is a useful instrument for an objective performance comparison of statechart execution mechanisms. The performance benchmark suite is novel work and we are not aware of the existence of other benchmarks for measuring BM runtime execution.

Verified concepts for the interpretation of BMs We demonstrate that the interpretation of statechart-based BMs, with support for modification during execution, is possible at runtime. This result supports very recent research results. To arrive at this goal, we devise a number of concepts, algorithms and guidelines for implementing statechart-based BM interpreters. These concepts can be considered mature, as they are backed up by a number of implementations, which where each validated in regard to applicability. The research community can benefit from the insight into the technical intricacies of such mechanisms which is provided by this thesis. Furthermore, for the UML interpreter we implement a wide range of advanced concepts (for example storing and re-establishing of a deep state history, dealing with deferred events or processing compound transitions). All of these have been tested and are practically proven to work. As there is very limited research material at hand regarding these topics, the lessons learned during the implementation process are useful as a best-practice reference for other implementors of graph- or automata-based runtime model interpreters.

Studies on interpretation performance We conduct a quantitative assessment of the performance of the BM interpretation approach for a number of different implementations. The result data paint a clear picture of the performance that the BM runtime interpretation approach has. Due to the detailed specification of the benchmark, it is also possible to investigate specific aspects in more depth, e. g. the evaluation speed of conditional expressions of a certain complexity or the memory consumption in relation to BM size. These results provide empirical values that can serve well for impact assessment purposes, for example for software engineers who plan to integrate BM execution facilities into their projects.

Framework for an application to the network and systems management domains A qualitative assessment of the BM interpretation approach is investigated by employing four use case scenarios in the context of the network and systems management domains. These scenarios demonstrate the practical relevance of the approach by giving concrete examples of applications of the approach. This is useful for understanding the benefits of the BM interpretation approach, such as BM optimisation at runtime or the reduction of effort for managing code artefacts that encode system behaviour. It is also useful for network researchers or engineers as a blueprint for engineering future management infrastructures.

1.4 Document Structure

The thesis is structured in seven chapters, plus an appendix. Each chapter contains a summary at its end, except for the introduction chapter and the conclusion chapter, which start with a summary of the complete thesis. The chapters are:

1. **Introduction** The current chapter, which explains the chosen research subject and the motivation for the thesis. We state the research problem, formulate a research hypothesis, summarise the key scientific contributions of our work and describe the employed methodology.

2. **Concepts** The chapter aims at creating a common understanding of BM specification by explaining the basic principles involved. We investigate novel concepts, algorithms and general guidelines used for the interpretation of BM at runtime. The chapter also contains studies on integrating BM interpreters

with an underlying platform and explores the management of BMs within a larger IT infrastructure.

3. **Related Work** The chapter contains a survey of the relevant state of the art, structured by research field. There are five fields: state-transition systems, BMs, systems engineering, network and systems management and performance benchmarking.

4. **Implementations** We describe our understanding of a BM interpreter and subsequently introduce four implementations of the concepts, each having different characteristics and its own motivation. The four implementations are: an engine for the Template Matching Processor Language (TMPL), which employs interpreted state machines for pattern matching on eXtensible Markup Language (XML) data streams; the Autonomic Communication Element (ACE) toolkit, a component-based framework for creating autonomic applications using interpreted state machines; a BM interpreter for UML State Machines; and finally a BM execution platform that uses a State Chart XML (SCXML) engine.

5. **Use Case Studies** In this chapter, we are using four use case scenarios to assess our approach from a qualitative perspective. The service supervision scenario demonstrates how the ACE toolkit can be used to create a supervision infrastructure that is able to reconfigure in response to failing system components. In a *management in the network* use case, we present a scenario that describes the use of BM interpretation as part of a troubleshooting process within the system and network management domains. A part of the scenario (monitoring a network element) is demonstrated using the SCXML execution platform. The intrinsic monitoring use case describes how BM interpretation can be used to implement a novel paradigm for monitoring paths in a network using the Internet Protocol, version 6 (IPv6). The last use case scenario investigates the feasibility of our approach for embedded systems by presenting an experimental implementation of a BM interpreter on a resource-limited platform, along with a documentation of the system performance.

6. **Performance Benchmark** We specify a benchmark suite for evaluating the performance of a BM execution engine in regard to speed and memory consumption, based on the generic platform. Subsequently, we specify mappings of the generic benchmark suite to three specific target technologies: Java [266], C++ [271] and the Rational Rhapsody tool (see page 3.2.3). We then compare the performance of the UML interpreter and the SCXML execution platform with the performance of generated C++ code using the previously defined benchmark.

7. **Conclusion** At the beginning of the chapter, we give a summary of the thesis and describe its potential impact on the research field. We critically discuss

the results of our work and describe the lessons learned. The chapter concludes with an outlook on future work.

Appendices The appendix is also a useful part of the thesis. It contains short descriptions of the features of the three main languages used to describe BMs (UML, SCXML, ACElandic). This helps readers that are unfamiliar with a particular formalism or feature. We also describe the BMs used within the employed use case scenarios and provide a listing of the complete data values acquired by application of the benchmark as part of the performance comparison in chapter 6.

2 Concepts

As the builders say, the larger stones do not lie well without the lesser.
Plato

This chapter describes the foundational concepts of our work, divided into three sections. The first section is dedicated to explaining the modelling of a system's runtime behaviour using state-transition systems. It is oriented along the basic concepts of UML State Machines: states, transitions, transition labels, state composition, partial BMs, regions and the history feature. The second section is concerned with introducing and discussing issues that arise when implementing runtime systems for interpretation of BMs that follow the principles outlined in Section 2.1. It encompasses the following principles: the stepwise processing of a BM using Run-To-Completion (RTC) semantics and the determination of active transitions[1], a discussion about the problems associated with concurrent control flows in a single BM, expression evaluation, the invocation of FCs and an investigation of scalability aspects of message-based communication paradigms. In the third section, we will propose a theoretical infrastructure for BM interpreters. Even though it is possible to use BM interpreters in a standalone scenario, we believe that it is more beneficial to employ a number of distributed interpreters. This serves also as a blueprint for the infrastructure employed within most of the use case studies in Chapter 5. Thus, the topics discussed in the third section are about the management and maintenance of a collective of interpreters. In addition to the concepts discussed here, an introduction to state-transition systems can be found in the description of related work in Section 3.1.

2.1 Modelling Runtime Behaviour

State machines in one form or another will be familiar for most people with a computer science background. This section serves both as an introduction to readers unfamiliar with the subject and as a general overview. It contains a discussion of state machine principles (based on UML Behavioral State Machines) and their relation to BM interpretation.

[1] Including an identification of the correct entry and exit actions during firing of a transition as well as their invocation order

2.1.1 States as Fundamental Building Blocks

The most significant concept is the notion of "state" itself. In the following chapters, we will only refer to state in the context of BMs, but for now, it is sensible to understand the word in a broader context: as a distinct, abstract condition of a system.

Figure 2.1 shows that a wine-filled chalice can be modelled using three system states: Full, Half-Full and Empty. Note the abstraction that takes place: although wine contained in the chalice could take a wide range of different volumes, only one out of three discrete symbols is used at a given time to represent the system state.

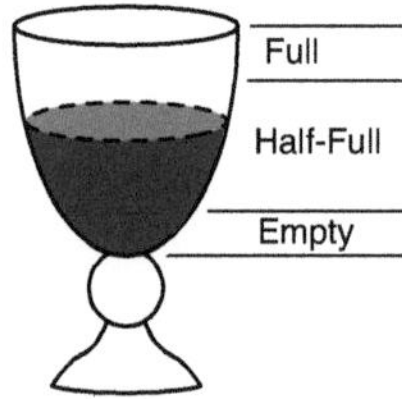

Figure 2.1: An optimistic model of a wine-filled chalice

The design of an appropriate set of states for modelling a given system requires a thorough understanding of both the system itself and of the purpose the model is created for. This type of captured expertise enables us (humans) to deal with the behaviour of very complex systems in a reasonable time[2], and we think that an application of this principle could also be an advantage for automated processing. In general, states are reflecting a situation with a valid invariant [28, p. 170] in either a static way ("the chalice is empty") or as a dynamic process or activity ("someone is drinking from the chalice").

Over its lifetime, a system would usually go through a sequence of states. For example, a chalice would be taken empty from a cupboard, filled with wine and subsequently depleted by a thirsty congregation. It is useful to distinguish two special states concerning the lifetime of a system. Initial states are the states that a system starts in. For the physical world, concrete manifestations of such initial states seldom exist[3], but when interpreting a BM, it is necessary to completely define the initial conditions that a system starts from. The same is true for final states, which are states that denote that a system has finished its operation. In the case of the wine-filled chalice, an apt choice would be to use the Empty state as both the initial and final state of the system. This is reflected in a typical scenario where a chalice is

[2]Humans are relying on mental models to cope with the complexity of their environment. This argument is supported by the "Theory of Mind" of cognitive neuroscience, see [21].

[3]What is the initial state of a door? Open or closed?

taken empty from a cupboard, used and cleaned before being returned to the storage shelf. The initial state is often referred to as being a *pseudostate*. Pseudostates are transient – they are processed during interpretation, but a system does not remain in them. Commonly, the initial state merely references a state as the first one that the model occupies when interpretation commences.

2.1.2 Changing States: Transitions

To describe a series of state changes, we use *transitions* that connect states with each other. Possible successor states to a given system state are determined using transitions that lead from one state to another. We call all transitions that leave a given state *outgoing* and all transitions that arrive at a given state *incoming*. Transitions that connect a state with itself are called *self-referencing*. Sometimes transitions are also termed *edges*, as the generated state-transition structure forms a directed graph consisting of nodes and edges.

One of the major tasks that all execution mechanisms for state-transition systems need to solve is the selection of active transitions, also called *transition matching*. The result of transition matching is the determination of a successor for the current system state. Figure 2.2 shows the problem using the familiar wine-filled chalice.

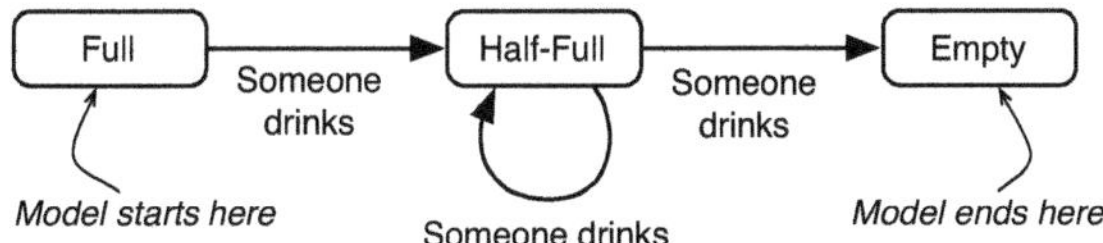

Figure 2.2: Transitions specify a series of system states

Initially, the model dictates that the chalice is Full. After the first sip (indicated by the Someone drinks label under the transition), the chalice is considered Half-Full. This state is maintained while further drinking takes place until someone takes the last gulp. Afterwards the chalice is considered Empty, which is the final model state. A problem appears at the Half-Full state: it is obvious, that using only the given information (Someone drinks), we are not able to figure out if the successor state should be Half-Full or Empty. Such a model is referred to as a *non-deterministic* model. In addition to an *event* label, it is therefore common to further annotate transitions with a conditional statement, often referred to as a *guard condition*, to allow a deterministic selection of a transition.

2.1.2.1 Events

State-transition systems are called *reactive* in the sense that they are reacting to events observed in the environment. The process of observation is usually conducted by mechanisms external to the BM — the model contains only a reference to a standardised notification message that signals the occurrence of a certain event. Due to this close relation between the event and the notification message, we also refer to them as *events*. For practical reasons, events are supplied in a sequential manner and typically stored using a suitable buffering mechanism (queueing or pooling) before being matched with the outgoing transitions from a current state. The event message itself is *consumed* during the matching operation. Events may carry additional information (referred to as the *payload* of the event), which is often used in communication between a state machine and its environment.

Event labels are used to determine which transitions are becoming active in reaction to the events provided as input to the BM. Usually, only one event is used for determination of the active transition, but there are formalisms (e. g. UML State Machines) that also allow the usage of more than one event as a transition trigger. Events are not only used as input to the system, but can also be send to the environment from the BM or can be used for system-internal triggers. There are many different types of events that might occur in a state-transition system, and the following classification collects major types of events in use (compiled from [120][255]):

Signal An event that declares an asynchronous, one-way communication signal.

Call Events that are used to imitate (a)synchronous operations. These events include triggering an invocation of a function and delivery of the operation's result (a return value).

Timed It is common to reference an absolute or relative point in time as an event (e. g. *after 1 minute*). If used in a relative way, this refers to the time of entry in the state that the transition is leaving.

Deferred In some state-transition systems, events are allowed to be deferred, meaning that they remain stored when they cannot be handled in the current state. They are then reconsidered for transition matching upon state changes.

Change This type of event is raised each time that a previously established condition becomes true. A change event might be revoked if the condition changes to false before the event is consumed.

Completion Such events are raised once any activities defined as part of a state are completed.

Failure An event type that represents a system failure. It can be beneficial to differentiate failure events from regular events, as failure events may need to be handled very differently (depending on the employed fallback strategy of a system).

Input Events that are used for matching transitions.

Output Events that are generated by the state transition system. If an output event is dispatched internally to the system, it will become an input event. This distinction in terminology will become more clear when regarding event transmission mechanisms in detail.

Internal Events that are used only within the state-transition system. Such events will not be transmitted to the environment.

External These events are used to communicate with the environment.

Epsilon Notationally denoted as ε (also referred to as λ or *null*), such a transition label does not specify a concrete event, but rather a successful transition match without consuming any of the input events, given the case that no other transition matches. Transitions that are labelled with this kind of event will activate if no input event is available to the system.

The presented classification of events is not a strictly disjoint taxonomy (e. g. a signal might also be an input event at the same time).

2.1.2.2 Context

For theoretical purposes, it is usually sufficient to define the model state space purely through the model structure. In practice, this is seldom done. Execution mechanisms use a separate data space that holds additional variables along with other information, such as the current input event. We refer to this data space as *context* or *session data*. It is possible to transform a context into a model structure by representing every potential configuration of a context within the structure, but such an approach is unsuitable for behaviour modelling. For example, a context containing a single 32 bit-wide integer value could be represented as a model containing 2^{32} states. Clearly, such a state explosion is impractical, hence the separation of context and structure[4].

The context structure is defined by the underlying data model of an application domain. It can range from simple, untyped {*key, value*} pairs to full-fledged implementations of object-oriented (OO) information models.

As explained before, a single event label might not be sufficient to unambiguously select the active transitions. A boolean expression can be attached to any transition, which further affects the matching behaviour through the evaluation of context conditions.

[4]On a side note: The decision for state separation impacts a possible application of pre-deployment model-checking techniques, as the context is unavailable before execution and any context references are therefore opaque to an evaluation.

2.1.2.3 Guard Conditions

Once a transition has been preselected due to an event label that conforms to the current input event supplied to the system, an optional guard condition might be evaluated. Depending on the outcome of the conditional test, the transition is selected (when the outcome is *true*) or rejected (when the outcome is *false*), in which case the transition matching process continues. The syntax and semantics of guard condition expressions are not fixed; they are prescribed through the language that is chosen, based on the application domain. Among popular languages for specification of conditional expressions are the Java Expression Language (JEXL) [217], ECMA Script [231], OCL for Execution (OCL4X) [242] and the XML Path Language (XPath) [288].

Expression languages have very different capabilities, but despite their variety, the usual programming language constructs are supported by most of them. The supported features include: literals, comparison operations, arithmetic operations, boolean operations, context references and structured data types. Some languages even employ OO principles or allow for the execution of method invocations within an expression. It is also not uncommon to have looping constructs and branching statements, making an expression language Turing-complete. This is due to the fact that such languages often have a heritage of general programmability, with the formulation of conditional expressions being only a part of it.

2.1.3 Executing Actions

If one would capture every detail of system behaviour on a model level, it would hardly be justified to refer to models as an abstraction of the actual behaviour. In such a case, BMs would become glorified programs, detailing the computational algorithms employed. We want to hide the extensive programmatic details needed to encode system behaviour on a platform within a Functional Components (FC) and to trigger the FCs from behaviour logic encoded in the model. This is accomplished through the use of *actions* (sometimes also called *effects*). Actions are attached to a transition and execute once the transition successfully matches. Most BM formalisms support specifying actions that are not executed when a transition fires, but when entering, exiting or while staying in a state.

The syntax for specification of actions depends on the application domain. In the simplest case, they take the form of procedure call statements known from imperative programming languages, e. g. `function(1`st`parameter, 2`nd`parameter, ...)`, with the parameters supplied as literals or context references. To allow for passing of return values from an FC back to the calling mechanism, it is common to provide context assignment statements that can handle the return value, i. e. `var := function(...)`. For convenience, it is possible to allow for more complex expressions, either as parameters for a call to an FC or as the action itself. The exact nature of interaction between actions and FC depends on the technology used for implementing FCs (e. g. by using a dynamically bound library, remote service invocation, method call on an object, stored database query, etc.). Figure 2.3 shows an example for a BM that counts to ten using the invocation of an increment function with a reference to context variable a.

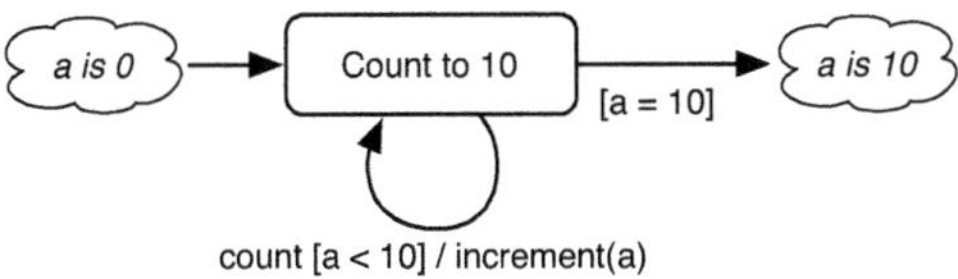

Figure 2.3: Example for a simple counter

Note the syntax structure for the label on the self-referencing transition: the event name comes first, followed by the guard condition in square brackets and the action statement after a separating forward slash. Basic actions like the incrementation of a are commonly specified directly using the expression language, which then serves as glue-code between FCs and the model structure. The final transition in the example is an ε-transition, triggering as soon as a has reached a value of 10.

If not mentioned otherwise, we consider a single action trigger as executing synchronously with the calling mechanism. In the case of an FC execution, it is required that no context is shared with the model, except through parameter and return value passing. The functionality called by the action is regarded as a black box; it is opaque to the triggering mechanism.

One of the most basic actions is the sending of one or more output events. In fact, this action can be generic enough to be used for execution of arbitrary functionality through the dispatching of suitable command events. Such an approach relinquishes all "procedure-call" characteristics in favour of a pure message-based communication approach and can be beneficial in environments that strictly de-couple FCs and BMs; for example, in cases where the underlying hardware supplies several concurrent functional execution units.

The concept of a transition that is selected by an event, activates at a positive condition evaluation and executes an action as a result is one of the most basic building blocks not only for state machines, but for event driven architectures in general. In the wider field, this concept is known under the term Event-Condition-Action (ECA), with applications in Policy-Based Management (PBM) [32, 122], Active Databases [60] and Rule-Based Programming [211]. State Machines add an additional level of structure by enabling the composition of ECA structures, for example by aggregation or parallelisation.

2.1.4 Creating Structure by Composition

As previously established, state machines can be used to break down complexity by creating a model that defines triggers on a set of FCs. Although this makes it possible to greatly reduce the effort involved in understanding a system behaviour, a single abstraction step might not be enough to allow individuals to comprehend and manage a system's behaviour. In addition to conventional automata theory, statecharts introduce two further features, which can be employed to reduce complexity in a model: composition and parallelism.

A compound state consists of a set of states, which is combined under a single symbol. This process is also commonly referred to as *composition*, *nesting* or *aggregation* of states. Applying composition to a BM defines a hierarchy of states, where the most abstract state is at the root and the most concrete ones are at the leaves of a tree. Figure 2.4 shows an example of state composition using a structural model for a door.

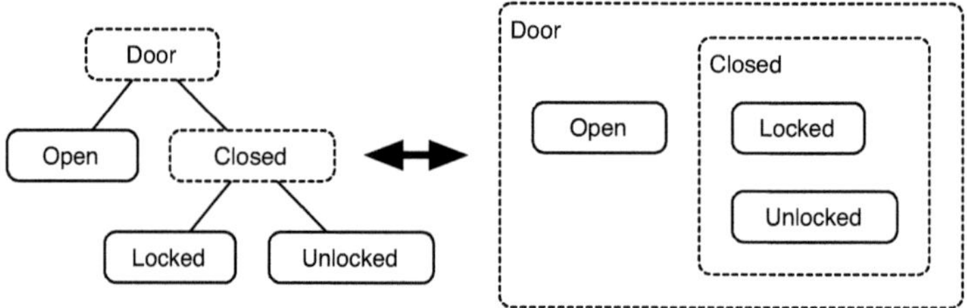

Figure 2.4: Composition of states: two views of a structural model for a door

Shown is a hierarchical view of states (left) and a containment view (right). The root state Door is composed of two substates Open and Closed. The Closed state is composed of two substates Locked and Un-locked. In this figure, the compound states are emphasised using a dashed outline. It is common to specifically mark compound states to differentiate them from atomic, non-compound states[5]. Both views are equivalent.

By representing a BM as a black-box that can be entered and exited like a state, a sub BM can be integrated within another (super) BM. To re-use common BMs, it is possible to specify partial models that can serve as building blocks and that can be integrated with other models. The idea is simple: a suitable subset of states is selected (a *partial model*) and all transitions that leave or enter this set are identified. The state set can then be re-used in another model by re-connecting these transitions.

[5]This is mostly important when using graphical tools for description of BMs, as visual clues are necessary to tell atomic states apart from compound states with hidden substates.

It is also necessary to determine which part of the context and which events are used by the partial model to later re-instantiate these in the context of the new model. To mark the transitions that leave or enter a partial model, two new pseudostates are introduced.

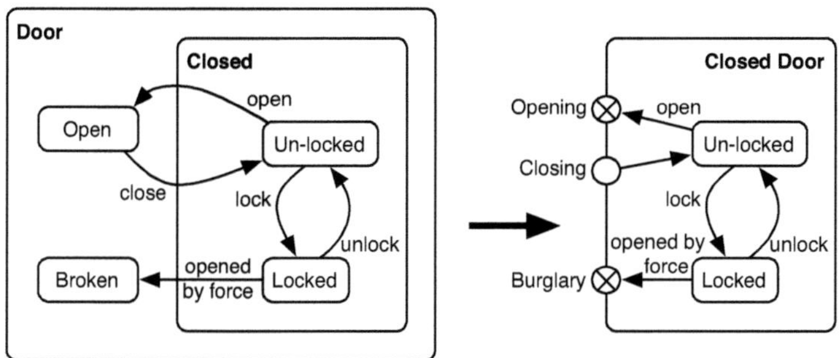

Figure 2.5: Example for breaking-out a partial model using entry and exit points

When breaking-out a partial model from an existing behaviour, the transitions that are leaving the partial model are assigned new destinations; these are referred to as the *exit points* of the partial model. In a similar fashion, incoming transitions to the partial model are assigned new source states, the *entry points* of the partial model. As partial models can have many entry and exit points, it is common to identify these by names. Figure 2.5 exemplifies the breaking out of a partial model (on the right side) from an existing BM (shown on the left side). This example is an extension of the door model with an additional state Broken that is entered when a locked door is opened by force. The partial model state set consists of the Closed compound state and its substates. When breaking-out a compound state, it is only possible to select complete trees of the composition hierarchy for a partial model. Entry pseudostates are usually depicted using a circular symbol, while exit pseudostates are marked by a circle with a cross. Both carry symbol names that help to identify the state change that the transition implies. The **Closed Door** partial model can be re-used by inserting it into a different BM and by connecting transitions with all of the entry and exit points.

2.1.5 Manipulating the Control Flow Cardinality

Statecharts enable the specification of more than one control flow where a control flow is understood as an independent series of state changes. Concurrently executing control flows are enabled through *Parallel Regions* (also referred to as *Orthogonal*

Regions, *Parallel Components* or *Concurrent Regions*). We differentiate between active and dormant parallel regions. A system is in a number of concurrent states equal to the number of active parallel regions at any given time. Parallel regions are dormant by default; they are activated when entered by the control flow and dormant when the control flow leaves the component. Parallel regions are always grouped by a mutually shared superstate, but if the superstate is left, then all contained parallel regions are dormant. There are a number of features in the form of pseudostates that enable the description of concurrent control flows with parallel regions.

A terminal pseudostate forces all control flows of a BM to an end once it is reached and terminates all activities that are currently executing. It is semantically similar to a BM reaching the final state configuration, but in a less coordinated fashion as other control flows are not allowed to finish properly. A fork pseudostate enables splitting a single control flow into two or more concurrent ones. It is used as the last state before entering a number of parallel regions. The counterpart of fork is the join pseudostate, which is used to combine multiple control flows into a single one.

An example, employing both join and fork constructs, is shown in Figure 2.6. It models the behaviour of a person counting and dancing at the same time using a superstate called **Active**.

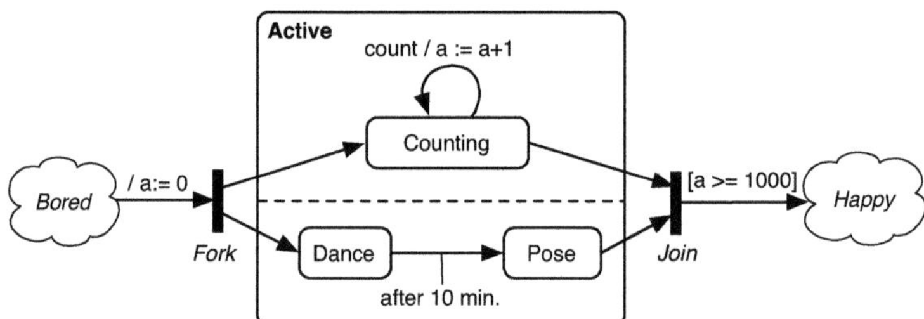

Figure 2.6: Example for parallel behaviour

A fork pseudostate splits the control flow into two orthogonal behaviours: counting and dancing. Note that only the single incoming transition to the fork pseudostate carries a label. Once this transition activates, the **Active** state (and all contained parallel regions of the **Active** state) are entered. Exiting the **Active** state is done via the join construct, as long as 10 minutes of dancing are completed and the person did count to at least 1000. The fork pseudostate is also restricted, as only the single outgoing transition can be labelled. The outgoing transition is only activated when the system is in each of the source states of the incoming transitions. In our example, the system needs to be in the states Counting and Pose at the same time for the transition to be selected. If in this case the variable a is also greater or equal to 1000, then the transition will be activated and the states will be left.

2.1.6 Remembering Control Flow State

The last feature that we will discuss concerns the *history* pseudostate. This feature can be used in conjunction with compound states to store an active state configuration when leaving a compound state. Figure 2.7 shows a BM for a person reading an article while eating a sandwich. In case that the person finished reading the article, the model goes from state Reading Article to state Article Read. In a similar fashion, an empty plate signals the model to change from Eating Sandwich to the Sandwich Gone state. Once both activities are complete, the model is left via the join transition. At any time during the execution, the model can be in one of three combinations defined by the innermost states (Reading Article and Eating Sandwich; Article Read and Eating Sandwich; Reading Article and Sandwich Gone). During the BM execution, the state **Reading & Eating** can also be left through a transition that fires on the reception of a phone rings event. In this case the person stops the current activities and answers the phone. On hanging up the phone, the person resumes the activities that were carried out beforehand.

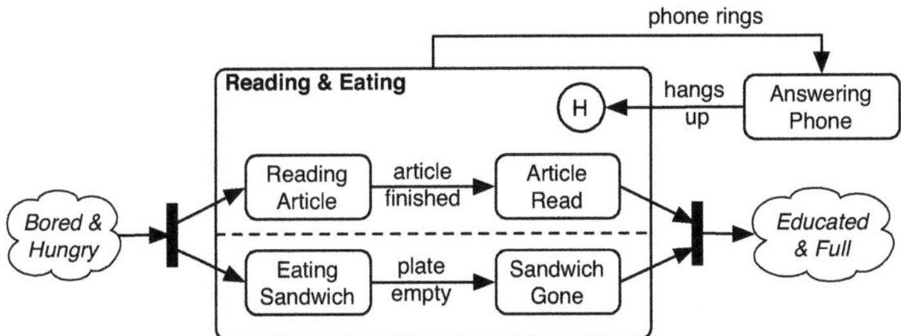

Figure 2.7: An example for remembering state configurations

The model describes this behaviour by entering the **Reading & Eating** state through a history pseudostate (denoted by a circle enclosing the letter H). The history state establishes the control flows as well as the state configuration that was in effect at the time that the superstate was left.

History pseudostates need to be taken with a pinch of salt: as they only restore the control flow state, it is up to the modeller to make sure that there are no side-effects regarding interaction with the context or with FCs when re-entering a state configuration.

2.2 Interpretation of Behaviour Models

We already stated before that the interpretation of BMs at runtime is fundamentally different from BM execution that employs code generation. With code generation, a traceable relationship between the executable representation (e. g. parts of an application binary) and the original model elements, which were used to generate the executable artefacts, is not given. Therefore, it is difficult to adapt the system at runtime. Often the only solution is to stop the currently running system instance and to restart the system with a different binary executable. With BM interpretation, the runtime format of the executable model is kept, and changes can be applied directly to the model at runtime. To demonstrate the differences between the two approaches, we are employing Figure 2.8, that shows the diverse formats and artefacts employed during BM execution, together with the relations between them.

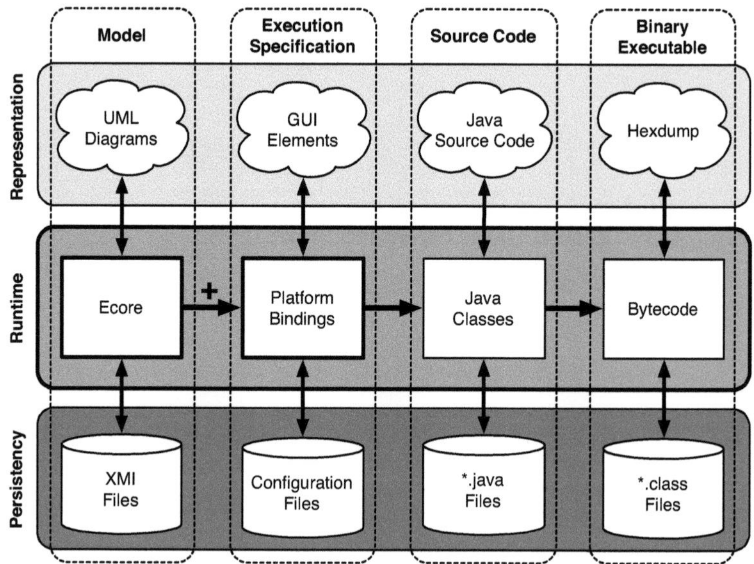

Figure 2.8: Formats and exemplary artefacts used with BM execution

The diagram is structured horizontally and vertically. While the three, grey-shaded, horizontal boxes represent the three different classes of employed formats, the four vertical boxes, depicted using dashed lines, represent the four different types of artefacts. For each combination of artefact type and format class, we are providing a concrete, exemplary artefact format, e. g. a typical **Source Code Persistency** format are *.java Files. The three different classes of formats are listed below.

Representation Formats solely exist in a human-readable form and are used for creation, visualisation and modification of system behaviour.

Runtime Formats are in-memory formats: they are used to hold the necessary information that allows runtime mechanisms to operate on a behaviour specification.

Persistency Formats are conventions on how to persistently store system behaviour information on mass storage media.

When using BM execution, the system behaviour goes through a number of phases from specification to execution and each phase employs specific artefact types. Artefact types of a single phase are kept closely synchronised. A change in one of them will trigger corresponding changes for artefacts of the two other format classes. For representation formats this happens implicitly, for example through the signalling in a Model View Controller (MVC) [75, p. 300] architecture, whereas for persistency artefacts it is common to explicitly trigger the alignment as part of the conversion process, e. g. during load or save operations of a BM. The four different artefact types are listed below.

Model Artefacts describe the behaviour encoded by a BM, without specifying how the behaviour relates to an execution platform. An example are UML Behavioral State Machines that are represented as UML diagrams to a user, stored in the Ecore in-memory format of the Eclipse Modelling Framework (EMF)[278] and serialised for storage using the XML Metadata Interchange (XMI) format.

Execution Specification Artefacts provide the necessary information to bind a BM to a concrete execution platform. For example, these could be Graphical User Interface (GUI) elements that allow a user to specify and configure the employed FCs. The **Execution Specification** artefacts complements the **Model** artefacts and together they carry sufficient information[6] to interpret a BM at runtime.

Source Code Artefacts are created using code generation with the platform independent **Model** and the platform dependent **Execution Specification** as input to the transformation mechanism. They are a representation of the BM in a programming language, e. g. Java [266].

[6]This fact is highlighted by the bolder outlines of the corresponding artefacts in the diagram.

Binary Executable Artefacts are necessary for executing the transformed BM on a target platform. The **Source Codes** are compiled to a format that is native to the execution platform. For example, Java source code is compiled into Java Bytecode [247, Chapter 4], which can be executed by a Virtual Machine (VM).

The Interpretation of BMs uses two **Runtime** formats: **Model** and **Execution Specification**. This approach maintains the model structure during execution. In contrast, BM execution that is based on code generation introduces a number of additional artefacts. The code generation process first transforms the model into **Source Code**, which is then compiled into **Binary Executable** artefacts. Although these transformations result in an execution mechanism that performs better, due to closer bindings to the execution platform, they effectively prevent model adaptation at runtime. Should a modification of the model or the execution specification take place, the code generation transformations need to be re-applied and the resulting **Binary Executable** artefacts would need to be re-deployed, necessitating a system restart. The benefit of BM interpretation is that it only relies on the closely linked **Model** and **Execution Specification** artefacts and modifications can thus be directly applied to the executing model during the runtime of the system, without the need for transformations or generation of further artefacts.

2.2.1 Initialisation from Model Specification

At the start of a BM interpretation process, BM specifications are usually provided in a **Model Persistency** format to the interpreter. The interpreter has to first parse the given format in order to construct a runtime representation of the BM, which is a task that is normally accomplished through libraries, provided as part of the **Runtime** or **Persistency** format implementations. At this stage, a check of the BM's syntax is employed, to make sure that a BM conforms to the declared **Runtime** format.

After successfully creating an in-memory, **Runtime** representation of the model, an interpreter has to make sure that all dependencies of the model are met. This includes satisfaction of dependencies regarding any required resources (such as FC) as well as parametrisation of the model and setting up of support for the expression language used in guard conditions and action statements.

To determine the resource dependencies of the model, an interpreter has to analyse the transition labels found in the BM for use of platform resources in the guard condition or action expressions. The interpreter can also make sure that these resources are available, i. e. that all necessary FCs have been instantiated from storage. An alternative way for dependency resolution is to explicitly provide the dependencies as part of the BM specification within the **Persistency format**. An example of this technique is the use of the UML ElementImport feature to define the platform bindings. In this case, the interfaces to the platform and of all of the utilised FCs need to be modelled within the UML, as well. If the dependencies are gathered implicitly from the transition labels, a suitable query language for the **Model Runtime** or **Model Persistency** formats provides an advantage here. For EMF, there is an in-memory query language provided under the name *Model Query*. For the **Persistency** format, an XPath statement could be used to isolate the necessary statements. Once the transition labels have been isolated, they need to be analysed within the context of the employed expression language to identify statements that rely on platform bindings, e. g. the invocation of an FC.

Resolution of the required platform dependencies is only a part of the initialisation process. BMs might also require the manual specification of model parameters. For example, if a BM is used to query a remote service that requires user credentials for authentication, these credentials need to be provided to the BM interpreter as parameters at initialisation time. The result of the initialisation process is a **Runtime Model** with a matching **Execution Specification** that specifies the resource bindings to the execution platform, along with a binding of values to required BM parameters. Before commencing interpretation, an interpreter has to prepare the runtime system by creating a BM instance. The interpreter needs to allocate and initialise context data objects, hook up communication channels for internal and external event transmission, create message queues for buffering events, create the bindings to instances of FCs and set up the runtime data structures for managing the active and historical BM state configuration.

2.2.2 Event Processing

Once an **Execution Specification** has been provided and the BM has been instantiated, processing of the BM can start. Interpretation of the model occurs step wise, with the model returning the control flow to the interpreter after each step. A single step is triggered by an external event and processed completely, including all raised internal events, before the next external event is retrieved — this is known as the RTC semantics [255, p. 565] [289, Appendix B]. The following text describes event processing in detail, but leaves out the specifics of event dispatching and transmission, which are covered later (in Section 2.2.6).

RTC Semantics A general algorithm for processing events using RTC is given as pseudo code below (Algorithm 1 describes the RTC step and Algorithm 2 the selection of an enabled transition), note that ∅ marks the *null* element.

At the beginning of each RTC step, an event is received from the environment and added to the tail of the event queue (line 2). The *getNextExternalEvent()* operation does not return until an external event is available and interpretation of the BM is suspended until then. Once an event is available, the interpreter will continue to process all events in the queue (lines 3–13). In each iteration, an event is removed from the queue and stored in a local variable (line 4); the algorithm then proceeds to

Algorithm 1 Stepwise processing of events with RTC semantics

```
1: loop
2:   eventQueue ← getNextExternalEvent()
3:   while eventQueue.size() > 0 do
4:     event ← eventQueue.removeHead()
5:     for all activeState : ActiveStateConfiguration do
6:       transition ← selectEnabled(activeState, event)
7:       if transition ≠ ∅ then
8:         exitStates(transition)
9:         execute(transition)
10:        enterStates(transition)
11:      end if
12:    end for
13:  end while
14: end loop
```

determine transitions that are enabled by the given event. When a runtime model contains active parallel regions, the active state configuration will consist of one state per active parallel region. Transitions can be enabled for each of these active states; therefore the interpreter processes each of the active states separately (lines 5–12). For every active state, the interpreter selects up to one enabled outgoing transition. The algorithm for selecting an enabled transition is given as Algorithm 2 and explained below.

Once the interpreter is able to determine an enabled transition, the transition is *triggered* and will be *fired* (lines 8–10). Firing a transition consists of exiting a number of states, execution of optional transition behaviours and entering a number of states. It is important to realise that a large number of states can be exited and/or entered with one transition. When exiting a *leaf* state in a BM instance, an interpreter might need to exit a number of super states, as well as enter into nested states within a hierarchy of new states, e. g. when the transition leads to a disjunct part of the composition hierarchy of states. There are also some specific pseudostates (e. g. History) that require a number of subsequent states to be entered within a single transition. Entering and exiting states can be complex operations and their functionality depends on the set of features available to the BMs. Usually, these operations execute an optional behaviour and update the active state configuration. Exactly which states are exited or entered depends on the source and target states of a transition and their position in the composition hierarchy of the BM. This will be explained after detailing the selection algorithm of the *selectEnabled()* function.

The algorithm for selection of an enabled transition goes through all of the outgoing transitions of a given state (lines 2–6), in an order that is determined implicitly by the in-memory storage format of the BM. Each transition is checked to see if it is

Algorithm 2 Selection of an enabled transition

```
Require: state, event
1: while state ≠ ∅ do
2:   for all transition : state.getOutgoingTransitions() do
3:     if transition.isEnabled(event) then
4:       return transition
5:     end if
6:   end for
7:   state = state.getParent()
8: end while
9: return ∅
```

enabled by the current input event. Again, this test depends on the features of the implementation and can be quite complex. As a minimum, an interpreter would check if the transition is triggered by the given event and evaluate an optional guard condition. Once an enabled transition has been found, it is returned to the caller (lines 3–4). If there is no outgoing transition enabled for a given event, we are not finished with processing: outgoing transitions of superstates might also be enabled. The algorithm therefore needs to re-iterate through the tests for every superstate found from the initially given state, up to the composition hierarchy root (lines 1–8, with the modification of the current state in line 7). In case that no enabled transition is found, the *null* element is returned. Processing semantics prescribe that a single active state can have at most one active outgoing transition. Algorithm 2 uses an implicit prioritisation based on the definition order of transitions in the in-memory storage format, together with a bottom-up traversal in the composition hierarchy to solve the issue of conflicting transition.

A Note on ε-Transition Loops Line 3 of Algorithm 1 decides on the termination of the inner loop, which processes a single, internal step of the BM. In the case of transitions triggered by completion events, it is possible that a cycle of ε-transitions is entered and the step function would never return. Imagine a state A left by an ε-transition to State B. State B has an outgoing ε-transition leading back to the state A. As soon as one of these states is entered, it will add a new completion event to the event queue, which keeps the internal loop running and the BM oscillating between the two states A and B. This is called a "life-lock", as the **while** loop will continuously be executed without termination. Life-locks can be avoided by means of model construction, but we also found an engineering solution by introducing a second queue for outgoing internal events, which is drained to the event queue after each step is completed. One also needs some additional logic to determine if both of the queues are empty when making the potentially blocking call in line 2.

Determination of Entered and Exited States The state-transition paradigm seems to be simple, but when combined with state composition, it can become complicated to determinate the set of entered and exited states. Figure 2.9 depicts the major variants of transitions between states embedded in a composition hierarchy.

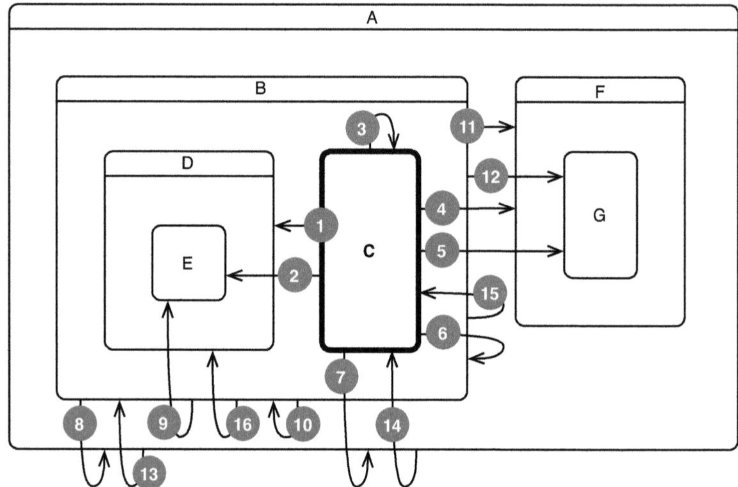

Figure 2.9: Variants of transitions between compound states

The Diagram displays a single active state **C**, within a composition hierarchy. Although the syntax is UML, we abstain from showing any pseudostates that regulate the entering of control flows within compound states (e. g. initial). For our conclusions, it is only necessary to be aware of the position of source and target states within the composition hierarchy. That being said, it is good to keep in mind that the set of entered and exited states might be modified during transition execution, depending on encountering certain pseudostates.

When determining the sets of exited and entered states, both an identification of the state itself is needed as well as an ordering between states needs to be established. During exit, states that are located nearer to the composition tree leaves (*lower* in the hierarchy) are exited first. During entry, states that are located nearer to the composition tree root will be called before the ones nearer to the leaves. Table 2.1 shows the source (SRC) and destination (DST) states for the 16 transitions of Figure 2.9, together with the exited and entered states in correct execution order.

No.	SRC	→	DST	Exited States	Entered States
1	C	→	D	C	D
2	C	→	E	C	D, E
3	C	→	C	C	C
4	C	→	F	C, B	F
5	C	→	G	C, B	F, G
6	C	→	B	C, B	B
7	C	→	A	C, B, A	A
8	B	→	A	C, B, A	A
9	B	→	E	C, B	B, D, E
10	B	→	B	C, B	B
11	B	→	F	C, B	F
12	B	→	G	C, B	F, G
13	A	→	B	C, B, A	A, B
14	A	→	C	C, B, A	A, B, C
15	B	→	C	C, B	B, C
16	B	→	D	C, B	B, D

Table 2.1: Entered and exited states for the transitions in Figure 2.9

All of the transitions shown are considered external transitions (see pages 218 ff. in Appendix A). Internal transitions neither exit nor enter states. Local transitions exit and enter states in a similar fashion as external transitions, but do not consider the direct SRC or DST state depending on its position in the composition hierarchy. When trying to classify the different transitions, we can identify three different groups, as detailed below. We discovered, that within these groups, we can determine the execution order of the entered and exited states solely by calculating a range of states along a single path between two nodes in the composition hierarchy. For calculation of these ranges we will also need the notion of the current (CUR) active state, which in our example is always **C** and the concept of a least common ancestor (LCA). The LCA is the lowest node in the composition hierarchy, which is parent to both SRC and DST.

Source state is a superstate of destination or both states are the same This constraint is valid for transitions 3, 9, 10, 13, 14, 15 and 16. The exited states are then given by the range [CUR, SRC] — whereas each state is only allowed to be included once into this list. For example, if CUR := C and DST := C, then exited states = [C]. The entered states are given by the range [SRC, DST].

Destination state is a superstate of source This constraint is valid for transitions 6, 7 and 8. The exited states are calculated using the range [CUR, DST]. The entered state is always only a single element [DST] and any further nodes would need to be added according to the various pseudostates that regulate the initial entry to a state.

Source and destination states are in disjoint parts of the hierarchy This constraint is valid for transitions 1, 2, 4, 5, 11 and 12. For the calculation of the range, one needs to first determine the LCA, which is B for transitions 1 and 2; and A for transitions 4, 5, 11 and 12. The exited states are then given by the range [CUR, LCA[and the entered states are calculated by]LCA, DST] — the reversed brace symbol is used to indicate that the LCA is excluded from the calculated range.

2.2.3 Concurrency

Concurrency aspects in BM interpretation can be distinguished in two distinctly different classes: the parallel interpretation of multiple BMs and the concurrent execution of control flows within a single model.

Behaviour Model Parallelism Depending on the use case, a single program might be applied to interpret multiple BMs in parallel. Concurrency issues within this kind of approach can be solved with mechanisms for conventional multi-threaded programming. For an introduction, see the section on thread synchronisation in the "Advanced Programming in the UNIX Environment" book [181, Section 11.6] and the concurrency and synchronisation patterns from the 2nd volume of the "Pattern-Oriented Software Architecture" (POSA) series [169]. An example of such mechanisms has already been encountered within Section 2.2.2: the blocking *getNextExternalEvent()* operation in Algorithm 1, used to separate a synchronous process (the RTC step loop) from an asynchronous one (receiving an external event). In reactive event systems, queues are typical data structures for this kind of task. Event dispatching between environment and BMs constitutes one of the situations that calls for synchronisation between threads of otherwise unrestrained parallel execution. An implementation of synchronisation mechanisms might also be needed when accessing shared resources, such as global variables in the BM context or mutually utilised FCs.

Generally speaking, the interpretation of BMs is a task that is well suited to parallelisation, due to the low and well-defined number of synchronisation points between models, although there are constraints regarding the event dispatching mechanism. The dispatcher usually executes in a single thread. Should the overall time for dispatching the event to the separate execution threads take longer than the time that it takes a single thread to execute a RTC step, then this dispatching thread will determine the overall speed of execution, independent of the number of concurrent threads that will process the BMs. Such a situation might occur when a larger number of BMs are supplied with the same external event. We cannot devise a one-size-fits-all concept for efficient parallel interpretation of behaviour models, as there are too many factors influencing the performance, e. g. the underlying hardware architecture, the feature set of the interpreted BM formalism, the BM structure, the frequency of dispatched events, etc. Some of these factors will be explored in the following chapters in the context of concrete interpreter implementations and use case studies.

Concurrent Control Flows Within a Single Model The second form of parallelism that we discuss concerns the execution of parallel regions in a single BM. Each active region within a BM corresponds to one control flow with a single active state. One might be tempted to also model control flows with a thread model to facilitate the parallel processing capabilities of an underlying platform, but we found that this approach fits badly to the reactive, RTC semantics used for state machine execution. To reach a quiescent state of the system between each processing step, all threads would need to be synchronised at the beginning and at the end of each step. Furthermore, parallel control flows in a single model are much closer coupled than concurrently executing BM instances, because they are relying on the same execution specification. For example, they will access the same input event[7] and use the same context data. For these reasons, the processing of parallel control flows should be done in a sequential manner. This course of action is feasible, as the execution order of orthogonal control flows should be irrelevant, as long as model consistency is given at the end of each interpretation step.

Maintaining a set of active control flows during model interpretation is a non-trivial task, as BMs can include elements that explicitly or implicitly influence the set of active control flows during a step. BM features that can influence the control flow are the following ones:

Final states and terminal pseudostates Final states will trigger a termination of a control flow on entering. Terminal pseudostates will trigger a termination of all control flows within the current BM.

Fork constructs A fork node splits a single control flow into n parallel ones. The current control flow continues in one of the forked target states and $n+1$ new control flows are created. Alternatively, fork terminates the current control flow and creates n new ones. We refer to the first option as having *retained* control flow continuation semantics, whereas the second option exhibits *separated* continuation semantics.

Join constructs Join nodes merge n control flows into a single one. One of the control flows continues in the target state, while the other $n-1$ are terminated (retained continuation). Alternatively, all n control flows are terminated and a single new one is created (separated continuation).

[7] As long as one does not employ per-control-flow event queues with event duplication during dispatch

Transitions entering or exiting orthogonal states Such transitions trigger an implicit creation, respectively termination of the control flows corresponding to the parallel regions of the orthogonal state. BM formalisms that do not have fork or join features solely rely on this for handling concurrent control flows (e. g. SCXML). Fork or join constructs might also be mixed with implicit control flow modifications (e. g. a fork that only enters two parallel regions of an orthogonal state containing three regions — the third parallel region would be entered implicitly via an initial pseudostate).

Shallow or deep history constructs Upon re-instantiation of previously captured history information, a number of control flows might be created, leading to different active states in the composition hierarchy. A precise semantics for doing this is prescribed by the "temporal fork" concept of A. Derezińska and R. Pilitowski [52], who propose to enter these active states as if through a fork construct with outgoing transitions ending in each of the active states to restore.

Apart from the calculation of the set of active control flows and the engineering task of supporting the dynamic adaptability of this set during execution of a processing step, there is another issue that needs to be considered when implementing model interpreters that support control flow concurrency, which is the correct determination of entered and exited states. Section 2.2.2 describes finding the correct number and order of states to exit and enter for a transition leading from a single source state to a single destination state. Unfortunately, with control flow concurrency, this is not correct anymore. Transitions might leave multiple source states and might end at multiple target states. The task to determine the number and order of entered and exited states becomes more difficult, as it is not possible to determine the correct solution merely by examining single transitions. Take, for example, Figure 2.10.

There are two transitions leading from States C and D to States F and G via join and fork pseudostates. The calculation of exited states, when carried out for each of the transitions separately, leads to the results C, B and D, B. This is wrong, as State B should only be left once, even though this seems to be counterintuitive to the diagram's syntax. We found that a solution to this problem can be achieved by following a divide-and-conquer approach. One starts by determining the active state configuration C_{active}, as well as the target state configuration C_{target}. We define a state configuration as an N-ary tree with states as nodes.

The active states form the leaves and the LCA of all active states defines the root of the tree. C_{active} constitutes the state configuration before the current step, whereas C_{target} reflects the state configuration after the current processing step finishes. Figure 2.11 shows both the active as well as the target state configuration for the example depicted in Figure 2.10.

After determination of the two state configurations, it is possible to establish the overall exited and entered states by means of an exclusive or operation (we

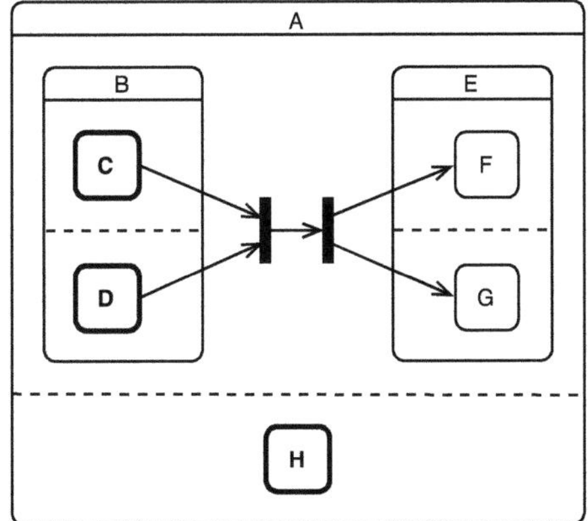

Figure 2.10: Which states should be entered or exited?

use the symbol $\oplus$ to denote this) between the two trees; exited states are given by $C_{exit} := C_{active} \oplus C_{target}$, entered states are calculated using $C_{enter} := C_{target} \oplus C_{active}$. C_{exit} can be determined as the configuration depicted in the emphasised part (bold outline) of the state configuration of C_{active} in Figure 2.11 and C_{enter} is emphasised in the C_{target} configuration, respectively.

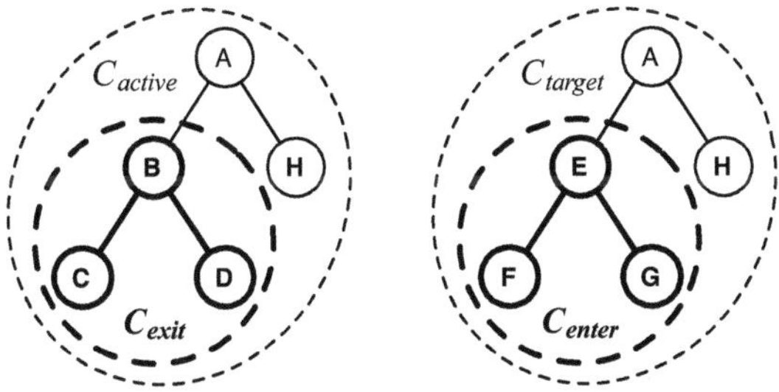

Figure 2.11: Active and target state configuration for Figure 2.10

Algorithm 3 Calculating $\oplus$ for two state configurations

```
Require: OverlapStartNode, Result, Flag = false (global)
Require: FirstNode, SecondNode (local)
if FirstNode = SecondNode then {Conjunct part of the tree}
  if FirstNode = OverlapStartNode then
    Flag = true
  end if
  if Flag then
    {Append current node to result tree and set as new leaf}
    Result.children ← shallowCopy(FirstNode)
    Result ← Result.getSimilarChild(FirstNode)
  end if
  {Continue with children of current node}
  for all FirstChild : FirstNode.children do
    if SecondNode.hasSimilar(FirstChild) then
      {Node does exist at second node}
      SecondChild ← SecondNode.getSimilarChild(FirstChild)
      Re-enter with FirstNode ← FirstChild, SecondNode ← SecondChild
    else
      {Subtree does not exist at second node}
      Result.children ← deepCopy(FirstChild)
    end if
  end for
else {Disjoint part of the tree}
  Result.children ← deepCopy(FirstNode)
end if
```

We implement the $\oplus$ operation according to the re-entrant Algorithm 3. The required arguments need to be initialised as follows: The argument *FirstNode* holds the root of the state configuration that is used as first operand, *SecondNode* references the root of the second operand state configuration. *Result* needs to be initialised with an empty node; it will contain the result of the operation upon completion of the algorithm. The arguments *OverlapStartNode* and *Flag* are used to take care of cases where a transition is self-referential within a composition hierarchy. With compound states, a self-referencing transition is not only a transition that leads back to the source state, but also each transition that leads to a superstate or substate of the source state.

Generally, the algorithm performs a top-down traversal of the state configuration tree, composing a new result tree consisting of the nodes of the first given tree, as long as they are disjoint to nodes in the second tree. Thus, if *OverlapStartNode* is not set, the algorithm discards all overlapping parts of the state configuration tree.

When the argument is initialised with a node, the algorithm includes overlapping parts of the tree from the position of the *OverlapStartNode* downwards in the *Result* state configuration. *OverlapStartNode* needs to be initialised with SRC when DST is a substate of SRC, and to DST when SRC is a substate of DST.

By a subsequent partitioning of the two resulting state configurations C_{enter} and C_{exit} into disjoint fragments that correspond to a single control flow each, one not only obtains a set of paths that each begins and ends in a single state but has also determined the control flows that need to terminate and the ones that need to be created. The employed partitioning algorithms depend on the control flow continuation semantics and can also take the form of a simple tree traversal. E.g., for a retained continuation semantics, we successfully used a depth-first traversal strategy. Results for a control flow partitioning of the BM shown in Figure 2.10 could be the following:

Using separated continuation semantics An existing flow that exits C and terminates; an existing flow that exits D and terminates; a newly created flow that exits B, enters E and terminates; a newly created flow that enters F; and a newly created flow that enters G.

Using retained continuation semantics An existing flow that exits C, exits B, enters E, enters F; an existing flow that exits D; and a newly created flow that enters G.

2.2.4 Expression and Action Evaluation

BMs use conditional expressions and action statements. When evaluating a conditional expression, an interpretation process will need to return a boolean value and is only allowed read access on the context. Contrary to this, the interpretation of actions will usually change the runtime state and does not return values. Conditional expressions are merely used for guard conditions, whereas actions can be used in several places: when entering, staying in or exiting states, when firing a transition or as part of an initialisation or shutdown behaviour.

The characteristics of languages that can be used to specify expressions and actions within a BM are different from the characteristics of the languages used to express the BM structure itself. Both language types have different focuses: the BM structure is used to orchestrate functionality by defining the ordering and dependencies between function invocations, whereas expressions and actions are used for calling functions and performing arithmetic. A BM language does not only need to encompass these two unlike aspects but will also need to integrate them with a given data model and its particular type system. It would be possible for an interpreter to support the usage of different combinations of languages and types systems but as pointed out in Section 2.1.2.3, expression and action languages are usually prescribed by the application domain in which a BM will be used. The same applies for the data model.

Automated expression evaluation is one of the core areas of computer science. There is a large body of existing work regarding the design and implementation of expression evaluators for a variety of language types and technological platforms. We will therefore not investigate expression evaluation mechanisms any further in this chapter, but will concentrate on the aspects of integrating them with a BM interpreter. We mostly refer to the "dragon books" [3] when implementing evaluation mechanisms.

One has to always keep in mind that conditional expressions might be evaluated many times by the interpreter, while trying to determine an enabled transition. When designed carelessly, these evaluations can drastically impact the runtime performance of the overall BM. For example, the XPath language has features, which make it easy to unintentionally construct expressions that will traverse large parts or even the complete context, during each evaluation of the expression.

Although actions, as well as conditional expressions, could theoretically be complex programs, we recommend keeping them concise. Once an expression starts to resemble an algorithm, e. g. by using loops, rather than just a simple function call, test or assignment, it should either be moved to a dedicated FC or split into several steps and integrated with the BM structure. The choice for relocating a functionality to an FC also depends on the aspired visibility of the statement; it would be hidden from the model designer when integrated with an FC and otherwise visible (and modifiable). Keeping the model free from complex expressions helps understanding and visualising BMs.

The Role of the Native Interpreter Language From a performance point of view it would be ideal to use the same language for expressions as the one used to implement the interpreter, since actions could be directly bound and expressions would be interpreted natively. But there are downsides to such an approach; from a security perspective, there is a bigger potential vulnerability of the execution platform. Unless expressions are executed in a sandbox environment without access to the interpreter runtime, they would use the same local address space as the interpreter and could easily crash or influence the program itself. Furthermore, the native language syntax and semantics might not be well suited for BM designers, who are working on a different abstraction level than application programmers.

Using the interpreter implementation language for expression evaluation is trivial if the interpreter is programmed in such a language itself. The interpreter process could then utilise appropriate language features to directly execute the particular character sequences that make up expression statements. For example, both Ruby [249] and Python [284] provide an `eval(...)` statement that evaluates a given string as a conditional expression defined in the respective language.

For compiled languages, following such an approach is either very hard or not possible at all, as linking is done statically, before the interpreter process begins execution. This is different for languages that are using an intermediary representation format, like Java bytecode or the Common Intermediate Language (CIL) [233, Partition III]. As these technological platforms support late binding, it is possible to compile and bind expressions at runtime.

2.2.5 Functional Components

FCs provide functions (sometimes called *services*) of a platform to BMs. When regarding BMs as an abstraction, this is where one would "hide the details of what is being abstracted". FCs are not limited to certain types of functions, but typically cater for technical concerns, like communication protocols, hardware control or data conversion. Providing two places where behaviour can be defined (an FC and the BM itself) also has administrative implications; FCs should only be created by programmers familiar with the technical execution platform and they should pass through the usual quality assurance processes before being deployed in the target environment. We assume that this is different for BMs, since people with much less technical insight could create these for carrying out customised tasks. There should only be a fixed set of tested FCs available for binding with the BMs, thereby allowing a wider audience control of a technical infrastructure, while minimising the risk for abuse.

The creation of FCs might be carried out using any programming language or development tools — it is only necessary to ensure that an interpreter's implementation and an FC can interact via appropriate interfaces. We stipulate that the role of an FC is to serve as "function libraries" for BMs, sharing the view of C. Szyperski on the characteristic properties of components [193, p. 30]:

1. A component is a unit of independent deployment.
2. A component is a unit of third-party composition.
3. A component has no persistent state.

Characteristics 1 and 2 are central to the way that we propose BMs should be developed; a BM designer orchestrates existing FCs, which are independently created and maintained by system programmers. Characteristic 3 fits naturally to our approach, as we explicitly maintain context, which could then be passed to FCs as part of an invocation. Due to the tight coupling between an FC and the interpreter, both should execute in the same address space. It is also possible to regard FCs as independently executing services and some BM formalisms emphasise this by supporting constructs for invoking remote services, but we will only examine local communication within this thesis.

2.2.5.1 Calling FCs Using Procedure Call Semantics

Synchronous procedure call semantics are similar to procedure calls or method invocations as employed in higher-level programming languages. Figure 2.12 depicts the synchronous invocation of a single function call with a number of input parameters *param 1, ..., param n* from the step method of the interpreter, in UML sequence charts syntax. The FC executes a function identified by the given procedure signature and returns one or more output values. The interpreter's BM step processing resumes operation only after the return value(s) are received.

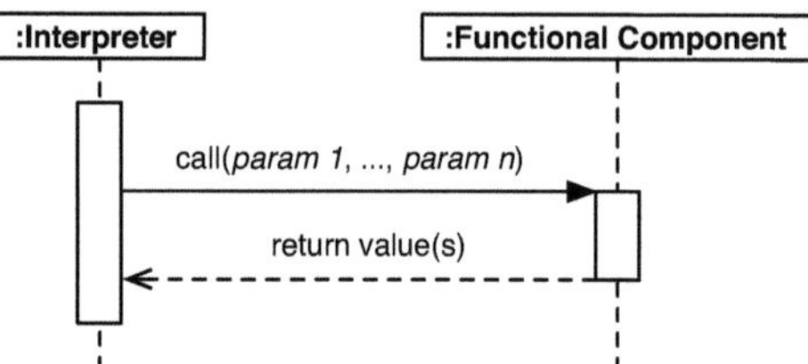

Figure 2.12: Calling a function using procedure call semantics

The thread used to execute this function is often the same as the one executing the step function in the interpreter. Consequently, if the given function executes for a long time, the complete BM execution will also be blocked for the whole duration. On the plus side, it is often possible to directly map such function calls to the native calling conventions of the underlying platform, making them fast and the integration simple.

Synchronous calls can also be mimicked using a purely message-based communication paradigm. In this case, there are two threads involved: one thread executes the step method within the interpreter, and the second thread executes the function of the FC. Synchronisation between these threads can then be done according to the strategy in Figure 2.13. After sending an initial command event 1 with the parameters as payload to the FC, the interpreter thread needs to be blocked, e. g. by entering a wait() statement. The FC thread would then receive the event, process it and send a corresponding result event 2. Upon reception of event 2, the interpreter thread would be unblocked and continue with processing of the results contained in the response event.

Although such an approach provides simple means of achieving synchronicity, it can easily end up in a deadlock situation, should the corresponding response event not appear. In this case, the interpreter thread would wait forever. A timed guard construct can ensure that a deadlock is circumvented and an error is raised but this only helps to identify errors and does not remove the underlying complexity (due to the multiple threads and matching of sent & received events).

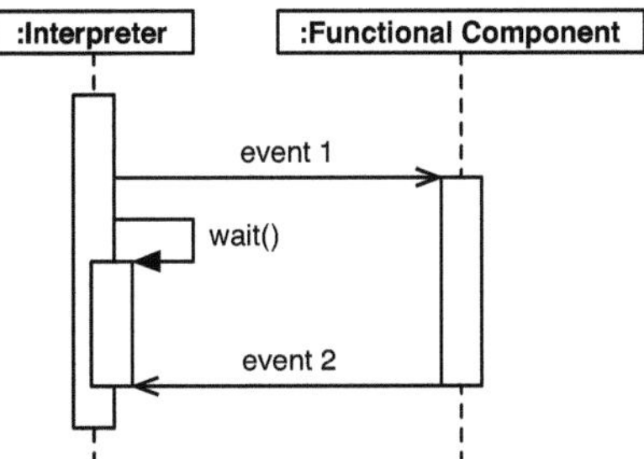

Figure 2.13: Using events to call a function with procedure call semantics

2.2.5.2 Asynchronous Communication Between FC and Interpreter

As communication within a BM is carried out using asynchronous event transmission, using this mechanism for function invocation is a natural solution. In this case, a service would be triggered using an event that carries the invocation parameters as payload. BM processing continues directly after submission of an invocation event. The FC would then receive the event and execute an appropriate function. During execution, a number of events might be generated, which are handled in the following interpreter steps, using the normal event processing mechanisms. Figure 2.14 depicts this approach.

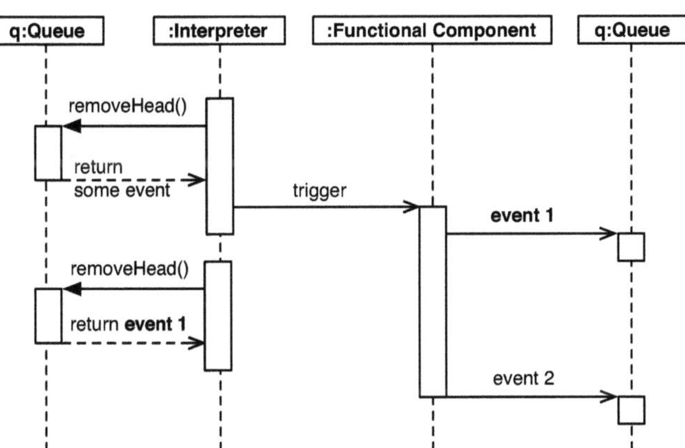

Figure 2.14: Asynchronously triggering a function

Analogous to Algorithm 1, the event queue is modelled as a passive structure and each interpreter step dequeues the first event stored in an external event queue (in the example this is some non-relevant event). Subsequently, a **trigger** event is send to an FC, e. g. as part of an action statement of a transition. The event carries enough information to select and call the appropriate function, which enqueues **event 1** during its execution and **event 2** at the end of it. With the next step of the interpreter, a new event is retrieved from the queue and processed by the model. In our example this would be **event 1**, which is the first of the events generated by the FC. Using events for asynchronous function execution integrates well with the event handling mechanism already in place, but demands more complex BMs, which need to explicitly represent the communication between the model and FC. Interestingly, by facilitating this approach the communication between model and FC and the communication between distributed models can be treated in the same way.

There are also several variations of these schemes known in literature. For example, the Common Object Request Broker Architecture (CORBA) specification defines two additional approaches: *Oneway* and *Deferred Synchronous* [67, p. 181]. *Oneway* refers to the special case, where a triggered function does not send any events in response, at all. *Deferred Synchronous* is more complicated: a client triggers a function and the control flow returns immediately. The function will now execute in parallel and the client can retrieve the result (or inquire about the completion status) with a subsequent event.

2.2.5.3 Key Aspects of FC

In addition to specific aspects dictated by the concrete technical foundation of a system, we identified a number of general aspects that one has to consider when creating FCs.

Introspectable Signatures FCs are employed as building blocks and composed using BMs. As already known by small children, only matching building blocks can be put together properly. To determine if an FC matches, one needs to at least conduct a syntactical check on the signatures of the interfaces provided by the FCs. One also has to keep in mind that even if a signature matches, there is no guarantee that an FC fits to a model: there has to be a semantic correspondence, which is usually established outside the interpreter, i. e. by convention.

Timely Execution FCs typically use external threads for execution of their functionality, blocking the original caller during that time. For a synchronous call, this would be the thread running the interpreter step method, and for asynchronous calls, this would be a thread of an event dispatcher. The consequence of blocking any of these is that the interpreter is not able to continue to operate during this time. Therefore, it is mandatory that functions either finish fast or employ an internal thread that allows for parallel execution of a function. Another solution would be to introduce multi-threading on the level of the interpreter step method or the event dispatcher.

Statelessness All state data that is used by FCs should be stored in the context and passed to the FC as part of an invocation. The idea is to only have a single place where state is stored. Having stateless components allows the system to relinquish the handling of FC instances and helps with FC management; this concept can also be found in server enterprise infrastructures, e. g. see the *Session Component* pattern described by M. Völter, A. Schmid and E. Wolff [203, p. 56].

Dispatch Interface An FC needs a dispatch interface if it should be able to react to incoming events. Dispatch interfaces are used to receive events that encode commands and to trigger a corresponding, component-internal functionality. Code that implements the dispatch interface also cares for type conversion between the event format and the internal function.

2.2.5.4 Requirements on the Interpreter

FCs are part of an overall framework, and they are missing some basic functions that need to be provided by the interpreter. The following is an overview of functions that an interpreter needs to provide when executing FCs.

Caller Identification Identification of the originator of a function call is needed if the function is triggered asynchronously. Broadcasting response events that are carrying the result of the function execution might not be a feasible strategy: a direct dispatching of the response event to the call originator using a suitable identifier helps to reduce the number of transmitted events as well as better insulating one FC from problems caused by other FCs.

Logging Application tracing or logging is an important administrative utility. As part of a framework, FC should not use a custom logging framework, but access logging functionality provided by the interpreter infrastructure. This also enables the setup of different logs for different FCs.

Configuration There needs to be a way to handle FC configuration, either statically as part of the FC packaging or as a service provided by the interpreter. It is also possible that BMs would want to alter the configuration of an FC, in which case the FC can provide a suitable configuration interface.

Error Handling When utilising a direct-bound, synchronous procedure call approach for triggering functions, error handling can be done using the native constructs of the platform, e. g. exception handling primitives. Otherwise, means need to be established for the communication of errors. There should also be a clear specification for the meaning of error codes/messages.

Providing Context Access during FC Invocations Already mentioned as a key aspect for an FC, statelessness requires the interpreter to provide an FC with the necessary context with each invocation. Alternatively, the FC could be provided with direct access to the context and poll the context data on demand. It has to be ensured that the context is either in exclusive use by one component or that concurrent access cannot lead to inconsistent data.

Accepting Events To send events, an FC needs access to the event dispatching mechanism of the interpreter. This can be done by providing a dispatch interface at the interpreter side. The interpreter dispatch interface enqueues received events at the input queue of a number of target BMs (e. g. selected by caller identification or event type), where they are processed as normal external events.

2.2.6 Communication Mechanisms

All communication is supposed to follow a message-passing paradigm, as this fits best to the interpreter event propagation semantics and to the reactive nature of BMs. Should a streaming paradigm be needed, one could divide a stream into segments that follow the underlying protocol granularity, e. g. packets, frames, requests, tokens, blocks, et cetera and conduct the processing on these segments.

The mechanism for acceptance and delivery of events is a crucial part of any interpreter implementation, and the task that such a mechanism has to fulfil is simple, which is to transmit events from a single sender to potentially multiple receivers. Usually a sender is unaware of the existence or number of receivers that an event will have; we refer to this as *sender-receiver decoupling*. Full sender-receiver decoupling allows the sender to relinquish addressing concerns: it can just initiate an event without considering who will receive it. Such a strategy helps to reduce configuration overhead and enables more dynamic system architectures, at the cost of additional communication. An issue arising with cases where explicit addressing is necessary concerns address resolution: addresses of distributed interpreters need to be known prior to sending an event. One could use either a static configuration of addresses or a discovery/directory mechanism, which allows to dynamically resolve interpreter addresses. Implementing such a mechanism is unnecessary when employing the sender-receiver decoupling strategy, but instead the key question becomes: how to determine the set of receivers for a given event?

The most simple answer to this question is: Send to everyone! For a low number of participants this is also a valid approach. However, for widely distributed or large numbers of communication partners, there are inherent performance and scalability limits. A solution to this problem consists of assigning a scope to certain events or categories of events and to only dispatch events to receivers within that scope. For example, typical scopes could be a single control flow, a BM instance, an interpreter, a Computational Unit (CU), a network segment, a local network or an administrative domain. Scopes might also be logical, in which case they do not refer to a concrete topological or technical feature, but to a group of communication partners using a common identifier (often called a *topic*). We will refer to this form of communication as *group communication*.

2.2.6.1 Communication with Interpreter scope

There are several possibilities for implementing one-to-many event communication with an internal interpreter scope, e. g. a shared message bus or the Observer pattern [75, p. 287 ff.]. Performance-wise, *internal* event dispatching seldom forms a critical part of an interpreter implementation, as message transfer times are small compared to the time needed to process an event, which is usually the opposite in *external* event communication. More important for internal communication is the format used to represent the events.

Choice of Event Format In most aspects, the distribution of an event and the format of the event data can be considered independent issues. Event formats depend on the concrete cases that an interpreter is used in; they might range from the most simple form, e. g. a single integer value, to rather complex data structures like the Common Base Event (CBE) XML format [258]. Contrary to external events, which might need to be compatible with various platforms and transmission protocols, internal events are usually stored and handled in the format of data structures native to an interpreter's programming language due to performance reasons.

2.2.6.2 Communication with Host scope

When running multiple interpreters on a single host, one can possibly make use of the mechanisms that operating systems provide for Inter-Process Communication (IPC) [181, Section 15] or alternatively employ mechanisms that are intended for larger scopes.

Each of the major operating platforms has its own proprietary message handling mechanism, which can be used for event dispatching between interpreters running on the same platform. We are deliberately using the term "platform", as this is true for operating systems as well as other platforms, e. g. Java 2 Enterprise Edition (J2EE) technology [266] or web browsers. For operating systems, platform independent event dispatching mechanisms are often implemented using *signals* and *shared memory*. Signals are used to notify running applications in an asynchronous fashion. This is achieved by registering signal handlers, which are executed by the operating system once a signal is raised by another process. Shared memory allows a number of processes to use the same part of Random-Access Memory (RAM). The same RAM region is mapped within the address space of each of the processes. When using shared memory to communicate, care needs to be taken regarding the consistency of the shared resource; usually, standard libraries are utilised that at least ensure that writing to the resource is an atomic operation.

2.2.6.3 Communication with Local Network scope

We consider local network scope as being characterised by either the existence of a single (logically) shared medium or the routing of multicast packets. These requirements enable the facilitation of the underlying transport protocol and the usage of hardware specific mechanisms for group communication. Being able to reach all of the nodes within a network scope supports a flexible topology without static Internet Protocol (IP) addresses by means of node discovery: the process of determining potential partners which participate in the group communication.

Communication in Clusters Server machines are often grouped in clusters for performance or robustness reasons. Cluster architectures often have dedicated hardware that provide fast data transport between the cluster nodes, but with the advent of fast IP networking it has also become common to create server clusters without dedicated hardware, relying purely on standard hardware components, e. g. Ethernet [241].

Event communication in cluster architectures is usually done in accordance with the Message Passing Interface (MPI) specification [252]. MPI has its roots in high-performance computing and it is the de facto standard Application Programming Interface (API) for message passing in cluster architectures. For maintaining a consistent state in clusters of J2EE application servers, it is common to employ TCP [43, Chapter 25] based clustering protocols like JGroups [19], which provides reliable group communication primitives. When using JGroups, one should be aware of the inherent limitations in regard to scalability and bandwidth as identified by T. Abdellatif, E. Cecchet and R. Lachaize [1].

2.2.6.4 Internet Wide Communication

Whereas in a Local Area Network (LAN) a shared communication medium and homogenous networking technology is employed, this is not true for the internet. These restrictions have an impact on the node discovery processes, which need to be substituted with either previously known, static IP addresses or by look-up mechanisms that employ service access points with static addresses, e. g. directory or naming servers.

Event Services Event services are often used in large enterprise networks. They exist in various forms, e. g. as specification for conventional distributed systems like the CORBA Notification Service [257] or as a more modern variation in the form of Message Oriented Middleware (MOM) [195, p. 108 ff.] or Enterprise Service Bus (ESB) infrastructures [223]. Such systems serve as a central location for storage and forwarding of messages and often add features like message persistence, access permissions or content conversion. An important group communication paradigm that has been shown to scale up to a large (but limited) number of participating communication partners is Publish-Subscribe (PubSub) [68], in which event senders publish events using a topic and event receivers process only events for topics that they previously subscribed to. Although event services can be set up between domains that are administrated by individual organisations, one often finds these types of systems within uniformly administrated domains.

With Unknown Communication Partners Even when there is no previously established scope, it is still possible to set up group communication infrastructures, e. g. by means of peer-to-peer technologies like Distributed Hash Tables (DHT) [15]. Besides bootstrapping[8], the main issues then revolve around trust: since no information is available on a communication partner, there are also no guarantees that the node will play along in correctly interpreting BMs. Towards this end, we applied the concept of *contracts* to group communication. Using contracts to ensure interaction between components in software systems goes back to B. Meyer's *Design by Contract* [139] principle, although we are omitting parts of his concept, specifically the specification of pre- and postconditions. In our case, a contract specifies the number and roles of collaborating parties as well as an invariant. It is established explicitly between all participants and will only be created if the necessary number of roles can be filled. Once the contract is in place, a group communication scope is formed, where role names can be used as message addresses. Violations of a contract invariant are detected and lead to a cancelation of the contract and notification of all collaborating parties. After a contract has been canceled, the role names cannot be used for addressing anymore. The monitoring of a contract's invariant requires technical components that are able to supervise the operation of the nodes and that can monitor the exchanged messages. We successfully tested this model using a *lifeliness* invariant, which specifies that a contract is valid as long as participants are accepting messages within a given timespan.

[8] Finding the first link to a DHT node

2.3 Distributed Model Management

In addition to the specification and interpretation of BMs, we are introducing processes for supporting the deployment of existent BMs. Deployment is not only considered as copying a BM in a persistent model format from one place to another, but we found that it is beneficial to adapt a given set of BMs, before supplying them to some interpreters. The difference to the previous text is that we are now talking about a number of collaborating BMs instead of a single BM executing at a single CU. For most use cases, managing a collective of distributed, cooperating BMs is an important aspect.

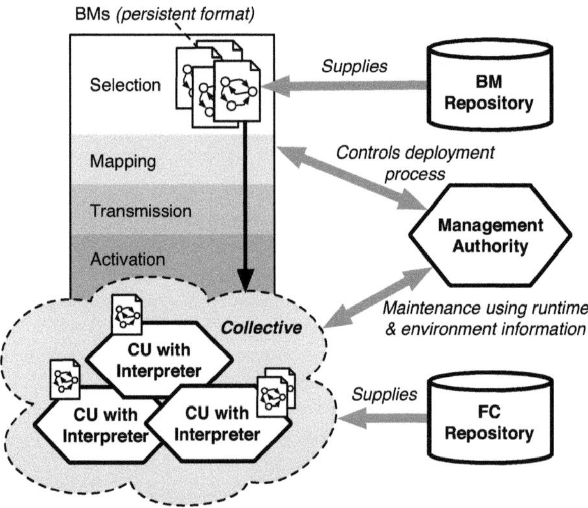

Figure 2.15: Entities involved in BM activation and maintenance

The deployment of BMs at a collective of CUs can be done in a multi-step process as depicted in Figure 2.15. Based on the analysis of use case scenarios (see our publications [56, 105, 106, 104] and Chapter 5), we identified four general components for the management of a collective of distributed BMs.

Behaviour Model Repository The BM Repository stores BMs in a persistent representation format and provides facilities for inspection and retrieval of BMs. Such an entity would also be a good place for versioning of the BMs and could serve as the data backend for BM specification tools.

Management Authority The Management Authority (MA) controls the overall deployment process and serves as the central coordination authority for any administrative operations or notifications in regard to the distributed CU collective. It maintains a view of the current runtime state of the collective. The MA is also a convenient place for evaluation of runtime environment data — such information can be used to influence the deployment of BMs in response to changes in the environment.

Functional Component Repository The FC Repository stores all FCs for a domain in binary format and provides facilities for retrieval and inspection of FCs. Similar to the BM Repository, the integration of versioning functionalities can be a good idea.

Computational Unit with Interpreter The CU with interpreter represents an individual instance of an interpreter running on a CU, which is able to exchange information with interpreters on other CUs or with the environment.

While it makes sense to logically centralise the two repository entities, as well as the MA, it is also possible to distribute these components, as long as content consistency can be kept. Besides introducing the four entities, we also identified a number of standard activities for deployment of BMs in a CU Collective. A typical deployment process, as shown in Figure 2.15, consists of four sequential activities.

Selection consists of identifying a number of BMs in the BM Repository. This step would be triggered by the MA. The trigger could be issued either by a human operator or through an automated mechanism, for example a scheduling process. The employed BMs should be formulated in a way that abstracts from a concrete environmental situation, e. g. through the use of model parameters instead of statically encoded identifiers, which is essential for the re-use of BMs.

Mapping assigns an interpreter to each of the selected BMs based on suitable criteria, i. e. proximity to a certain entity, utilisation or technical compatibility. Additionally, configuration parameters are mapped to concrete values, depending on information on the environment's situation. We refer to this as *static* configuration. The alternative is *dynamic* configuration, where configuration is defered until the BM has been activated and then triggered using a start event that contains the necessary configuration data. Although the mapping step can be automated to a large degree (depending on the concrete use case and availability of environmental data), the MA has to be consulted as a last resort to resolve any arising ambiguities. Results of the mapping step are BMs, ready to be interpreted in the context of a certain environmental situation and on a single, specific interpreter.

Transmission transfers the mapped BMs to the assigned interpreters, running in the distributed CU collective. Before interpreting a BM it has to be ensured that any necessary FC, which is used by a BM, is available at the responsibly interpreter. An opportunity for this presents itself at the end of the transmission phase, where an interpreter could analyse the model dependencies, retrieve the required FCs from the FC Repository and subsequently install them. Alternatives to this strategy are discussed subsequently.

Activation is the final activity, during which BM instances are created for the BMs that have been transmitted to the respective interpreters. On completion of this step, the collective is ready for operation. Operation usually commences by triggering the collective using a start event. The removal of BMs from the interpreters is not depicted in the process but could occur implicitly on termination of the individual BM instances.

Dependency Resolution of FCs Before a BM can execute an action provided by an FC, the FC needs to be available for the system. Activating the correct FC within an interpreter is a multi-step process: firstly, an identifier for the required FC needs to be determined. Then, the identifier needs to be resolved, which would include a query and retrieval process at a repository. Subsequently, the retrieved FC needs to be installed and started. It is also possible that FCs depend on other FCs, additionally complicating this process.

There are several places where dependencies on an FC could be declared, and there are several points in a BM lifecycle where dependencies could be resolved and FCs loaded. Useful strategies for the specification of FCs can be:

Use convention Calling of FCs can be done by convention. For example, using a previously agreed upon standard set of identifiers shared between execution platform and model.

Declared by BM FC dependencies can be explicitly declared as part of the BM persistent storage, in-memory or representation format.

Given by expression syntax The syntax for calling FCs can integrate an identifier for the FC to be used.

The times for resolving dependencies and loading are independent of how or where dependencies are specified, and the following points in time have been identified as feasible.

Interpreter startup There is a fixed set of FCs loaded during startup of the interpreter and available over its whole lifetime.

Model deployment time FCs are resolved at model deployment time and unloaded once the model is removed from the interpreter. In case that an interpreter shares FCs between executing BMs, an FC is unloaded once the last model with dependencies on the FC is removed.

Model start time FCs are resolved just prior to the start of the model and removed as soon as the model is stopped or when the last model, using the specific FC, stops.

Lazy Initialisation An FC is resolved on the first call issued by the model. The FC is unloaded after a certain time of inactiveness.

It might be beneficial to combine FC loading and unloading strategies. Using deployment time dependency resolving together with a lazy, on-demand loading and unloading approach can be suitable for models with a long running time. For example, if a model runs for half a year, with a single action being executed shortly before the model terminates, it does not make sense to keep the respective FC in-memory for the whole time.

Maintaining the Collective Maintaining a collective of interpreters in a purely decentralised manner is the approach advocated by the autonomic systems engineering community, and we demonstrated the feasibility of this strategy [56]. Although this scheme provides better support for dynamic network topologies, together with less configuration overhead than approaches based on static configuration, it can be beneficial to introduce centralised elements like the two repositories and the MA depicted in Figure 2.15. As the functions provided by these entities are required in either case, bringing them together in a common location might have operational advantages within large ICT infrastructures, e. g. for enterprise production networks or telecommunication operators.

In addition to discussing system architecture, we need to investigate how the employed entities communicate. The requirements for the communication mechanisms and protocols vary with the participating communication partners, e. g. they are different when communication takes place between interpreters, or when it takes place between an interpreter and a repository. In the following text, we characterise the different requirements in regard to the underlying communication mechanisms and protocols.

Between Interpreters BM instances are able to send external events to one another as well as to receive external events from other instances. This message exchange takes place between interpreters and requires a reliable message passing protocol, as with some networking technologies events might be lost. For scalability reasons, it might also be beneficial to choose a protocol that supports addressing and/or multicast delivery.

Between MA and Interpreter An MA can control various aspects of an interpreter's function. This encompasses the lifecycle of any interpreted BMs, activation of new BMs, retrieval of runtime status information (e. g. utilisation, active state configurations, deployed FCs, etc.) as well as interpreter lifecycle management (e. g. termination or restart). Therefore, a management protocol for the interpreter collective has the characteristics of a control protocol, combined with commands for runtime information retrieval.

Between Interpreter and BM Repository BMs need to be transmitted between the BM Repository and the interpreter, prior to activation. Protocols used between these two entities would typically fall into the category of file transfer protocols, possibly with a focus on XML, as this is a usual encoding employed for persistent storage formats of BMs. Using a dedicated file transfer protocol guarantees that larger amounts of text can be transmitted reliably between the entities.

Between Interpreter and FC Repository FCs are used by BMs during interpretation. They need to be deployed at the interpreter before being called. The protocol between the interpreter and the FC Repository needs to support binary file transfer as well as retrieval functions for FC identifiers and versions to properly resolve binding issues. Furthermore, the protocol needs to guarantee the correct transmission of large binary files.

Although we found four different kinds of communication mechanisms and each of these types might have its own protocol, it might also be sensible to adopt a single, universal communication infrastructure that fulfils all the necessary requirements. A more concrete advice cannot be given, as there is a large choice of suitable middleware products available and it all depends on the requirements of a specific use case. We will therefore re-visit this topic during the discussion on the use cases in Chapter 5.

2.4 Summary

At the beginning of this chapter, we described the necessary principles for modelling behaviour. We started by describing states and mention initial and final ones. Then we discussed transitions and transition labels, which specify events and expressions used for describing guard conditions as well as action specification. Building upon these basic concepts, we introduced two composition principles: compound states that enable the combination of multiple states in a superstate and partial models, which allow us to re-use parts of a model. The discussion then continued with a description of the *parallel region* principle that enables the specification of concurrent control flows. The description of basic principles concludes with an introduction of the history concept, which enables the storage and re-establishment of a state configurations. Following the description of the basic principles, more concrete aspects of BM interpretation have been investigated. This contains the novel part of our conceptual work, broken down into two sections.

The first section looked at the interpretation of BMs, beginning with the involved artefact types and formats, and continuing with an investigation of event processing and the details of RTC semantics on a algorithmic level. After that, the surprisingly complex mechanisms needed for determination of entered and exited states, while incorporating aspects of concurrency and state containment, are described. Subsequently, we discussed the evaluation of expressions and the role of the native platform language, before continuing with a discussion on FC invocation and the corresponding requirements on the BM interpreter. This section ended with a discussion of potential communication paradigms used for event transmission between CUs.

The second section placed the interpreter in a wider context and discussed questions of BM management. A high-level architecture for deployment of BMs is proposed and four general entities have been described, along with a number of required activities for BM deployment. The section closed with an investigation of the approaches for dependency resolution of FCs and a study of the requirements for communication protocols used to maintain a CU collective.

3 Related Work

Knowledge is of two kinds. We know a subject ourselves, or we know where we can find information upon it.
Samuel Johnson

Efforts from various research areas inspire and impact this thesis, and the following text contains a state of the art analysis of these topics, structured in five sections.

State-Transition Systems Discusses history and current use of formalisms for specification of state-transition systems. As we are employing statecharts as the main formalism for specification of BMs, it is not only important to understand the manifold developments that lead to the features found in the most current incarnations of the formalism (e. g. UML Behavioral State Machines), but also to understand related approaches that complement or extend the statechart formalism. This section is mostly relevant for the discussion of concepts in Chapter 2.

Behaviour Models A BM is more than just the formalism that specifies it. In this section we study approaches for the execution of BMs (interpreted or otherwise) and look at alternative means for modelling executable system behaviour. We are also investigating approaches for transforming and validating models, which is a necessary prerequisite for adaptation of BMs at runtime. This section is relevant in conjunction with the description of concepts in Chapter 2 as well as with Chapter 4, that discusses implementation issues.

Autonomic Systems Engineering Our goal is to support functional scalability by enabling BM adaptation at runtime using interpretation. Although our approach is a promising one, it is only one idea amongst others. People are working in AS engineering to solve the problem of system adaptability using a number of different approaches and we are investigating the relevant ones in this section. It is mostly relevant for the discussion of interpreter implementations in Chapter 4.

Network and Systems Management The use case studies conducted as part of the thesis are situated within the domains of network and systems management. To realistically apply our approach within these domains, we study state of the art management approaches, along with best-practices for modelling the system and network management domains. This section is mostly relevant for the use case studies in Chapter 5.

Performance Benchmarking Within this thesis, we are proposing a benchmark for the determination of the performance of BM execution mechanisms. Therefore, we are investigating existing benchmarks in regard to their applicability for our purposes and with the intention of using them as guiding examples. This section is mostly relevant in conjunction with the description of the performance benchmark contained in Chapter 6.

3.1 State-Transition Systems

In this section, we give an overview of state-transition systems, from the beginning of automata theory to OO formalisms for statecharts. We shortly describe Petri nets, as they are an important alternative formalism for describing state-transition systems. By exploring the foundations of the employed formalism, the reader is able to better place BM features in regard to their historic context and to develop an understanding of the major application areas of the formalisms.

3.1.1 Automata Theory

The roots of all state-transition systems are in automata theory, which stems from the field of switched circuit design. Based on the earlier works of A. Turing, C. Shannon and G. Montgomerie, it was D. Huffman who pioneered this area as part of his doctoral thesis [111] at the MIT in the early 1950s. There are many different kinds of automata, but the most interesting for us are Deterministic Finite Automata (DFA). These automata are called *finite* because they only have a limited number of states, and they are called *deterministic* because the selection of active transitions is done in a deterministic manner. In addition, there are probabilistic automata, Non-deterministic Finite Automata (NFA), and a wide range of other machines/automata that are outside the scope of this thesis. Often the term Finite State Machine (FSM) is used for a certain class of finite automata. The canonical definition of a FSM [109, p. 18] is given as a tuple $\langle Q, \Sigma, \delta, F \rangle$, where Q is a finite set of *symbolic states* (including the initial state q_0), Σ is the input alphabet, $\delta : Q \times \Sigma \rightarrow Q$ is a transition function and F a set of final states.

Building on FSMs, E. Moore and G. Mealy [144, 137] (both working under supervision of C. Shannon at the Bell Telephone Laboratories) developed their automaton concepts. Contrary to the FSMs that are known in formal language theory as *acceptors* or *recognizers*, Moore and Mealy researched *transducers*: machines that are able to transmit output information. Mealy's automata generate an output symbol solely depending on the state that they are in, whereas Moore's automata generate an output symbol based on the current system state and input symbol.

Introduction of Concurrency According to J. Hopcroft [108], the foundation of automata theory had already been laid in the 1960's, and over the course of the next decade a great deal of research emanated, focussing primarily on the areas of language theory and computability. Research in the 1970's was concentrating on the analysis of algorithms, rather than on compilers or programming languages. From a behavioural modelling perspective, the theoretical advances in these years gave rise to understand, calculate and proof the properties of graph-based BMs. An important development took place at the end of the 1970s, when people started to give thought to the possibility of distributed and parallel processing in conjunction with automata theory.

In 1978, C. Hoare wrote *Communicating Sequential Processes* (CSP)[99], in which he introduced the concepts of input guards and parallel commands[1], plus a mechanism for pattern matching on input messages. C. Hoare defined parallel commands, assuming communication between the processes via shared memory. Five years later, the idea of communicating concurrent processes was adapted to FSMs by D. Brand and P. Zafiropulo [33]. They were modelling the operation of communication protocols using communicating FSMs. This approach remains successful and is in wide-spread use today, for example for the specification and test of communication protocols using the Specification and Description Language (SDL).

Input/Output Automata Created as a tool for modelling concurrent, distributed systems, Input/Output (I/O) automata had been devised by N. Lynch and M. Tuttle in the late 1980s [130]. By providing means for specification of actions, automata composition and fairness considerations for execution of concurrent automata, the I/O automata formalism introduces a way to integrate automata with their respective environments.

The work of N. Lynch and M. Tuttle takes inspiration from CSP (such as the understanding that inputs are transmitted instantaneously) but there are differences. For example, I/O automata are not allowed to suppress input actions, as those are under the control of the environment. An automaton needs to explicitly handle such situations as failure cases. The main application of I/O automata is for correctness proofs of distributed algorithms using so-called "executions" – alternating sequences of states and actions, which constitute traces of the automaton execution. The main interest of N. Lynch and M. Tuttle was to decide on the fairness of specific I/O automata-based on given execution traces.

The work on I/O automata continued in miscellaneous directions; one concerned dynamic systems, where automata can be created or destroyed during operation and the set of events in use by the automata can change [9]. A different research direction studied the interaction of discrete and continuous behaviour using hybrid I/O automata [129].

[1]Both are based on concepts previously elaborated by E. Djikstra

Extended Finite State Machines The FSM formalism was generalised into the EFSM formalism in the 1990s by K. Cheng and A. Krishnakumar. The extension concerns the addition of a data space, guard conditions in the form of enabling functions that are evaluated on the data space and update transformations that modify the data space. The EFSM formalism also separates input and output symbols. In [39, Section 2], an EFSM is defined as the 7-tuple $\{S, I, O, D, F, U, T\}$, where S is a set of input states, I and O define the input and output symbols, D is an n-dimensional space $D_1 \times ... \times D_n$, F is a set of *enabling functions* f_i such that $f_i : D \rightarrow \{0, 1\}$, U is a set of *update transformations* u_i such that $u_i : D \rightarrow D$ and T is a transition relation such that $T : S \times F \times I \rightarrow S \times U \times O$. The EFSM formalism adds a basic definition of the ECA transition label discussed on page 23.

Petri Nets The Petri net formalism is a graphical tool that can be used to describe and analyse discrete, distributed systems. It was initially developed by C. Petri and published in his doctoral thesis [153] in 1962.

A Petri net describes a bipartite graph of places (a.k.a states) and transitions. There are so-called *markers*, which are assigned to the places. The dynamic aspects of a Petri net are described by the way in which the markers are changing places in the static graph structure. The definition [22, page 50 and 79] of a Petri net is based on a Petri net graph, which defines the net's structure. Petri net graphs are commonly defined as a triple (S, T, F), with S as a finite set of places, T as a finite set of transitions and F as a so-called *flow relation*, defining the edges of the graph $F \subseteq (S \times T) \cup (T \times S)$. The Petri net is then defined as a 6-tuple (S, T, F, K, W, M_0) by adding properties for marking the net. (S, T, F) needs to constitute a valid Petri net graph, $K : S \rightarrow \mathbb{N} \cup \{\infty\}$ describes the capacity (the number of markers that can be assigned to each place), $W : F \rightarrow \mathbb{N}$ determines the weights of the edges (how many markers are needed in a place for an outgoing transition to fire), and $M_0 : S \rightarrow \mathbb{N}_0$ determines the initial marking of the Petri net. Since its introduction, the formalism has not only been widely adopted with thousands of publications about the definition, application and uses of Petri nets, but it has also been standardised in ISO/IEC 15909. For more information about Petri nets, refer to the "Petri Nets World" web site [274], which serves as a central information repository for the Petri net research community.

3.1.2 Statecharts

The statechart formalism was invented in the 1980's by D. Harel to describe complex, reactive event systems [88]. The formalism builds on higraphs, which are defined in [89, Appendix] as a quadruple $H = (B, \sigma, \pi, E)$, where B is a finite set of so-called *blobs*. E is a binary relation on B defining a set of edges, $E = B \times B$. Composition is given through the sub-blob function σ, which is defined as $\sigma \rightarrow 2^{2^B}$ and assigns each blob x its set $\sigma(x)$ of sub-blobs. $\sigma(x)$ needs to be cycle-free. The partitioning function π is defined as $\pi : B \rightarrow 2^{B \times B}$ and associates with each blob $x \in B$ some equivalence relation $\pi(x)$ on the set of sub-blobs, $\sigma(x)$. Where σ is used to define a composition relationship between the blobs, π can be used to define parallel regions based on equivalence classes. In a recent article [107], we proposed a formalisation for higraphs that is better suited to our work on statechart execution for embedded platforms.

Higraphs can be understood as the main innovation that statecharts contribute to the field of automata theory. Statecharts, or other similar Higraph-based formalisms, contribute two very useful features: composition and concurrency. Both concepts were previously studied on the level of distributed processes, but the use of higraphs allows one to incorporate these aspects into a single automaton.

D. Harel later investigated the modelling of executable objects with statecharts, together with E. Gery [90]. O. Grossman and D. Harel published [84], within which they define syntax and semantics of higraphs in a way that minimises (but not circumvents) interpretation ambiguities. In the same report, they also investigate algorithms that calculate basic properties on statecharts, similar to the ones used in graph theory, e. g. shortest path or Hamiltonian cycles.

Object Orientation The proliferation of OO in the fields of programming languages and modelling techniques led to the study of various approaches that aimed to combine OO with statecharts. A straight-foward approach was carried out by S. Yacoub and H. Ammar, who published a pattern language for statecharts in 1998 [208]. The created language allows engineers to rely on standardised design patterns when implementing functionality as state machines using an OO language.

Other approaches concern the integration of statecharts and OO on a conceptual level. B. Paech and B. Rumpe specify the refinement of automata for behaviour modelling [150] with OO concepts like type specialisation. D. Coleman et al. describe a concept called *Objectcharts* [41], which adapts statecharts to describe the behaviour of objects by identifying transitions with state-changing methods of a modelled object, while states model the lifecycle of the associated object.

OO Statecharts also found acceptance in the field of real-time system engineering as part of the Real-Time Object Oriented Modeling (ROOM) methodology [172]. ROOM prescribes a three-layered architecture consisting of a system, a concurrency and a detail level. Behaviour is modelled on the concurrency level using ROOM-charts, which are based on statecharts. Individual behaviour is assigned to actors, which communicate by transmitting messages over *ports*. This explicit communication model is the main difference to statecharts, where the sending and receiving of events is specified implicitly (events arrive instantaneously). In the late 1990s, it became obvious that UML State Machines can benefit from the integration of ROOM charts [164].

UML State Machines Statecharts have been integrated with the UML under the name of "UML State Machines" [255, Section 15] since the first version of the language. Currently, they can be reckoned as the most feature-rich statechart formalism in use today, which is the reason why the discussion of statechart issues in this thesis is orientated along the set of features defined by UML State Machines.

3.2 Behaviour Models

Within this section we examine existing research related to BMs, including alternative formalisms for behaviour specification, as well as research on BM execution semantics, model checking and model transformation. We are looking at the different techniques for generating code from statecharts and survey the published execution semantics for statechart formalisms. We also take languages for the evaluation of expressions and execution of actions into account. This complements our own work on the concrete semantics of BM interpretation, highlighting issues with UML State Machine execution as well as providing inspiration for possible solutions. We then continue to look at work regarding model transformation and model checking. Both areas are important as a foundation for adaptation of BMs at runtime. Model transformations provide the necessary means to execute an adaptation, and model checking can ensure the correctness of manually provided BMs, or BMs that result from a transformation process. This section also contains a survey of software libraries and commercial tools for BM specification, simulation and code generation. Tool support is a major factor in software engineering; therefore, it is interesting to know which applications are available on the market and what they are able to do. Although we chose to solely adopt statechart-based formalisms, it is necessary to investigate other existing approaches. This section therefore contains an overview of alternative ways for specification of executable system behaviour.

3.2.1 Interpretation and Execution

We found a usage of the term "interpretation" in conjunction with statecharts in an article from the early nineties by J. Ebert [65]. The paper contains a discussion of the operational semantics of statecharts as well as a description of algorithms for their interpretation and validation. It does not explore the implementation from a practical perspective, but discusses the subject theoretically in the context of support for code generation using Computer-Aided Software Engineering (CASE) tools. Although the concept of statechart interpretation exists already for some time, it is only in the last two or three years that BM interpretation has become a hot topic. During the work on this thesis, we saw the emergence of three other interpreters for statecharts. On the one hand the MOCAS Engine by C. Ballagny [16], which interprets UML State Machines based on EMF in a similar manner to the UML interpreter that we created; on the other hand the Apache [215] and the QT [253] SCXML engines. From inspection of the source code, we can conclude that all are maintaining BM in dynamically modifiable runtime structure, as the BMs are completely allocated on the heap and build at runtime. Thus, they could theoretically support the adaptation of an executing BM at runtime, but only the MOCAS system does provide support for this feature. Compared to our implementation of a UML interpreter (see Section 4.4), the MOCAS engine is better integrated with UML, but less sophisticated in regard to the interpretation of conditions or actions. This is also true for the QT SCXML engine, where guard conditions have to be specified using new classes, which derive from a `QAbstractTransition` base class. The Apache engine is more flexible in this regard, allowing a user to change the language and interpretation mechanism for action and condition specifications. It is also the most mature implementation currently available. Due to these two properties, we decided to include this particular engine for one of the implementations, within the use case studies and the performance comparison (see Section 4.5, Section 5.2.2 and Section 6.3.2, respectively).

There is also a large body of research on the interpretation performance of programming languages, but we did not find it to be applicable due to the scope of our problem; the discussion of programming language interpretation performance is usually too closely related to a specific hardware or platform.

Code Generation Although interpretation of statecharts was discussed early in the 1990s, the vast majority of realisations of executable models have been implemented with automatic or semi-automatic code generation approaches, even when BMs are employed for simulation purposes only (as done by, for example, the Rhapsody tool). Code generation from statecharts itself is a well researched problem, e. g. see [119, 147], with applications of the formalism going back to the early 1990s [71] and an active ongoing research on, for example, runtime issues of extensibility and adaptation [167].

The Shlaer-Mellor Method and Executable UML Developed by S. Shlaer and S. Mellor in the late 1980s, this method introduced OO techniques for model-based system analysis and design [178]. Shlaer-Mellor uses FSMs for specification of behaviour, but lacks a single, standard expression language for specification of action expressions. This shortcoming was addressed with the specification of *UML action semantics*, which lead to the Executable UML (xUML). Considered a successor to the Shlaer-Mellor method, xUML was created within the MDA research direction as a UML profile. The profile restricts the UML to elements that have clear execution semantics, while adding the missing action semantics.

Although the employed UML action semantics prescribe the necessary details for integration of the UML with an expression language, they do not specify a concrete syntax (what Sunyé et al. describe as a *surface language* [191, Section 2.4]). This is still left to the user, with universal programming languages, such as C++ or Java or more specific solutions like OCL4X [242], Jumbala [230] or ASL [265, Chapter 10] being employed. Further information on xUML is available from a number of sources, e. g. [138] [265].

Regarding its relation to our work, xUML is an approach that employs BMs for specification of system dynamics, with the goal of generating code from these specifications. We demonstrated the general possibility of interpreting the complete set of features for UML State Machines in Section 4.4; thus, an adaptation of the interpretation approach to the restricted set of xUML features is also possible. The approach complements our work insofar as we did not examine the binding of other UML diagram types (especially ones for data & structural modelling) to expression language statements, and exactly this has been done in the UML action semantics research.

UML State Machine Execution Semantics The execution semantics of UML State Machines are commonly criticised for not being adequately formalised, and a substantial amount of effort has been invested into the identification of weak points in the standard, as well as in the creation of execution semantics using alternative formalisms. Using predicate logic, H. Fecher et al. formulated an execution semantics of UML for model checking purposes [69], although they omitted some pseudo-states (choice, junction, terminate) and nesting constructs (submachines). X. Than et al. [197] specify execution semantics in the Z language, but examine only core statechart constructs (states, transitions, state containment, concurrency). A treatment of the ambiguous semantics of the history concept within UML State Machines is provided by A. Derezińska and R. Pilitowski [52]. Execution semantics have also been studied by mapping to other existing formalisms, e. g. by applying graph rewriting techniques to statecharts [131] or by using Abstract State Machines (ASM) [115]. An exhaustive survey of these research efforts can be found in a technical report [45] compiled by M. Crane and J. Dingel from Queen's University in Ontario, Canada.

3.2.2 Operations on Behaviour Models

Employing an interpretation approach for BM execution is only sensible when making use of more advanced operations that go beyond the straightforward execution provided by generated code. One of the most interesting of such operations is runtime model transformation; by modifying models at runtime, system behaviour can be adapted to a changing operational context.

Model Transformation UML State Machines are commonly modified by means of graph transformations [212, 143]. H. Frank and J. Eder worked on equivalence transformations[2] on statecharts, which could be employed for runtime refactoring purposes [74]. N. Guelfi and B. Ries proposed the Statechart Transformation Language (SCTL) [85].

There are a number of languages available for model transformations on general UML: MOLA [245], UMLX (which has a graphical syntax for specification of transformations) [285], the textual ATLAS Transformation Language (ATL) [243], GReAT [227] and the popular Query View Transformation (QVT) language [246]. This area can currently be regarded as a hot topic, and work is carried out to unify some of these approaches (e. g. see [116] for a discussion on the integration of ATL and QVT). A comparative study on model transformation approaches using graph transformation has been conducted by G. Taentzer et al. and can be found in [194].

Model Checking When allowing for the dynamic runtime adaptation of BMs, it is also necessary to ensure that such a transformation yields correct, interpretable results. Applying techniques from the research field of model checking enables transformations to be verified, as well as model properties and constraints to be supervised at runtime. The Formal Methods & Tools Group at the Institute of Information Science and Technologies in Pisa conducts research on model checking of UML State Machines using the JACK environment [79]. They also investigated the runtime verification of a group of interacting state machines [80]. For a verification of UML 1 statechart core concepts the use of PROMELA and SPIN is described in [124]. An application of the Extended Hierarchical Automaton (EHA) formalism for state machine verification can be found in [61]. Algorithms for the verification of UML State Machines have recently been researched by C. Prashanth and K. Shet [158].

3.2.3 Tool Support

In the realm of BM execution, concrete execution semantics created through code generation seem to be more relevant than formally specified execution semantics. Thus, tool suites are of significant importance for the processes of behaviour design, validation and execution. We briefly describe major tools used for the creation of executable BMs.

Statemate The U.S. American company i-Logix created the Statemate development environment with the help of D. Harel. After acquisition of i-Logix by Telelogic in 2006 and subsequent acquisition of Telelogic by IBM in 2008, Statemate is now sold as part of the IBM Rational tool suite. Statemate is technically obsolete, but

[2]Transformations which do not change the semantics of a model

still relevant for legacy system support and due to its leading role as the first major product employing statecharts. A description of Statemate can be found in [92]. The tool can produce either C [268] or Ada [272] code.

Rhapsody As a successor to Statemate, the Rhapsody tool has a similar history; created at i-Logix and acquired first by Telelogic and later by IBM. Now sold as part of the Rational Toolsuite, it is IBM's flagship application for behaviour modelling. Similar to Statemate, the Rhapsody execution semantics are clearly defined [91]. The product is able to generate code for the C, C++ and Java programming languages.

StateWORKS Created by the swiss company SW Software, StateWORKS allows for visual modelling, simulation and code generation using FSM-based BMs. The product does not support statechart concepts and generates code in C or C++.

Simulink/Stateflow MathWorks Inc. publishes the Stateflow software, which provides a toolset for the design of behaviour using state machines. The tool is used mainly in conjunction with Simulink, a simulation environment for embedded systems, developed by the same company. Stateflow can generate C code from BMs and provides advanced features like concurrency and a history mechanism.

iUML Modeller and Simulator The iUML product from the U.S. American company Kennedy Carter is a toolset for xUML, providing a visual modeller, along with a simulation environment. The software generates code in C, C++, Ada and Java.

BridgePoint Is a toolsuite for xUML, sold by the U. S. American company Mentor Graphics. Targeted at the embedded system market, the product offers a visual development environment for UML models including state machines, along with code generation capabilities for C and C++.

ASADAL The Software Engineering Laboratory at the Pohang University of Science and Technology provides the ASADAL CASE tool [263] for specification and analysis of real-time systems. The tool utilises statecharts for simulation and can generate Java code for prototyping purposes.

Software Libraries The PauWare software is a library for creation of UML 2 State Machines using Java classes. Resulting programs can be executed as BMs, while the employed state machines are constructed at runtime using hard-coded Java statements.

V. L. Maout researches approaches for the integration of automata with the C++ language. The Automaton Standard Template Library (ASTL) is a C++ framework for the programmatic creation of automata [133], which adapts well-known concepts for data structures to automata, i. e. Cursors — an adaptation of the Iterator pattern [75, p. 88 ff.] for traversal of acyclic automata [134].

The Framework for Executable UML (FXU) can transform UML 2 State Machines (and classes) into executable C# code [155]. The authors claim to have complete support for all features of UML State Machines. It is interesting to note that multithreading is used for the execution of concurrent behaviour.

3.2.4 Alternatives for Behaviour Modelling and Execution

Employing UML State Machines might be the most popular method for specification of system behaviour, but there are other approaches that enable behaviour description on a more abstract level than source code. There are languages for directly expressing system behaviour; S. Lee and S. Sluizer created the textual SXL language [125], which is also based on state-transition systems, while Nordstrom et al. propose a combination of two languages: the Behavioral Modeling Language (BML) and the *Action* language [148]. This division into two languages is similar to using UML State Machines and a separate expression language; BML is state machine-based and plays the part of a generic modelling language, while the Action language is responsible for prescribing platform details, like the type system and event structure.

Behavior Trees A technique, mainly researched at the Griffith University's Software Quality Institute by G. Dromey et al., aims at deriving BMs from functional requirements, while keeping a traceable relationship [64]. Using behavior trees, system requirements are systematically refined until arriving at a level where a concrete functional behaviour can be created for the system's components. The formalism has been grounded upon CSP [206] as well as on a Meta-model [81]. A formal, operational semantics has been specified by R. Colvin and I. Hayes [42]. Z. Milosevic and G. Dromey also applied behavior trees to the specification and monitoring of contracts, using a collective of interacting entities in a scenario from the Business-to-Business (B2B) domain [141]. Behavior trees complement our work, as they offer a solid methodology for the creation of BMs from functional requirements. However, they are missing a more concrete elaboration in regard to model execution.

Control Theory Control theory has been used successfully for several decades to formalise the behaviour of dynamic systems. An introduction to the topic can be found, e. g. in the book by J. Hellerstein et al. [95]. Control theory is mainly used for time-continuous systems with a small number of variables and it was a popular topic within cybernetic research on self-organisation in the 1960s and 70s, e. g. as described in [8, 25]. It is still an active research area, as demonstrated by the more current works of M. Kokar et al. [121] and Y. Diao et al. [58] on self-control and autonomic computing. As already argued in the introduction in Section 1.1.1, control theory is a good example for controlling system behaviour using models, but not generally suitable for our purposes.

Software Agents The definition of behaviour is a central topic in the research on agent-based systems. M. Lötzsch et al. developed the Extensible Agent Behavior Specification Language (XABSL) [128], which uses hierarchies of FSMs to specify agent behaviour. A. Sharpanskykh and J. Treur propose a behaviour modelling approach for cognitive agents, which can be transformed into an executable format employing finite state-transition systems [174]. S. Donikian uses hierarchical and concurrent transition systems for the behavioural specification of autonomous agents [63]. Similar to the former approach, a BM is compiled into C++ code, which is then used for simulation of an agent's behaviour. Research in BM interpretation and software agents is considered complementary and both fields can benefit from each other.

3.3 Autonomic Systems Engineering

Many of the concepts examined or developed in this thesis are based on systems engineering research conducted in the autonomic communication [180] or autonomic computing [112] areas. This is particularly true in regard to the integration of BM interpretation mechanisms with network and systems management infrastructures, as presented in the use case studies in Chapter 5. Within this section we are surveying approaches for dynamic adaptation of system behaviour that can serve as guiding examples for our own work. On an architectural level, BM interpreters can be regarded as autonomic components, which is why we included a survey of the current work on component systems that support system adaptation. We also consider our approach as an adaptation of *programming in the large* concepts (e. g. as used for business process composition) to an *programming in the small* environment; therefore, a short overview of this area is also included. The passing of events between operating BMs is critical for the correct operation of a collective of CUs; thus, we investigate communication mechanisms that can be used to transmit events between CUs in various types of communication networks. The section concludes with a survey of a number of other frameworks and relevant architectures that can be used to engineer ASs.

3.3.1 Dynamic System Adaptation

Research on large-scale, distributed systems that can be adapted or are self-adapting to a changing environment has received a large amount of attention within the research community. An overview of adaptive software can be found in [136], and G. Serugendo et al. compiled a state of the art report in regard to self-organisation

[173]. Ö. Babaoğlu et al. describe biological mechanisms that could be utilised for self-organisation purposes in [10]. Self-organisation using software agents was researched by P. Marrow and M. Koubarakis [135] as well as R. Quitadamo and F. Zambonelli [159]. Communication mechanisms that support self-organisation can be found in [165] and [11]. The creation of BMs from an existing system has been researched by S. Uchitel et al. [199].

Autonomic Components There a several approaches to extend the existing body of work on software components [193] towards adaptive systems. We consider the work of C. Herring and S. Kaplan on the application of cybernetic principles to component systems [97] as an early (end of 1990s) ancestor of autonomic components. Autonomic Components are also proposed in [127], using a rule-based approach for component behaviour specification. More recent work by C. Ballagny et al. uses UML 2 State Machine execution for realising the runtime behaviour of adaptive components in the PauWare and MOCAS systems [17, 18].

Apart from research on adaptable runtime behaviour on the level of components, work is also done on the composition of components, supporting dynamic adaptation on the system level. For the field of pervasive computing, C. Becker et al. propose the PCOM system [23], and a similar approach has been developed by D. Sykes et al. [192], employing high-level goals to assemble a collective of interacting software components. A. Bailly et al. describe the hierarchical composition of components, while maintaining a behavioural specification for the whole aggregate [14]. An overview of current technologies and approaches for the modelling of component behaviour and compositions can also be found in the masters thesis of I. Ferdelja [70].

Service Composition There is an established body of research on *programming in the large* approaches for business process/work flow automation and scientific GRID computing [73]. Together with the Business Process Execution Language (BPEL) and the Business Process Modeling Notation (BPMN) standards, these are in wide-spread use for orchestration of services. Alternatively, services are composed without central control using choreography, with the Web Services Choreography Description Language (WS-CDL) as the prime specimen of this genre. The main difference to our approach is that we employ *programming in the small* principles, which require fundamentally different techniques. For more information on BPEL, BPMN and WS-CDL, refer to [244, 213, 287].

System adaptation is researched in the context of service composition by A. Bottaro et al. [29]. P. Michiardi et al. discuss adaptive service composition by means of overlay network rewiring [140], while M. Pistore et al. research Web Service (WS) composition by planning with state-transition systems [156].

3.3.2 Communication Mechanisms

The following examination of relevant approaches for the communication between BM interpreters is motivated by the necessity for a *broadcasting* mechanism that conveys events in a one-to-many fashion between orthogonal parts of a model, see [89, p. 523] and [208, p. 11]. Extending this mechanism to a distributed setting, where events are mediated between multiple models on a single machine or even between multiple distributed model interpreters, leads us to a discussion of group communication mechanisms. We also consider a category of mechanisms where event transport relies on one-to-one communication channels with guaranteed properties.

Reliable Multicast In IP networks, the simplest form of group communication is based on IP broadcast or User Datagram Protocol (UDP) multicast communication [43, p. 128 ff.]. These low-level primitives are provided for network layer communications and do not offer reliability or fragmentation features, i. e. packets can be lost and there is no support for datagrams of a bigger size than the network's MTU. To solve this issue, reliable multicast protocols have been introduced, e. g. [151, 126]. A major issue with reliable multicast concerns scalability, on which O. Ozkasap et al. did an investigation using two popular reliable multicast protocols [149]. Another issue is the protocol deployment within networking devices. To implement a reliable multicast protocol, each networked device within the domain of use needs to implement the protocol in question. Hitherto, none of the existing protocols gained enough clout to be widely deployed.

Application-Level Group Communication A possible solution to this problem are application-layer multicast mechanisms, i. e. [72, 110], where multicast routing, retransmissions and group membership is handled on the application level.

The Horus [162] and Totem [146] group communication systems have been designed in the mid-1990's to support the *virtual synchrony* paradigm. Virtual synchrony guarantees that the total order of messages is the same for all communication partners throughout the local network, which is a crucial requirement for consistency in distributed systems using group communication. A popular framework for group communication is JGroups [19], which is the default mechanism used for data replication in clusters of JBoss application servers. Although JGroups is successfully applied in production environments, its scalability in cluster replication scenarios is limited, as demonstrated by T. Abdellatif et al. [1]. Another popular framework is Spread [6], which concentrates on establishing security measures for the group communication paradigm. Spread scales on an Internet-wide level by using a static configuration approach, sacrificing the flexibility needed for context-adaptive and self-organising applications. Scalability of secure, reliable multicast has also been researched by S. Banerjee and B. Bhattacharjee [20].

We would also like to point out the work of our colleagues C. Reichert and D. Witaszek on the Group Event Notification (GEN) protocol [161]. GEN introduces primitives to select groups based on expressions with operators like $oneof(p)$, which selects exactly one member out of a set p, or $prop(x)$, which selects all members where x is true. We also contributed to the field with the Autonomic Reliable Multicast (AutoRM) mechanism that supports the $oneof(p)$ operator using a reliable multicast scheme with declarative group membership [102].

Message- and Notification Services Event dissemination can also be carried out using notification services, for example the ones that follow PubSub principles. These are well-understood, and there is a large body of work done on the subject. An overview of PubSub systems and approaches has been compiled by P. T. Eugster et al. [68].

In the enterprise computing domain, the task of event transport and dispatching is often left to a MOM. Typically, such systems support more advanced features, such as message persistence (useful when sender and receivers of a message are only sporadically connected to the network). Popular examples are the CORBA Notification Service and Java Message Service (JMS) [266, p. 610 ff.] compatible queueing systems like Apache ActiveMQ. Notification services are also a central component within an ESB or Cloud Computing infrastructure, i. e. the Amazon Simple Notification Service [214].

Contract Based Communication We deviate from the meaning of *contract*, as coined by B. Meyer [139] and being widely used in Software Engineering, as we do not use pre- and post-conditions. The goal is still similar: to specify constraints between interacting system components and to discover when these constraints are being violated. The usage of contracts for cooperating objects was researched by R. Helm et al. [96] as well as later by M. Schrefl et al. [170]. J. Strassner published an application of contracts in runtime system design to interacting components in telecommunication systems [185]. We later utilised contracts as a means of establishing trust and control for service collaborations in AS [55]. In our view, contractual connections are similar to the *managed communication channels* concept of E. Stoyanov et al. [182], where the channel is associated with metadata that captures mutual agreements between cooperating parties in a machine-understandable language.

3.3.3 Frameworks

A popular method for researching AS engineering concepts consists of the development of prototypical software implementations, either for proof-of-concept purposes or as a preliminary stage for software products. A typical example for this is the ACE Toolkit [222], which is described in Section 4.3.

One of the most important AS engineering implementations is the IBM Autonomic Computing Toolkit [113]. Its major use is the management of computing infrastructures in the context of IBM products. Management processes are specified and executed using JavaScript [113, Section 7.1], and communication is done using the CBE format, which defines the structure and content of exchanged events [113, Section 4][258].

Autonomia, also an autonomic computing environment, is presented by X. Dong et al. in [62]; a description of self-configuration using this system is given in [38]. In Autonomia, a user can edit application templates that define compositions of distributed components, along with management requirements. Mobile agents are used during the runtime of the application to monitor these requirements and adapt the system for self-healing and self-optimisation purposes. In [12], Ö. Babaoğlu et al. explain the AntHill framework that employs mobile agents to achieve adaptability and self-organisation in peer-to-peer systems.

The autonomic self-healing of J2EE clusters using the component-based JADE framework is described by S. Bouchenak et al. in [30]. The approach relies on the novel FRACTAL component model, which adds runtime introspection and reconfiguration capabilities to the components and aims at improving the self-repair capabilities of systems by means of architectural reconfiguration. The Rainbow framework [76] also enables an architecture-based runtime system adaptation. The approach understands architectures as models that are transformed into a more concrete operational representation of a system at runtime. M. Agarwal et al. describe the AutoMate framework in [2]. It can be used to compose and adapt GRID applications in a context-aware fashion. This is achieved on an architectural level by means of composition and reconfiguration of autonomic components and by employment of the so-called RUDDER deductive reasoning engine to control the process.

In [200], the authors propose a process-based approach for the adaptation of existing (legacy) systems, using an engine that is called WorkFlakes. The approach can be used as an external component to adapt existing systems. It relies on the existence of a set of suitable effectors (mobile agents) and sensors (so-called Probes and Gauges) with the target system. A framework for reconfiguration of component behaviour by means of statecharts is proposed by X. Elkorobarrutia et al. under the name *FraC* [66]. In FraC, statecharts define the runtime behaviour of system components, which are encoded as Java classes and instantiated during runtime. The authors also investigate the adaptation of such systems by means of class inheritance. This enables them to change a component's BM at instantiation time, but does not allow them to adapt BMs on the level of model elements while they are executing.

3.4 Network and Systems Management

In this section, we are studying research that is relevant to the application of our approach in the network and systems management domains. We first look at current research in regard to systems supervision and monitoring, which are the major areas picked for the use case studies. We then take a look at Information Models (IM) and Data Models (DM). This impacts several aspects of our work: the event format that is used by CUs to communicate, the context format that is used to store local data, the definition of the expression language, the definition of the action language, the process of mapping the BMs to a CU collective, and a potential usage of BMs for describing dynamic aspects in IMs. The idea of shifting management processes into the network itself is not novel; therefore, we survey existing *management in the network approaches* in relation to our approach, which is called *Model Based Integrated Management* (MBIM). The section concludes by looking at the field of policy-based network management, which is considered as having the biggest impact for current research on autonomic network management.

The current state of the art in network management is captured from a historical perspective in an article by G. Pavlou [152], while A. Gupta describes developments with a forward-looking perspective [86]. Research challenges are detailed in a 2007 article from A. Pras et al. [157].

3.4.1 System Regulation

A general background for system supervision can be taken from cybernetics. Within this field, the connection between system regulation and BMs had already been explored in the 1960s and 70s [8, 44].

Supervision The planning of system supervision using BMs was thoroughly investigated by P. H. Deussen et al. [53, 54]. The determination and adaptation of an FSM-based BM to a running system has been researched by G. Denaro et al. [51], while A. Schumann and Y. Pencolé researched supervision of event-driven systems based on a state-transition model [171].

Monitoring Monitoring is the primary means for observing the operation of a network. Although the basic mechanism for monitoring IP networks seems to be set in stone (SNMP), there is still a considerable amount of research conducted on the subject. A novel paradigm known as On-Demand Monitoring (ODM) has been researched by R. Chaparadza. The approach uses a composition language that allows to flexibly program monitoring sessions [37]. M. Andreolini et al. examine a number of models for monitoring network load with regard to their applicability for systems with autonomic decision making capabilities [7]. The monitoring of networks using mobile agents has been researched by S. Manvi and P. Venkataram [132]. Besides our own work on intrinsic monitoring [104], L. Shi and A. Davy from the TSSG[3] are also researching this subject [176, 175], and we recently wrote a shared paper on the subject [177].

3.4.2 Information and Data Models

There are clear differences between an IM and a DM. For example, in [264] an IM is described as "[...] primarily useful for designers to describe the managed environment, for operators to understand the modeled objects, and for implementors as a guide to the functionality that must be described and coded in the DMs. [...] IMs can be implemented in different ways and mapped on different protocols. They are protocol neutral. An important characteristic of IMs is that they can (and generally should) specify relationships between objects", whereas "Compared to IMs, DMs define managed objects at a lower level of abstraction. They include implementation- and protocol-specific details, e. g. rules that explain how to map managed objects onto lower-level protocol constructs." (Changes to the original text are set in [square braces].)

A BM is typically interpreted in conjunction with context data. In the network and systems management domain, this data would usually conform to a DM, which in turn might have been derived from an IM. The idea is to use a single IM for the overall network and to map this model to the different implementations used for the individual subsystems, thus creating a number of data models. For model integration purposes, the usage of ontologies has been researched by a number of groups, e. g. see [49, 186]. Employing a metamodel for model integration is discussed by B. Zakaria et al. [210].

Common Information Model (CIM) The CIM has been standardised by the Distributed Management Task Force (DMTF) as a general model for managing complex IT systems. It is structured using OO concepts and has an XML format [228], which is used with the Web-Based Enterprise Management (WBEM) standard technologies [229]. WBEM has particular significance, as Microsoft products conform to this standard.

Directory Enabled Networks – next generation (DEN-ng) The DEN-ng IM is being actively developed and is currently at version 7.1. It aims at capturing all necessary aspects of network management, from business requirements to the control of concrete router configurations using OO techniques and design patterns — this includes capturing dynamic characteristics as well as the behaviour of managed entities using FSMs. DEN-ng has been created by J. Strassner in UML, and a number of publications on the subject exist, for example [183, 189].

[3]Telecommunications Software & Systems Group at the Waterford Institute of Technology, Ireland

Shared Information and Data Model (SID) An IM standardised by the TeleManagement Forum (TM Forum) [273], the SID provides business and system view definitions for designing and managing telecommunications networks. SID is based on an early version of DEN-ng (version 3.5), and Z. Boudjemil et al. criticise the model as not adequate for autonomic management [31, p. 14–15] with the following words: "*[...]* the SID is limited with regard to modelling autonomic environments in four main areas. First, the SID policy framework is inflexible compared to that of DEN-ng; see *[59, 184]* for more details. Second, the business-to-network translation (and vice versa) was not realised in any tangible form in the SID. Third, important concepts such as context are completely missing from the SID. Finally, the SID does not provide artefact *[sic]* for the design of the entities behaviour such as state machines." (Changes to the original text are set in *italic* font and in [square braces].)

Structure of Managed Information (SMI) The IETF created SMI [250] as a DM for usage with the SNMP Management Information Base (MIB). It is one of the most widespread DM, but also one of the most simple ones. SMI is tightly coupled to SNMP, and research has been conducted on a protocol-agnostic language as a successor to SMI, called SMIng [270]. However, the working group closed, and this work was abandoned.

3.4.3 Management in the Network

Shifting network management from a centralised system to decentralised components located within (or close to) the network core is an idea that has been examined in various other contexts than BM interpretation. A similar approach as Intrinsic Monitoring, but without the BM interpretation aspects, has been studied by D. Pezaros under the term In-Line Measurement [154]. In [36], K. Calvert et al. propose the Ephemeral State Processing approach, which facilitates a lightweight programmable service within routers to achieve management in the network. The usage of mobile agents for network management has been widely researched by various groups, e. g. [168, 198]. Work has also been carried out in the area of active networking regarding the application of programmability to individual network nodes, see for example the article of D. Tennenhouse and D. Wetherall [196].

3.4.4 Towards Autonomic Network Management

As communication networks become more and more complex, engineers and researchers aspire further automation of network management by incorporating higher levels of abstraction within the management processes. This supports humans to take decisions on management actions or even allow machines to decide, instead of human operators. R. Cronk et al. researched the application of expert systems for short term as well as long term planning operations within a network, specifying an autonomic, context-aware scheme [46] as early as 1988. Researchers in the field of Artificial Intelligence (AI) also consider network management as an application domain. For a discussion of various approaches, refer to the article by G. Kumar and P. Venkataram [123]. From our perspective, the area of autonomic network management emerged from the PBM field around 2005–2006. The following text is structured in two parts, with the earlier work on PBM in the first one and recent approaches in the second part.

Policy Based Management According to the article by R. Boutaba and I. Aib [32], the work of a group lead by M. Sloman at the Imperial College of Science and Technology, University of London, did create the PBM concept. For an explanation of the original work, refer to [179]. A more current overview of the field can be found in J. Strassner's book on PBM [184]. An analysis of the manifold PBM models and languages can be found in [4], and a specific investigation of the popular Ponder language can be found in [47]. The use of policies for automated configuration management has also been studied in the context of active networks by A. Konstantinou et al. [122].

Approaches for Autonomic Management In a "lessons-learned" article [145], R. Mortier and E. Kiciman discuss some general considerations regarding autonomic approaches, based on studying previous techniques employed for automation and adaptation in network management. S. van der Meer et al. strive for a clarification of terms and concepts in a 2006 article [202]. J. Strassner created the concept of the Policy Continuum; this was then formalised in the TSSG enabling the integration of policy languages using DEN-ng [48, 114]. A prototype of the policy continuum has also been created [201], and work on this subject lead to the Foundation, Observation, Comparison, Action and Learning Environment (FOCALE) [187]. The DEN-ng policy model used within FOCALE is described in [190, 189].

Based on PBM research, R. Bahati et al. created a system to manage an Apache web server using autonomic principles, facilitating policies for the control operations [13]. The JADE [30] successor TUNE uses policies to specify deployment and reconfiguration processes based on components [35]. We also contributed a publication [103] in this area that proposes an autonomic regulation approach for AS. The mechanism makes use of TMPL for monitoring a system and policies for controlling a resulting adaptation within the system.

3.5 Performance Benchmarking

To compare the performance of different methods for solving a single problem, it is common engineering practice to exercise the different methods in question using a set of standard examples. Collections of such standard examples, or data sets, are usually referred to as *benchmarks suites*. There is a large body of work on the usage of state-transition systems in benchmarks, with a wide spectrum of applications. We will survey the existing work by investigating three distinct areas: benchmarks used for logic synthesis, the utilisation of statecharts and general performance benchmarks. This work is of importance for our quantitative assessment of the interpreter implementations. Most of the publications on state-transition systems for benchmarking are referring to quite simple automata or are using a single, exemplary statechart. As we will see, this is not sufficient for the thesis, as we strive to investigate very specific aspects of an execution system in far greater detail as provided by the current state of the art.

Usage for Logic Synthesis The usage of FSM-based benchmarks has a long history in the field of logic synthesis. This research area is concerned with the mapping of logical expressions, usually formulated in a higher-level language like the Very High Speed Integrated Circuit Hardware Description Language (VHDL)[240], to connections of transistors using a given hardware technology. Benchmarks suites for application in this area usually contain one or more FSMs because of the importance of the formalism for designing control systems. Besides employing FSMs, such kinds of benchmark suites encompass designs for standard elements (e. g. shift-register or adder).

The most popular collection of benchmarks of this type is referred to as the Association for Computing Machinery (ACM) Special Interest Group on Design Automation (SIGDA) benchmarks, or as the Microelectronics Center of North Carolina (MCNC) benchmarks [209]. They are somewhat dated[4], but still widely referenced. The ACM/SIGDA benchmarks are archived by the North Carolina State University at the Collaborative Benchmarking and Experimental Algorithmics Laboratory site [254]. The benchmark suites have been compiled at meetings of the International Symposium on Circuits & Systems (e. g. the ISCA89 benchmark suite); at various High-Level Synthesis workshops (for example the HLSynth91 benchmark suite); or at the Logic Synthesis Workshops (e. g. LGSynth93). For the usage in the area of Field-Programmable Gate Array (FPGA) hardware, the Programmable Electronics Performance Corporation (PREP) benchmark suite is often utilised, which contains, among other benchmarks, two definitions of state machines [118, Table 1].

The Utilisation of Statecharts in Performance Benchmarks There is no widely accepted benchmark suite that uses statecharts for performance assessment and we found only a very small number of publications documenting the utilisation of statecharts for this purpose. Among the employed statecharts is the calculator

[4]Most of them are older than 15 years

example from the book on statecharts by M. Samek [166] and a statechart that is constructed from the *Generalized Railroad Crossing* problem [158, 94].

General Performance Benchmarks For the general performance assessment of computing systems, there are a number of well-known standard benchmark suites. For example, the SPEC-cpu2000 benchmark suite [269] or the Dhrystone benchmark [204]. Such benchmarks will asses the performance of a hardware platform and are not suitable for evaluating software execution mechanisms. For this area, other benchmarks have been devised, e. g. the DaCapo benchmark suite [277], which is intended as a tool for benchmarking the runtime performance of the Java programming language in relation to implementation aspects like memory management and the binding to the underlying computer architecture.

An interesting approach for designing benchmarks is to generate them. S. Ramesh reports on using a statechart generator to achieve this, but does not disclose further details [160]. A similar approach is followed by L. Jóźwiak et al. by generating FSMs based on user-supplied parameters [117], which allows them to customise certain aspects of the generated benchmark (e. g. number of states, relation of states to transitions, etc.) and to generate a wide variety of FSMs. Within the proposed benchmark, we are also making use of generative approaches for creating some of the employed models.

We did not find any suitable benchmark suite that will allow us to assess the performance of a statechart execution engine accurately and in necessary detail. Either the benchmarks are defined too simple, without taking statechart specific features into account (e. g. the ones that are based on FSMs) or they are using statecharts, but only in the form of a single, exemplary model. This is not sufficient for an in-depth study of the various aspects of an execution system. General performance benchmarks are interesting as a documentation of the current best-practices for benchmark design, but, again, these benchmark suites are not specific enough for our purposes. The current state of the art in this area forces us to create our own, more suitable benchmark, and this is where our work most obviously advances the current state of science.

3.6 Summary

This chapter captured the state of the art of research related to the thesis, structured into five sections.

We are using the statechart formalism, which has been influenced by a number of other formalisms and the first section gave a historic overview of state-transition systems, from automata theory to UML State Machines. Current state of the art for such formalisms are UML Behavioral State Machines, which is the paradigm that we employ throughout the thesis, although not all of the implementations that we discuss are using its complete set of features.

The second section discussed research related to BMs, in regard to interpretation, execution, transformation, the available tools and specification alternatives. We are significantly contributing to the current state of the art of BM interpretation through the concepts established in Section 2.2 as well as through the quantitative assessment of our approach as described in Section 6.3. The discussion on model transformation and model checking is included to complete the picture in regard to the use case studies in Chapter 5, as is the description of the state of the art tooling. The overview of alternative approaches for BM modelling and execution is included to allow readers to clearly separate our approach from others.

The third section investigated AS engineering topics by discussing recent advances in the area of dynamic system adaptation and composition. Our work contributed novel insights in this area, especially in the area of interpretation performance. It also provides novel tools (the performance benchmark described in Chapter 6, that can be used to evaluate AS). An important aspect of BM-driven systems is communication, where we adopt state of the art approaches and technology for the interpreter implementations. Therefore, this section contains an overview of the area. It also contains an overview of implementation technologies and frameworks.

A survey of the network and systems management application domains is contained in the fourth section. This is relevant for the qualitative assessment of our approach within the use case studies in Chapter 5, as we directly utilise the described best practices and state of the art research for information modelling and system management. We are advancing the current state of science in these fields and our work contains novel contributions to the areas of system supervision and monitoring as well as autonomic network and system management.

The fifth section contains a discussion of the state of the art research on performance benchmarking. We found no suitable benchmark for assessing the performance of BM interpretation or execution systems. Thus, the benchmark defined in Chapter 6 constitutes a novel contribution to the field of performance benchmarks.

4 Implementations

What I cannot create, I do not understand.
Richard P. Feynman

Four different implementations have been carried out, and the resulting prototypes have been used to study aspects of our approach. Each of the prototypes has a different focus. Our earliest implementation serves mostly as an inspiration and primer for the later interpreter prototypes. It is used as an engine for the TMPL runtime system and employs interpreted state machines for matching patterns in XML streams. The TMPL engine shows the feasibility of the general BM interpretation concept and demonstrates how BM adaptation can be used to optimise system behaviour at runtime.

The second implementation is the ACE toolkit, a component-based framework for creating autonomic applications using interpreted state machines. Component behaviour results from runtime interpretation of BMs, which are adapted by ACEs in reaction to changes in the environment of an ACE. The ACE toolkit implementation demonstrates the communication facilities needed to operate a CU collective, along with sophisticated mechanisms for FC binding and invocation. Furthermore, our work on the toolkit helped us to more clearly identify the general software architecture that such an approach requires.

For the third implementation, we created a BM interpreter for UML State Machines. The reason behind this is found in the richness of the UML State Machine formalism, which covers a large number of features beneficial for state machine execution. To gain insight into the implementation of mechanisms for the widest range of possible features, we implemented the complete set of features for UML 2 Behavioral State Machines based on an Ecore representation of the UML models.

The final implementation is a BM execution platform that uses an SCXML engine. This prototype concentrates on issues of BM initialisation, FC dependency resolution and CU management. The motivation for this prototype is to enable applications for *management in the network* — we want to shift the responsibility for network and systems management processes from dedicated and centralised network management systems to the elements that constitute the network itself. Thus, this prototype supports the thesis by demonstrating potentials paths for the integration of our approach with systems that are common to the infrastructure found in the network and systems management domains.

To better explain the differences of the various implementations, we start by establishing a basic set of BM features and a generic software architecture for an interpreter. The implementations can then be compared with this generic model, allowing us to not only highlight the focus of each prototype, but also to help us with the definition of a performance benchmark suite in Chapter 6.

4.1 An Interpreter for Behaviour Models

For comparing the different implementations, it is useful to first have an understanding of the general functionality that a BM interpreter needs to fulfil. Therefore, we are establishing a set of basic BM features and then continue to discuss the generic architecture of such runtime interpretation mechanisms. We will start by reviewing the basic properties that characterise BMs.

Graph Properties As discussed in the previous chapter, the state-transition structure of BMs forms a graph. This graph has certain properties: it is usually sparse, meaning that the real number of edges is much less than the possible number of edges. BMs often contain cycles, which are the equivalent of loops in traditional programming languages. Transitions are always directed. These properties directly impact the data structures used for model storage and we suggest to use a storage model based on referencing (e. g. a linked structure of objects).

BMs as Composition Glue for FCs The reason for introducing BMs is to capture the application logic in a format that is meaningful for humans and accessible to machines. By abstracting from detail, complexity can be hidden: this is done by encapsulating technicalities into FCs, which, in turn, are used by the BM. We see BMs as a lightweight orchestration mechanism on top of the FCs that do the *heavy-lifting* in regard to computational operations. Therefore, most processing time would be spent within the FC, not in the interpretation of the BM and the BM specification language should cover orchestration-like statements, rather then statements geared towards programming.

Explicit Control Flow The control flows within an application should be expressed explicitly in a BM. This allows the use of parallelism within the application logic but also ensures that we have a reactive system, which enters a quiescent state[1] at regular intervals during the interpretation. Quiescence is a crucial property for runtime adaptation of BMs and also necessary for model serialisation, i. e. for migration or persistent storage of a model during its interpretation.

The Application Domain Although an understanding of the application domain is not required at this point in the text, it is helpful to be reminded of the

[1] A system state where no active processing takes places

professional field in which the approach is being applied. Most of our research has its roots in autonomic systems engineering, and we apply BM interpretation to the field of network and systems management. The following text therefore puts an emphasis on non real-time, loosely-coupled communication mechanisms and should be read keeping a distributed systems setting in mind.

4.1.1 Fundamental Behaviour Model Features

A BM needs to be uniquely identifiable and the format has to be understandable by the interpreter. The following text provides a set of BM features that we found to be fundamental for runtime BM interpretation. These features should be reflected in any BM format used for specification of runtime-interpretable BMs.

States The employed BM format has to support the basic notion of States and has to uniquely identify states with a name. Initial states and final states need to be marked explicitly (see Section 2.1.1).

Compound States States are allowed to be contained within each other. There exists a composition hierarchy similar to the one defined by the higraph formalism [84, Section 2.1]. A state is considered active once a system has reached the state or any of its substates (see Section 2.1.4).

Transitions need to support the specification of ECA transition labels. Transitions are triggered by a single event, can be constrained through a single guard condition and might contain a single action specification (see Section 2.1.2 – 2.1.3). We need BMs to be deterministic; thus, event labels on the outgoing transitions of any state have to be unique. All of the ECA label components (event, guard condition and action) are optional. In case that an event trigger is omitted, the transition is considered an ε-transition, which is active as soon as the interpreter has finished entering the transition's source state. They can be self-referencing, might run laterally to the composition hierarchy and connect states in different parts of the hierarchy tree (e. g. the transition labelled **14** in Figure 2.9 that crosses the composition hierarchy between A and B, as well as B and C) and might connect more than one state, for example when forking a control flow (see Section 2.1.5). The state-transition graph that is defined by a BM has to be directed and traversable in a deterministic fashion[2].

Events Messages that are transmitted between a BM and its environment or internally within a BM are required to have a name and might optionally include a payload. The use of timed events needs to be supported (see Section 2.1.2.1).

[2]The selection of the transition that fires when a state has been completely entered needs to be unambiguous.

Conditions Guard Conditions are used as part of the transition labels and formulated in a suitable language as expression statements that evaluate to a boolean value (see Section 2.1.2.3). A suitable expression language needs to support arithmetic, boolean and comparison operators, as well as the specification of evaluation prioritisation using parentheses. The language also needs statements for accessing data in the context and for specification of literal values.

Context Features for the access to context information (see Section 2.1.2.2) must be available in the language employed for condition and action statements. We require that variables in the context data are identified by name and can be read and written to. Context data should be typed with support for boolean values, integer numbers, floating-point numbers and at least a primitive *list* data type for the dynamic insertion and removal of values.

Actions There are three distinct activities that can trigger the execution of actions: firing a transition, entering a state and leaving a state. Action statements are specified in a suitable language and we postulate the existence of two default actions for each interpreter. The first action concerns the ability to send and parametrise[3] events, while the second action concerns the invocation of FCs, including the binding of input parameters and storage of the return values in the context (see Section 2.2.5.1).

Parallelism Specially marked regions of the composition hierarchy have to be interpreted in parallel. There exists a disjoint partitioning of the composition hierarchy similar to the one in [84, Section 2.1]. We require the use of constructs that manipulate the control flow cardinality, like the fork and join constructs, to specify this (see Section 2.1.5).

History We require the deep history construct, which supports the storing of an active state configuration and the re-establishment of a previously stored configuration (see Section 2.1.6). The history mechanism is supposed to store the complete state configuration from a given root state down to all leaf states of the composition hierarchy.

4.1.2 Generic Interpreter Architecture

Building upon the fundamental set of BM features introduced in the previous section, we are now able introduce a generic architecture for a BM interpreter. Although each of our implementations employes a different set of technologies and is created with a different goal in mind, we found that their architectures are largely similar. Using this experience, we created Figure 4.1, which depicts a breakdown of an interpreter application into distinct subsystems, showing the connections between the different

[3] E.g. set a payload or a destination address

parts and the responsibilities of each of the components. We will use this diagram when investigating the features of each of the concrete implementations and while discussing how they are different from one another.

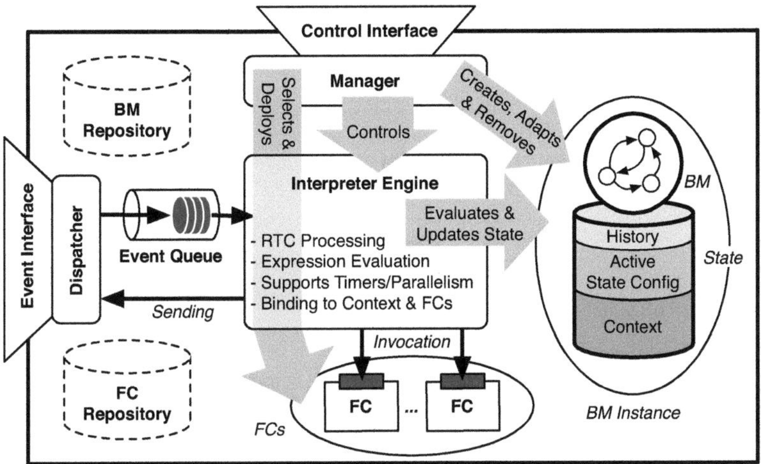

Figure 4.1: Generic BM Interpreter Architecture

The figure shows a CU running a single interpreter application. It is a system with two interfaces to the environment: the Control Interface and the Event Interface. For illustrative purposes, we show only a single BM instance where instances of several BMs could be used. The following text explains the architecture in more detail.

Event Interface Communication messages that pertain to the behaviour of the BM and that are exchanged with other entities in the environment (e. g. BMs that are part of a collaborating collective) are transmitted using this interface. The interface acts as a gateway between the environment and the locally active BMs and thus has to to be compatible with the messaging protocols and formats employed within the overall BM collective (see Section 2.2.6).

Dispatcher The Event Interface establishes a connection to the environment, but this is not sufficient in cases where the CU collective is widely spread and internet-wide communication technologies need to be employed (see Section 2.2.6.4). The Dispatcher subsystem enables the use of routable event messages by taking care of event addressing. When accepting events for sending, the

Dispatcher needs to differentiate between internal and external events and transmits the external ones via the Event Interface, whereas the internal ones are added to the interpreter's Event Queue.

Event Queue BMs are interpreted in a stepwise fashion, one event at a time. The event queue buffers external events until they can be processed by the Interpreter Engine. It offers the *getNextExternalEvent()* method used by Algorithm 1 as discussed in Section 2.2.2.

Interpreter Engine The Interpreter Engine executes the logic for a stepwise evaluation of the BM, by following the RTC semantics described in Section 2.2.2. It evaluates conditional expressions, action statements (see Section 2.2.4) and the context data associated with BM instances. It also provides support for timed events (see Section 2.1.2.1) and the BM concurrency features (see Section 2.2.3). To conduct BM interpretation using RTC semantics, the Interpreter Engine needs to maintain the state associated with each BM instance. This includes the context data, the active state configuration and the history state configuration (see Section 2.2.3). Functionality that is contained in FCs is triggered by action statements evaluated in the Interpreter Engine. The invocation process (see Section 2.2.5) relies on previously established binding information (see Section 2.2.1).

Control Interface Management access to the BM interpreter is given through the Control Interface, allowing an MA (see Section 2.3) to control the interpreter. It is understood as a gateway between the environment and the interpreter, which transmits messages that pertain to the management of the interpreter, not the behaviour of the BMs.

Manager The Control Interface establishes a connection to the MA, but does not implement the concrete logic needed to control the interpreter. This is done by the Manager subsystem, which provides lifecycle management capabilities for the interpreter as well as handling BMs and FCs.

An interpreter application can potentially execute a large number of BM instances in parallel. These instances need to be created, might be adapted during runtime and have to be removed when finished with execution. During runtime, the MA might also be interested in utilisation data and information about the progress of certain BM instances. Thus, the Manager needs to provide information about all existing BM instances and the active state configuration of BMs.

Similarly, a Manager needs to maintain the FCs used by the BMs instances. It needs to resolve the dependencies by analysing binding information and subsequently selecting and deploying the appropriate FCs (see discussion on dependency resolution in Section 2.3).

BM Repository BMs are stored in a repository that is accessed by the Manager to retrieve the BM prior to instantiation (see Section 2.3). We included the BM Repository in the diagram as a local subsystem, but in a larger setup it might also be beneficial to retrieve BMs from a central, remote BM Repository (indicated by the dashed lines).

FC Repository FCs are also stored in a repository that is accessed by the Manager when solving the dependencies of a BM (see Section 2.3). Again, our architecture proposes to use a local subsystem, with the option of using a distributed setup.

4.2 The TMPL Engine

The TMPL [238] has been devised for the specification of structured patterns that are to be identified in a stream of XML data. As a technical basis for executing the pattern matching, we initially chose to use a simple Pushdown Automaton (PDA) [109, Chapter 5], but it soon became clear that we will need to use a full-fledged EFSM, with separate access to a stack that stores nesting level values and some additional context data.

4.2.1 Architecture and Operation

Our first approach involved code generation, and TMPL patterns (called templates) were compiled to Java classes implementing the state machines [101]. An XML data stream is separated into tokens, e. g. using Simple API for XML (SAX) events [251] and each token is supplied as an input event to all state machines. Upon a successful match, an event is raised to inform an application.

We found that the inflexible structure of the compiled EFSM classes not only forced us to go through the code generation and deployment steps for each change in a template, but also that the approach does not scale well. Imagine a system that matches not a couple, but several thousand of templates against an input stream. Each token would need to be supplied to all of the thousands of templates. To solve this issue, we created an interpretation mechanism based on a runtime execution specification, instead of compiling the state machine structures into Java classes. This allowed us to combine state machines in one large automaton that needs to be supplied with only a single event. The resulting toolchain takes the form depicted in Figure 4.2.

TMPL templates are provided in a textual format to the parser, which does syntax checking and generates automata representations, one for each template. The automata can be stored using the Graph eXchange Language (GXL) [205] persistency

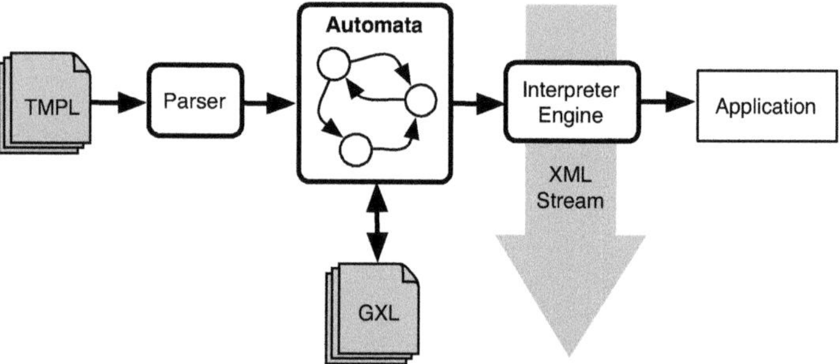

Figure 4.2: The TMPL toolchain

format. An interpretation engine uses the templates to match patterns on an XML data stream. Once a pattern has been identified, an application is notified with the identified variable values. To clarify this process, take a look at the following example template:

```
1 template ab {
2   <a>
3     <b>["hello"]</b>
4   </a>
5 }
```

This template identifies all occurrences of an `<a>` element, containing a direct child element `<b>` with the textual content `hello`. When compiling the template source given above, one obtains the automaton depicted in Figure 4.3.

The syntax of TMPL looks like, but is not, XML. This pseudo-XML is interspersed with square braces that contain predicates. Apart from matching the structure of an XML input stream, all predicates need to evaluate to *true*. For example, the predicate in line 3 checks that the content at the indicated position equals the given string `hello`. TMPL defines many more predicates (e.g. access to context data structures or regular expressions matching) and an overview of the language features can be found in [98].

As seen from Figure 4.3, TMPL automata use guard conditions as well as action statements (written in curly braces) during the interpretation process. Generated automata make use of a stack data structure for tracking XML element nesting levels. During a successful matching process, the TMPL automaton will be traversed from START, through the various MATCH states, to the END state, where it will signal a successful match and return to the START state. This path is shown using thicker arrows in the diagram. In case of an incorrect token in the input stream (e.g. a closing element tag, where content was still expected), a previous system

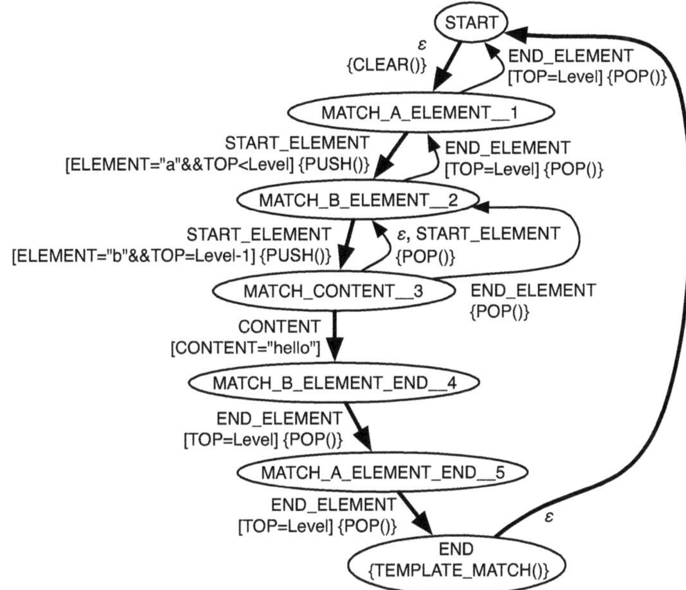

Figure 4.3: An example for a generated TMPL automaton

state is entered. The example uses a number of token types for the transition event labels: START_ELEMENT, END_ELEMENT and CONTENT; these are signalling an encounter with an opening tag, a closing tag or content data in the XML stream. The employed guard condition statements include ELEMENT (a variable holding the name of an element), TOP (a variable that holds the topmost value on the nesting level stack), Level (the current nesting level in the XML stream), a number of operators (the logical "and", comparison operators and the arithmetic minus operator) and literal values (e. g. "hello"). There are also some action statements used: CLEAR() (Resets the nesting level stack and level counter), PUSH() (Stores the current nesting level on the stack), POP() (Removes the topmost stack element) and TEMPLATE_MATCH (Reports a successful match for the template). The Level variable is updated automatically before firing a transition with a START_ELEMENT event and after firing a transition with a END_ELEMENT event. Using the TOP and Level variables is necessary when matching nested templates on an arbitrary depth: the example template will not only find patterns where <a> is a direct child of the root element, but also any occurrence of the pattern when nested below other elements (see the condition part of the transition from MATCH_A_ELEMENT__1 to MATCH_B_ELEMENT__2). In contrast, the <b> element will only be matched if it appears as a direct child of the <a> element (see the condition part of the transition from MATCH_B_ELEMENT__2 to MATCH_CONTENT__3).

4.2.2 Major Challenges and Key Results

Using state machines with an interpretative approach, instead of employing code generation techniques to create the executable matching logic, enables us to investigate an interesting optimisation technique: facilitating the state machine product based on the cartesian product of two graphs.

Optimisation using the cartesian product Calculating the cartesian product of two graphs is a standard procedure used in graph theory and the following definition is taken from [87, p. 22]: "The Cartesian graph product $G = G_1 \Box G_2$ of graphs G_1 and G_2 with disjoint point sets V_1 and V_2 and edge sets X_1 and X_2 is the graph with point set $V_1 \times V_2$ and $u = (u_1, u_2)$ adjacent with $v = (v_1, v_2)$ whenever $[u_1 = v_1$ and u_2 adj $v_2]$ or $[u_2 = v_2$ and u_1 adj $v_1]$."

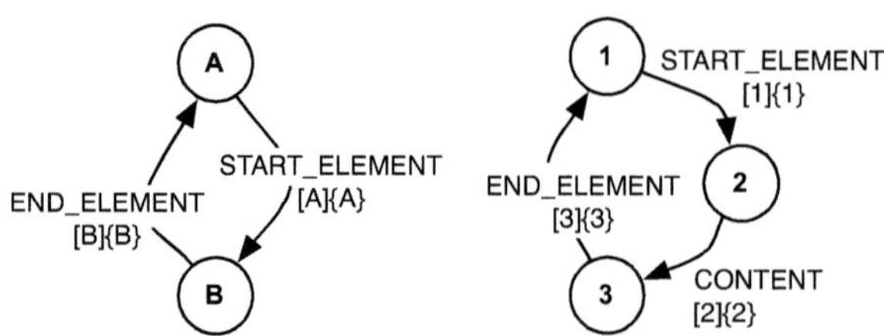

Figure 4.4: Two simple TMPL automata A_{ab} and A_{123}

As an example, take the two automata A_{ab} and A_{123} shown in Figure 4.4. These automata are structured in a simple manner and do not possess an actual function. The automaton A_{ab} uses only letters for states, conditions and actions, whereas the automaton A_{123} uses only digits. When calculating the combination $A_{ab} \Box A_{123}$, one ends up with the automaton shown in Figure 4.5.

The resulting set of states consists of all combinations between the original state sets: **A1**, **A2**, **A3**, **B1**, **B2** and **B3**. For example, when the resulting state machine A is in state **A2**, this would be equal to A_{ab} being in state **A**, while A_{123} is in state **2**. Transitions between the states are also handled accordingly: each of the transitions between the original states now exists multiple times, connecting each of the combined states with each possible destination. The problem with this approach

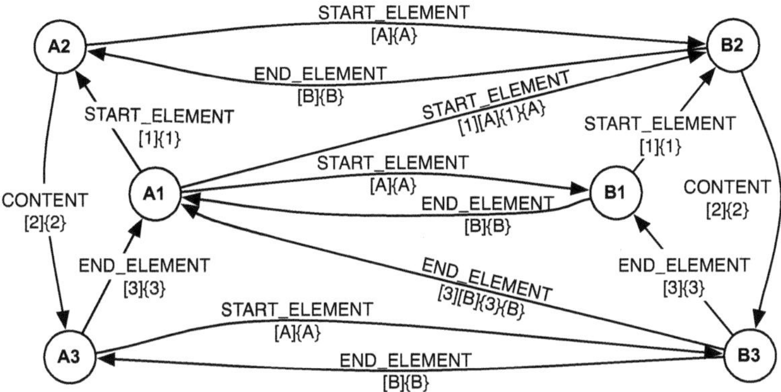

Figure 4.5: Combination of the automata A_{ab} and A_{123}

is in the exponential increase in states and transitions, which can be solved by using lazy construction as described by us in [98, Section 4.2.1 ff.]:

"A combination of ten EFSM with ten states each (e. g. templates having three elements and two content predicates) would end up with 10 billion (10^{10}) states and far more transitions. As the authors of [83] point out, a possible solution to this dilemma is to use lazy construction principles for the automata.

Even if the hypothetical number of states of a combined EFSM seems to grow to exorbitant numbers, only a very small portion of these states would ever be used. If an automaton is built in a lazy fashion by constructing new states at runtime only when they are needed, this number may be decreased dramatically. For example, we combined twelve templates with a total of 350 states using a lazy construction principle and ended up with an EFSM of only 169 states for a specific data stream after further optimisations that reduced redundant or empty states and transitions."

The potential for optimisation lies within the transitions that trigger state changes on the same event, but in both of the models. For example, see the transitions that trigger on START_ELEMENT in state **A** and **1**. These two transitions can be merged into a single one, as seen in Figure 4.5. In addition, both of the guard conditions still need to be evaluated to true, and both of the action statements must be executed on firing of the transition. This allows us to evaluate similar structures of different state machines only once, which leads to a substantial performance gain.

Performance We found that the approach proves to be not only successful, but that it also constitutes the fastest approach for template matching on XML streams that we know of [98]. This is due to the potential optimisations that are made possible by the dynamic properties provided by an interpretation mechanism. For example, with generated code, a lazy construction of the automaton cannot be implemented, which makes it effectively impossible to use this optimisation technique in combination with code generation. The success of this technique is also indicated in Figure 4.6, which compares the throughput of the previous, compiled version of TMPL with the interpreted one, as well as with the fastest library for pattern matching on XML data that we could find, called Streaming Transformations for XML (STX) [24]. Other XSLT engines are considerably slower than STX, which is why we choose to not include them here.

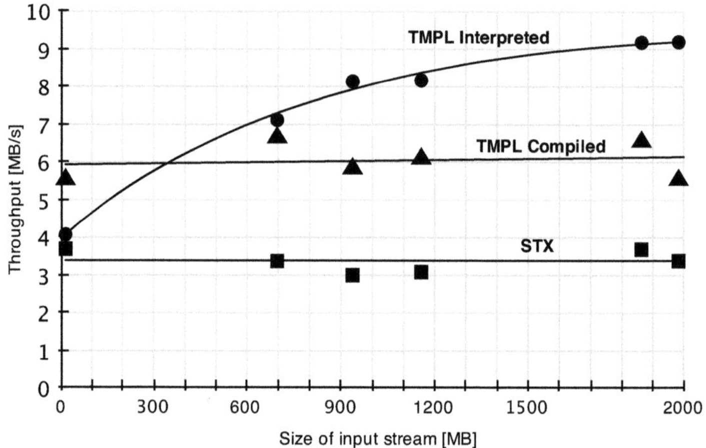

Figure 4.6: Throughput of TMPL implementations and of STX

The general conditions, employed data sets and templates for obtaining the shown results are described in [98, Section 5.1]. It is interesting that the interpreted version can be faster than the one using direct compilation. This happens gradually while the combined automaton is constructed internally. Over time, the combined automaton will be more and more complete and at some stage yield a higher throughput than the compiled approach. In the given example, the TMPL interpreter processes a 2 GB stream of data in less than half the time that its STX counterpart needs — for large volumes of data its throughput is more than 3 MB/s higher than the compiled version and almost three times as high as the one provided by STX. It needs to be pointed out that the interpreted approach only makes sense for large amounts of fairly redundant data.

Relation to the Generic Interpreter The interpretation of TMPL automata constitutes our first application of the interpretation principle to state machines. TMPL excels in the domain that it has been engineered for (pattern matching on large streams of XML data), and we have been employing it successfully in a number of projects. Although the templates are processed in a similar fashion as EFSM-based BMs, their purpose is to serve only as recognisers for a sequence of input tokes, not as interpreted BMs. This is most obvious when comparing the supported BM features to the generic BM format as laid out in Section 4.1.1. Both state machine formats support the notion of states and use ECA transactions, but the TMPL interpreter does not support compound states, nor does it have features for parallelism. The nesting level stack can be regarded as a history mechanism and TMPL is able to identify and store values in variables that are kept in a context data structure. Nonetheless, state names are generated automatically and have only limited informational value. The generated automata are rather hard to understand when read by a human.

From an architectural perspective (see Section 4.1.2), one can already identify most subsystems that a BM interpreter should have. The Control Interface is used to deploy the automata and to notify an application about the matching of a certain template. Logic for managing the Interpreter Engine exists, and the Engine itself conducts a form of reactive, stepwise RTC processing. The Event Interface and Dispatcher are boiled down to a tokenising mechanism that does not support the queueing of events, nor allows for sending of events from the automaton. FCs are hard-coded into the Engine, and there is no FC Repository as such. A BM Repository exists, which stores the templates that the Engine uses. Templates are instantiated, not on a one-instance-per-template basis, but as one, lazily-constructed instance that is a cross-product of all of the active templates.

4.3 The ACE Toolkit

A major influence for our current work on BMs has been the participation in the creation of the ACE toolkit. During development of the TMPL interpreter engine we needed to look closely into the details of runtime EFSM interpretation; working on the design and implementation of the ACE toolkit complemented this research. We investigated the dynamic composition of BMs, created a sophisticated event infrastructure and explored the concept of using FCs to provide additional functions to a BM.

ACE Self-Models The primary focus for ACE development has not been in creating a performant or feature-rich state machine executor, but rather in the engineering of a software architecture that enables the development of component-based, autonomic systems driven by BMs. One of the key aspects about ACEs is the ability to automatically adapt their runtime behaviour to a changing environment. This is achieved using so-called *self-models*. A self-model contains a set of rules that defines all possible ACE behaviours and that enables the ACE to construct concrete BM instances (referred to as *plans*) at runtime. The ACE continuously evaluates its self-model in regard to the environment, and creates new plans or adapts existing ones if necessary.

As the generation of BM instances from a set of rules is a challenging task on its own, we are employing only a simple BM format with only a limited set of features. The format uses EFSMs and does support states, transitions with ECA labels and context access features. It does not support parallel regions or state containment on a model level, although it is possible to spawn the execution of new plans parallel to existing ones. The defined expression language has nine default predicates for logical comparison and boolean operations, but is extensible by allowing the declaration of custom predicates. Actions are restricted to the invocation of FCs (which include functions for sending events). Context data can be accessed and stored in local data structures, either with a global, session or FC invocation scope. The session data structures are shared between the model and any invoked functions.

4.3.1 Architecture and Operation

An exhaustive discussion of the ACE architecture is found in [34, Section 3]. In the following text, we will only give a short overview of the architecture and describe the central elements that make up an ACE. The following description of components is adapted from one of our publications on the ACE toolkit [26, Section II].

ACEs are basic building blocks for creating autonomic services in distributed environments. An ACE can be seen as a general-purpose abstraction for communication services, which collaborates with other ACEs in order to fulfil certain goals while adapting its behaviour to changes observed in the environment. The ACE architecture is derived from the simple biological model where an entity consists of multiple *organs* and where each organ fulfils a certain purpose in order to keep the entity alive. As presented in Figure 4.7, an ACE consists of six organs that each fulfil a certain purpose, and in the following text, we will shortly describe these organs.

Gateway organ A subsystem responsible for the inter ACE communication. The ACE communication model is event-based and distinguishes between internal and external events. It corresponds to the Event Interface and Dispatcher subsystem of the generic interpreter architecture introduced in Section 4.1.2. The gateway supports two modes of communication. On the one hand, one can use the connection-less Goal Needed (GN) – Goal Achievable (GA) discovery protocol for retrieval of addresses of ACEs that implement a certain service. On the other hand, one can establish direct connections between a group of ACEs

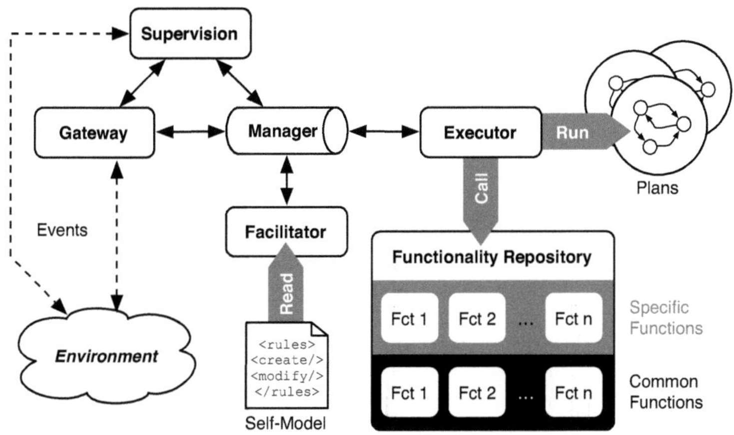

Figure 4.7: ACE architecture

using a software contract paradigm (the concept of a contract is introduced in Section 2.2.6.4).

Manager Organ This organ manages the ACE lifecycle (start, stop, migrate) and handles the internal ACE communication. Lifecycle management comprises scheduling, controlling and executing any operation that influences the lifecycle of an ACE. If a lifecycle operation is requested, the manager will inform all other organs about the upcoming lifecycle action and will execute the action after all organs have confirmed their readiness. The Manager organ corresponds to the Manager subsystem of the generic interpreter architecture. Besides management of an ACE's lifecycle, the Manager organ also handles the internal ACE communication using an elaborated version of the generic interpreter's Event Queue subsystem. The internal ACE communication model also implements a PubSub messaging paradigm: ACE organs can publish events to the *event bus* and can subscribe for receiving events from the bus.

Facilitator Organ The Facilitator is responsible for creating ACE plans and adapting the ACE behaviour with respect to new requirements. The ACE plan is a BM instance that is interpreted to yield the runtime behaviour of an ACE. All possible ACE behaviours are defined by the developer within a self-model, which contains a set of rules that enable the Facilitator to construct concrete ACE plans. The facilitator loads the self-model on ACE start up and continuously evaluates it in regard to the ACE environment, creating new ACE plans or adapting existing ones, when necessary. The Facilitator loosely corresponds to the BM Repository subsystem in the generic interpreter architecture as it provides behaviour specifications that the Manager organ uses to create BM instances.

Executor Organ This organ is a BM interpreter: it executes the ACE plans and requests the invocation of FCs. Multiple plans can be executed in parallel, which allows ACEs to fulfil multiple goals and serve multiple other ACEs at the same time. The executor maintains all active plans, along with their state configuration and context data.

Functionality Repository An organ that is responsible for maintaining FCs. It corresponds to the FC Repository component of the generic interpreter architecture. In the ACE toolkit we distinguish between common and specific FCs. Common FCs are an integral part of the ACE toolkit. They comprise a set of required functions, e. g. sending event messages, creating contracts, accessing the context, etc. In contrast, FCs can be custom defined; in this case, they are provided by an ACE developer and used to fulfil the specific requirements of the target domain within which the ACE is used. The functionality repository will load FCs on ACE start up and will invoke them when requested by the executor.

Supervision Organ The Supervision organ monitors and logs the ACE operation and enables access to the internal supervision system. It provides the supervision system with current events, the self-model, the active state configuration and the context. Using this information, the supervision system can control an ACE that entered an error state, leading it back to a normal operational state. The supervision organ does this by monitoring (and optionally modifying) the message flow over two monitoring points within the manager and gateway organs. We are regarding the Supervision organ as an implementation of the Control Interface subsystem of the generic interpreter architecture. The supervision concepts have been researched extensively (see Section 5.1).

4.3.2 Major Challenges and Key Results

The operativeness of the ACE toolkit has been shown successfully and the toolkit is provided as an open source project available from sourceforge [222]. We took a series of performance measurements for observing the toolkit performance and discussed the findings in an article [27, Section 5] that is currently under submission to the ACM journal *Transactions on Autonomous and Adaptive Systems.*

The development of the ACE toolkit helps us to prove that interpretation is a well suited strategy for creating adaptable runtime behaviour. We especially gained insights into the engineering of groups of autonomic components that collaborate towards a common goal. In comparison to the other interpreter implementations, there a four areas where our research on the ACE toolkit contributes novel findings to the research field. These are described in the remainder of this section.

The Communication Infrastructure ACEs interact by providing services to other ACEs and by consuming services from other ACEs in order to fulfil a certain goal. ACEs discover collaboration partners through the GN–GA protocol and subsequently form groups using software contracts. The process of forming and maintaining aggregates is highly dynamic: ACEs can migrate between hosts and ACE addresses used within existing contracts are maintained.

Most of the programmatic support for this functionality is provided by two communication mechanisms that are used for transmitting external events over the gateway. The event-based, connection-less mechanism is based on the REDS PubSub middleware [226], which is employed for service discovery purposes using the GN–GA protocol. Following this protocol, an ACE A publishes a GN Message with a goal identifier, and its own address to the REDS middleware. All subscribed ACEs will be supplied with the GN message. In case that an ACE B can fulfil the requested goal it will answer back to A with a GA message, containing its own address. By employing the addresses from the received GA, the ACE A can then proceed to establish point-to-point connections with B. As PubSub supports one-to-many communication (see Section 2.2.6.4), a single GN can result in a number of GA messages, where the originating ACE is free to select the most suitable communication partner(s).

Contractual connections are based on the DIET framework [248] which is used for creating dedicated communication channels between ACEs. A collaboration contract can be established upon a successful negotiation via GN–GA between the ACEs (see Section 2.2.6.4). A group of ACEs that has a contract in place exposes their services to each other and can invoke them. The contracting mechanism provides a form of reliable group communication with guaranteed notification on contract infringement[4]. These features are mainly responsible for enabling the engineering of robust, distributed applications using the ACE toolkit. Using a combination of a connection-less, non-routing message passing protocol for service discovery with dedicated point-to-point connections for service usage is also a central topic of [100].

The Functionality Repository The idea of using a BM together with a number of FCs emerged during our work on the ACE toolkit. There are some functions that are either too complicated or that need to be formulated too optimised to be expressed in terms of the BM format. FCs are considered as software components that encapsulate such functions. They are *orchestrated* by the operational logic contained in the plans executed by an ACE. FCs offer functions that can be called

[4]The invalidation of the contractual invariant

during the processing of the self-model and these functions are bound[5] to action statements contained in the plans. The mechanisms that trigger the invocation of FCs are supporting a binding to existing Java code using configuration files for specifying parameters, method mappings and type conversions. This enables software developers to easily create FCs for use by the ACE toolkit.

The Facilitator and Supervision Organs Both, the Facilitator organ, as well as Supervisor organ implement novel concepts. Until now, we argued that BM interpreters rely on manually-specified models. In the case of the ACE toolkit an additional indirection layer is introduced: behaviour is not specified in the form of a deterministic process but rather as a set of rules to describe the parameter space in which the behaviour should take place. A concrete behaviour is then determined with respect to an ACE's environment, using deductive reasoning on a given rule base. This is an interesting research venue and we would like to investigate it further as a topic in our future work. The creation of the Supervisor organ is a direct consequence of employing the Facilitator to create new behaviours in response to changes in the environment. Due to the complexity of runtime behaviour adaptation; it is very complex to assure that a BM always operates in a manner intended by an MA. The supervision organ supports truly autonomous systems by allowing errors and less than optimal behaviour. Once an intolerable situation occurs, the Supervisor is used by an external MA to adapt an ACE plan to conform to a more appropriate operational behaviour.

The ACElandic High-Level Language The self-model syntax uses an XML format to describe the rules that are used to create the concrete state machine BMs for the executable plans. Thus, manually specifying a self-model is a tedious undertaking. To ease this task, we developed the ACElandic language. With ACElandic, self-models can be created using appropriate higher-level language statements while the matching glue code and configuration files, which enable a binding with the required FCs, are generated by the ACElandic compiler. We can follow a compilation approach, as the tool only needs to produce the self-model XML file read by an ACE at startup. The adaptation of the runtime behaviour is achieved through the interpretation of the plan by the Executor organ and the plan adaptation by the Facilitator. The ACElandic language, as well as the toolset, have been used very successfully to demonstrate the approach [56]. A comprehensive presentation of the language is contained in Appendix C.

[5] In the sense of programming language binding of functions

4.4 The UML State Machine Interpreter

The following section discusses an implementation of a BM interpreter for UML 2 Behavioral State Machines. The intention is to investigate the performance impact of the corresponding mechanisms as well as to gain insight into the aspects that dominate the runtime performance characteristics of the approach. The use of UML for BM representation also has a second motivation: using a graphical symbology is beneficial to humans for understanding and developing BM specifications. While the specific representation format is irrelevant for machines, humans usually grasp the meaning of a graphical BM representation more easily, as when supplied with a textual representation. It is not our goal to develop general execution semantics for UML State Machines. This has already been done by several other parties, and information on this can be found as part of the discussion of related work in Chapter 3.

We picked UML 2 Behavioral State Machines, as they are the most feature-rich formalism for state machines that we know of. As UML aims at integrating all existing modelling languages within a single syntax, its current version (2.2) contains a very rich set of features for the specification of state machines [255, Section 15]. UML can be regarded as the current state of the art for BM representation. Both, the TMPL engine as well as the ACE toolkit, provide only a limited set of BM features and, most notably, they do not support compound states and parallelism. UML State Machines implement all of the fundamental BM features listed in Section 4.1.1, along with many others.

Besides state machines, UML provides three alternatives for the specification of behaviour: activities, interactions and use cases. We choose to not investigate these other UML constructs. Use cases are too abstract for our purposes and interactions only allow the modelling of black box behaviour. Activities might be an option for runtime behaviour modelling, but we choose to restrict ourselves to the use of state machines.

Whenever UML is mentioned in the following text, we are referring to version 2.2 of the specification. We restrict our description to UML behavior state machines and ignore the UML Protocol State Machine formalism, as we are interested in expressing behaviour only. An overview of UML Behavioral State Machines can be found in Appendix A.

Adaptive Systems Profile For runtime interpretation purposes, we found it useful to extend UML State Machines with a proprietary profile, which we termed the Adaptive Systems Profile (ASP). The ASP contains additional information that enables a UML interpreter to construct an execution specification of the BM (see Section 2.2). It currently consists of four stereotypes, which are extending the UML meta model as depicted in Figure 4.8.

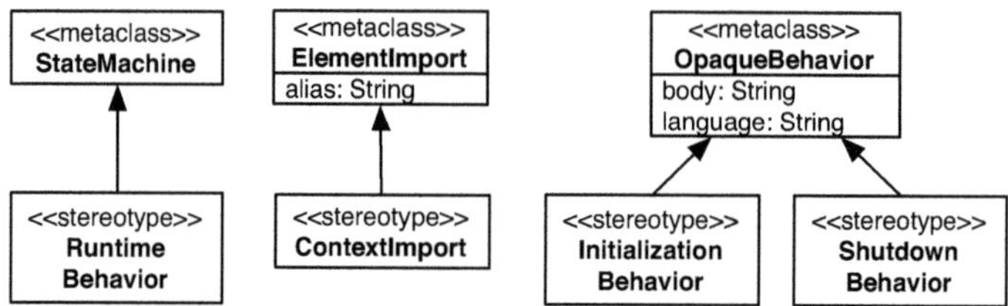

Figure 4.8: Structure of the Adaptive Systems UML Profile

RuntimeBehavior Extends the *StateMachine* class, allowing a BM interpreter to identify which state machines are designed for runtime interpretation (rather than being analysis or design artefacts).

ContextImport An association that is used to reference instance specifications as part of the context. An *alias* property is used to assign a local name to the imported instance and this alias can be used as an identifier in guard conditions or action statements. Extends the *ElementImport* class. This stereotype is evaluated by the interpreter prior to BM start to determine and instantiate the classes used in the context.

InitializationBehavior Extends the *OpaqueBehavior class.* Using the *body* and *language* properties one can directly specify a behaviour employing a programming language that is supported by an interpreter implementation. This allows the interpreter to execute an initialisation behaviour before the interpretation of the BM.

ShutdownBehavior Used in a similar manner as *InitializationBehavior*, but the specified function is executed after the state machine terminates. This enables the interpreter to execute the indicated clean up code after the interpretation process commences.

4.4.1 Architecture and Operation

We implemented an interpreter encompassing all of the features of UML 2 Behavioral State Machines, except for redefinition (see Appendix A on page 222). The support of state machine redefinition at runtime possesses only limited relevance for our approach. In the words of H. Fecher, M. Kyas and J. Schönborn: "The concept of redefinition *[...]* is not a behavioral issue."[69, page 2]. As we pioneer the basics of runtime BM interpretation, we choose to leave the treatment of UML State Machine redefinitions at runtime as an open task to the research community. We still regard state machine redefinition as a useful tool for model specification at design time and suspect that it could also be a beneficial structuring mechanism for runtime BMs.

The software architecture for the prototype is focussed on BM execution and integration with the Java platform. More sophisticated infrastructure aspects (remote messaging, logging, graphical user-interface, configuration, etc.) have been ignored. The core classes used for BM execution are depicted in Figure 4.9.

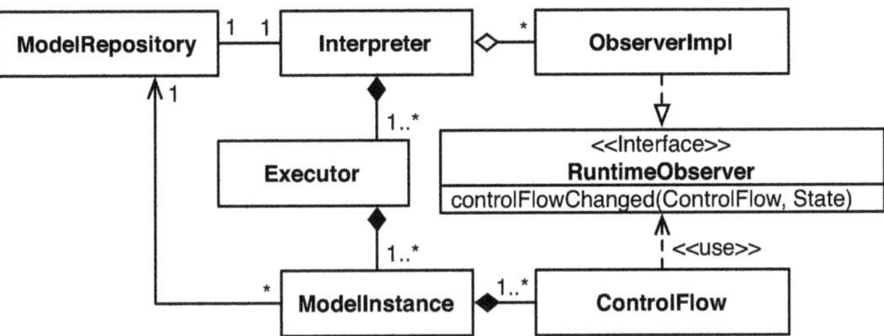

Figure 4.9: Architecture of the UML interpreter – execution aspects

There are seven central classes in the design that care for execution of BMs. The **ModelRepository** provides storage facilities and access functions for BMs, it corresponds to the BM Repository in the generic interpreter architecture (see Section 4.1.2). BMs are loaded from persistent storage and retained in dynamic memory. They can be accessed element-wise using query functions. BMs contained in the repository can be changed during runtime, resulting in a different execution behaviour of the interpreter implementation once the modified elements are encountered. From a user's point of view, the **Interpreter** class is the central point of interaction with the application. It offers lifecycle management functions and provides methods for inspection of running BM instances and the dispatching of events. For tracing BM state changes, the **Interpreter** allows other classes to register as observers for given models by using the **RuntimeObserver** interface. This design follows the *Observer* pattern [75, p. 287 ff.]. The **Interpreter** class combines the Control Interface, the Event Interface, the Dispatcher and the Manager subsystem found in the generic architecture.

A single **Interpreter** holds one or more **Executor** instances. These are active classes that use a separate thread for sequentially executing a number of BMs, which are referenced using the **ModelInstance** class. For all applications relevant to this thesis, we used only a single **Executor** and a single **ModelInstance**. The idea behind supporting several **Executor** instances is to be able to better utilise an underlying hardware platform's multitasking capabilities by adapting the number of executors to the numbers of available processing cores. Each **ModelInstance** object stands for a single running instance of a BM and contains all necessary information needed to interpret the model (e. g. the current active state configuration or the associated context). A **ModelInstance** accesses data stored in a **ModelRepository** when conducting model traversal and evaluation operations during the event processing steps. The **Executor** maintains an Event Queue for external events.

The logic for processing events is found in the **ControlFlow** class, which is instantiated once per control flow in the model. It largely corresponds to the Interpreter Engine subsystem in the generic architecture. Peculiarities of the UML State Machine model (support for deferred events) demand that the **ControlFlow** class also implements an Event Queue. Management of **ControlFlow** instances is done by the related **ModelInstance** class using using retained continuation semantics (see explanation on page 37 ff.). A **ControlFlow** uses the **RuntimeObserver** interface to update observers on state changes by triggering an invocation of the controlFlowChanged method for any registered observer classes. This enables the easy determination of the active state configuration in parallel with the BM interpretation. Additionally, it can be used to assure that a model is in a certain state before supplying it with further events. During event processing, the **ModelInstance** class's processing functionality needs to evaluate expression statements within guard conditions or action directives. The designed architecture, with the relevant classes shown in Figure 4.10, enables the interchange of platform bindings for the employed expression languages by means of an interface-based variation of the *Abstract Factory* pattern [75, p. 107 ff.].

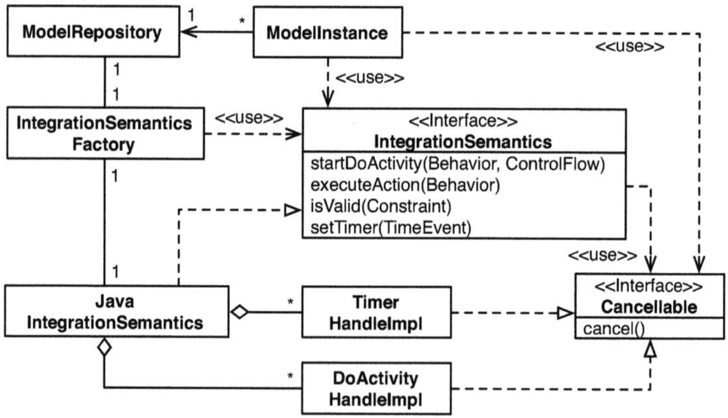

Figure 4.10: Architecture of the UML interpreter – integration aspects

The **IntegrationSemanticsFactory** provides the functionality to retrieve an object that adheres to the **IntegrationSemantics** interface. Within the scope of this document, we are only using a single integration semantics, the **JavaIntegrationSemantics**. This particular class employes native Java for the evaluation of expression statements using the MVFLEX Expression Language (MVEL) [275]. The motivation behind this is the usage of an on-the-fly bytecode compiler for MVEL. The resulting code executes very fast — the authors of MVEL claim that it is the fastest expression evaluator on the Java platform [276]. As the UML interpreter is able to directly bind its expression statements to the execution platform, we are omitting any features that relate to FCs. Instead, a BM invokes Java objects that have been specified using the ASP *ContextImport* Stereotype.

Apart from the platform-dependent evaluation of expression statements, **IntegrationSemantics** implementing classes are responsible for managing concurrent activities and handling timers. Concurrent do-activities (see page 220) are triggered as in-state behaviour. Timers are set once a state has been entered, when the state has an outgoing transition that is triggered by a timed event (e. g. *after 1 minute*). Should a state be left, before a timer expires, then the timer needs to be cancelled to suppress firing of the timed event. This is done using the **Cancellable** interface and the corresponding **TimerHandleImpl** class, which is instantiated for every started timer. A similar mechanism is used to cancel do-activities on state exit.

The UML interpreter has been implemented from scratch in Java language (version 6). We use version 3.0.1 of the UML 2 Ecore format provided by the EMF Model Development Tools (MDT) project [280] for the in-memory storage format. An Ecore version of the ASP was created to easily identify interpretable BMs and context data imports. The utilisation of Ecore is motivated by the large number of tools that can be used with this technology and the same reason applies for the selection of UML in the first place: it is a standardised representation format, widely understood and supported by a large set of tools. The following list enumerates additional components used by the UML interpreter, which are provided by [278], except the ASP and MVEL, which is provided by [275]. The mentioned version numbers are the ones used for executing the performance benchmark.

Ecore The Ecore libraries are used as the underlying framework for the model runtime format. Persistent storage is achieved using the XMI import and export facilities. The employed version of the libraries is 2.5.0.

UML 2 An implementation of the UML 2 meta model in Ecore. We use two libraries: the common functions in version 1.5.0 and the UML library itself in version 3.0.1.

ASP An extension to the UML 2 libraries, we use the initial version of this profile.

EMF Query A library for querying Ecore models, used for convenient access to the BM elements. The utilised version is 1.2.100.

MVEL We employ version 2.0.14 of the library.

We also use the EMF Compare tools for determination of model differences and merging of BMs at runtime. For graphical representation and modification of BMs the IBM Rational Software Architect (RSA) tool suite and the UML editor from the Topcased project [282] are employed.

4.4.2 Major Challenges and Key Results

Implementing the UML interpreter is an important and challenging task. Although the general mechanisms seem to be simple to engineer, correctly integrating the many features of UML 2 State Machines requires attention to detail regarding potential side-effects of the implemented mechanisms. Engineering the UML BM interpreter implementation forced us to look deeper into the involved complexities as for any of the other implementations. In the subsequent text, we will highlight the major lessons learned while creating this proof-of-concept prototype.

Processing Compound Transitions in UML 2, a transition is not limited to consisting of a single edge leading from a single source state to a single target state, but can be made up of an arbitrary number of segments leading from a number of source states to a number of destination states, eventually branching and merging via choice and junction constructs. To determine the correct sets of entered and exited states, we identify a set of paths through this graph of transition segments. Depending on these identified paths. it is possible — under consideration of orthogonality, history and initial pseudostates — to establish the target state configuration of a compound transition. Using the current active state and the target state configurations, the entered and exited states can be calculated as elaborated in Section 2.2.

Determination of Exited States in Transitions Using the Choice Construct A particular problem with determining the proper set of exited states is encountered when combining choice constructs together with transitions that trigger actions. Figure 4.11 shows a model that demonstrates the issue.

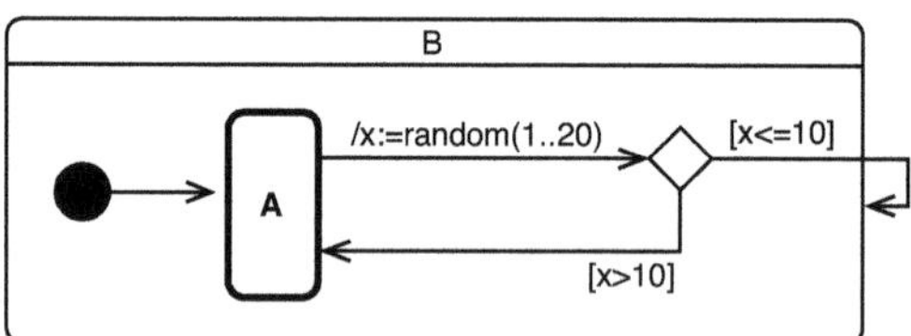

Figure 4.11: Demonstration of a problem with the UML choice construct

Imagine that the system is in state A and exits via the ε-transition, assigning a random value in the range 1 to 20 to the variable x. On the subsequent processing of the choice construct, a path is taken depending on the value of the variable x. Assuming that the transition is an external one, the exited states are either only A or A,B.

The UML standard, on the one hand, dictates that states need to be exited prior to executing any transition actions: "Once a transition is enabled and is selected to fire, the following steps are carried out in order: The main source state is properly exited. [...] If a choice point is encountered, the guards following that choice point are evaluated dynamically and a path whose guards are true is selected. [...]" [255, p. 576] (ellipsis added). On the other hand, it demands that "In a compound transition where multiple outgoing transitions emanate from a common *choice* point, the outgoing transition whose guard is true *at the time the choice point is reached*, will be taken." [255, p. 574] (emphasis in original text). The problem is that the individual states of a compound main source state might not be determinable before processing the choice — at this point in time, the states would need to have already been exited. This issue has already been reported on the 7 December 2000 issues list; it is tracked under issue number 4110 at the OMG and a solution has been deferred to UML 2.4. By convention, our interpreter exits states up to the level of directly nested children of the parent vertex of the choice pseudostate: in the example, this would only be state A.

Completion Events The UML standard introduces ε-transitions as transitions that trigger on completion events. Completion events are either dispatched once a state has been entered and eventual do-activities are completed, or once all substates of a compound state have completed. Understanding state completion as solely represented through events is an elegant approach for combining the state completion mechanisms and the mechanism that processes event triggers on transitions. Unfortunately, this approach is problematic in conjunction with guard conditions; imagine a transition that is triggered on a completion event and that is labelled with a guard condition relying on context data. Once the source state of the transition is completely entered, a completion event is generated. At this point in time, the guard condition could evaluate to false: the transition would not fire and the completion event would be discarded. At a later point in time the context changes and the condition could now evaluate to true. As the completion event would already have been discarded, the transition could not be triggered anymore. Such a behaviour is perceived as contrary to the semantics connected intuitively to such a transition. This problem is also obvious with internal transitions: as these do not exit or enter a state when firing, they do not generate completion events on processing — therefore, internal ε-transitions would only work once at the initial entering of the state.

We found that state completion needs to be characterised as a persistent situation and that it cannot properly be mapped to transient events, as one needs to retain per-state completion information. Our solution is to maintain an additional runtime data structure, which contains the completion information. This runtime data structure is evaluated and completion events are generated, even in a recurring fashion, if necessary.

Fork & Join The aforementioned completion data structure is also useful for determining the preconditions (completion of source states for all incoming transition segments) for join pseudostates. We found that a major obstacle for implementing UML features regarding to control flow handling is found in the non-exclusive usage of fork and join pseudostates for manipulating the control flow. For example, contrary to SCXML[6], UML allows us to mix fork/join nodes with transitions that implicitly enter or exit parallel regions: i. e. two regions of a state might be entered through a fork pseudostate, while a third region is entered by means of an initial pseudostate. Such a situation is depicted in Figure 4.12.

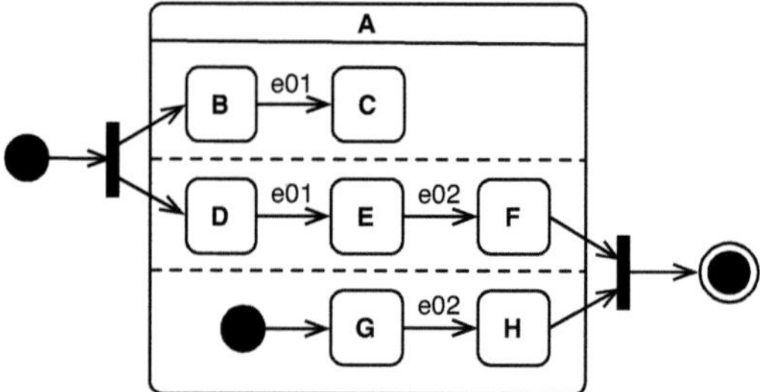

Figure 4.12: Implicit control flow creation and termination

The shown BM can be executed from start to end, by processing the two events e01 and e02. It can be seen that the initial fork pseudostate only specifies entry in the states **B** and **D**. State **G** is entered implicitly by means of an initial pseudostate. A similar issue can be observed when finally joining the control flows: once the BM enters the states **F** and **H**, the superstate **A** is left and the control flow with the active state **C** needs to be terminated implicitly.

Due to such combinations of constructs, an interpreter is required to check each exited, orthogonal state for control flows that need to be implicitly terminated and to check each entered, orthogonal state for control flows that need to be implicitly

[6]Which does not use join or fork and solely uses implicit handling of parallel regions

created. This information can be determined by calculations based on the active and target state configuration using the instructions given in Section 2.2.3.

Another issue concerns how the graphical representation of transitions outgoing from a fork pseudostate relates to the entered states of the individual control flows. For example, take the fork node depicted in Figure 2.10 on page 39: the graphical visualisation suggests that a control flow entering the fork node would split into two and that both of the control flows would enter state E individually, before entering their target states F and G. As discussed in the related text, this is not the case, as state E is supposed to be entered only once.

History and Regions As recognised by others [52], the semantics of the history pseudostate is not clearly defined with respect to orthogonal states. The UML standard states that "A composite state can have at most one [deep/shallow] history vertex." [255, p. 542] (square braces added, these are two separate statements). If the respective composite state is also orthogonal, the history pseudostate needs to be contained in one of the regions. This is confusing, as the history functionality refers to the composite state, not the region. There are also no clear specifications on how control flows should be created upon restoration of a previously stored state — as mentioned on page 38, we are entering parallel regions from a history pseudostate as if through a fork construct.

Storing the History To be able to restore a historic state configuration when processing a history pseudostate, this state configuration has to be saved beforehand. Saving the state cannot be done in-line with the regular state exit process, as nested states would already have been exited upon encountering the history pseudostate (exiting states requires a bottom-up traversal of the composition hierarchy). The state infomation would need to be saved before commencing any exit process, necessitating detection of any existing history pseudostates prior to transition firing. We are employing a top-down scanning functionality prior to state changes for this purpose, but more optimal approaches are imaginable (e. g. marking nested states on entering during a regular top-down traversal of the composition hierarchy or a preprocessing of the model at deployment/adaptation time).

Transition Kinds and Segments The UML *Transition* class exposes an attribute that assigns a *kind* to the transition which can be either *internal*, *local* or *external* (see page 218 ff.). Compound transitions consist of transition segments, where each one corresponds to the *Transition* class; therefore a compound transition could potentially consist of several segments with differing kinds. This is a conflict, as a compound transition should only be of a single kind (necessary for correct determination of exited and entered states). Our solution is to only consider the attribute of the first transition segment, assuming that it represents the overall transition.

Deferred Events and Message Storage Allowing states to be annotated with a set of deferred events entails the need for storing deferred events. This storage structure for the accumulated events has to exist separately for each control flow, as the sets of deferred events might vary from flow to flow. To allow for this, we implemented event queues on a per-flow level. If this feature is not to be supported, a single input queue could be used for all control flows, as events could be discarded right after their processing.

Fast Expression Evaluation As we will show in Section 6.3, the performance of expression evaluation is of utmost importance for the overall performance of the interpretation approach. By pre-compiling expressions in the native execution format (in our case Java bytecode) for the BM action and condition statements, we demonstrated a feasible path to implementing fast interpreters while still supporting BM adaptation at runtime.

Runtime Model Adaptation We conducted some simple experiments to confirm our hypothesis that BM interpretation allows us to modify the BM at runtime. We found that we can add and remove transitions and states without any problems, while the system is dormant between the RTC executions. The EMF supports runtime adaptation of models by providing *diff* functionality that enables us to create a second version of the BM and then to automatically calculate the changes needed to transform the original model into the new one. These changes can be executed as a series of basic transformations (e. g. remove a transition, rename an identifier, etc.). Thus, theoretically, BM runtime adaptation is feasible. Practically though, an implementer needs to take care not to introduce inconsistencies. For example, a saved history state configurations also needs to be taken into account when changing a BM structure or precompiled expression statements might require to be updated. There are also situations, where arbitrary BM modifications might be invalid, e. g. the removal of a state that is currently active.

Concepts that go beyond fundamental BMs UML State Machines provide many concepts that go beyond the fundamental features described in Section 4.1.1. With the UML interpreter we implemented all of them, including: support for partial models, evaluation of arbitrarily segmented transitions, handling of deferred events, support for multiple event specifications on transition labels, taking transition kinds into account, supporting concurrently executing do actions (and their termination on exiting the declaring state), termination of the BM by the corresponding pseudostate, handling the choice and junction features and support for completion events.

4.5 The Model Processing Unit

We created the previously described three implementations and although each of them has a different focus regarding its functionality and intended use, they all have something in common: they all have been written from scratch with only little utilisation of existing technologies. Thus, the goal of this, fourth, implementation is to create a robust interpreter application that utilises only mature technologies, which have been proven to be applicable for production use. By carrying out this implementation, we can explore the real-world[7] requirements for such an application and can investigate how well our approach fits to currently available technology.

The most important decision is the selection of an appropriate BM runtime format. We decided to use SCXML, which is a working draft [289] that is being maintained by the World Wide Web Consortium (W3C). SCXML does not only prescribe a XML persistency format for statecharts, but also specifies concrete RTC interpretation semantics. The employed SCXML specification supports all of the fundamental BM features as discussed in section 4.1.1. An overview of the language is provided in Appendix B. For the model runtime format, we adopt the Java-based SCXML engine from the Apache commons project [215]. Both, the SCXML standard document as well as the Apache engine, are commonly used for runtime statechart execution, which is the main reason for selecting them.

Based on the Apache engine, we create a comprehensive CU that is able to deploy, execute and maintain BMs within a network and systems management context. We refer to this implementation as the Model Processing Unit (MPU). The MPU employs the OSGi platform [262] for providing the fundamental framework and the services (e. g. logging, configuration, event dispatching) needed for its operation. OSGi is chosen due to its popularity, maturity and conservative resource usage. Compared to the bare-bones UML interpreter implementation, the MPU is feature-rich, in the sense that it provides many of the necessary features needed for real-world applications, like a web-based management interface or proper logging mechanisms.

The Plan Format SCXML has been devised with an arbitrary, but fixed and pre-established, set of external services (FCs) in mind. This can be concluded from the lack of language features for specification of FC bindings. We created a specific XML persistency format (the *plan* format), which incorporates plain SCXML for the description of behaviour, but additionally enables the specification of dependency information for FCs that a BM is bound to. This information is used by the MPU to make required FCs available and to create the runtime binding for invoking the FC-contained functions. The plan format is specified using XML Schema and its structure is depicted in Figure 4.13.

[7] We understand "real-world" requirements as related to the production use of systems, as opposed to employing a technology for academic research or as a prototype.

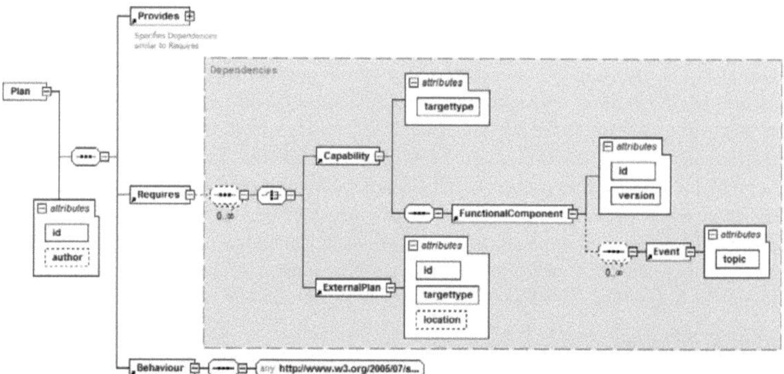

Figure 4.13: Structure of the plan format for BMs based on SCXML

Each plan starts with a top level `<Plan>` element, with a mandatory `id` and an optional `author` attribute. It has three child elements: `<Provides>`, `<Requires>` and `<Behaviour>`, where `<Behaviour>` contains content from the SCXML namespace. The two other children adhere both to the Dependencies structure, which allows an arbitrary number of children of either `<Capability>` or `<ExternalPlan>` elements. `<Requires>` specifies the dependencies needed for a BM to run, whereas `<Provides>` specifies which features the BM contributes to the interpreter. The motivation behind this structure is to handle the invocation of BM instances with similar calling conventions as the invocation of FCs; therefore, a plan could be treated as an FC and vice versa.

The `<ExternalPlan>` tag is used for addressing purposes. Its attributes `id`, `targettype` and the optional `location` are used by an SCXML interpreter in conjunction with an underlying transport technology to communicate with other BMs. The `<Capability>` element defines the interface to a single FC. It contains an attribute `targettype` that identifies the calling conventions used, along with a single `<FunctionalComponent>` child that contains the information for identifying an FC in the `id` and `version` attributes. FCs can be triggering by invocation or through event dispatching. Therefore, to specify event scopes, the plan specification stipulates a set of `<Event>` elements with assigned `topic` identifiers.

The following code fragment shows an example plan used in the MBIM monitor router-load use case (see Section 5.2.2).

```
<?xml version="1.0"?>
<Plan id="Example">
  <Provides/>
  <Requires>
```

```
5      <Capability targettype="x-mbim-event">
6        <FunctionalComponent id="SomeCapability" version="1.0">
7          <Event topic="monitoring"/>
8        </FunctionalComponent>
9      </Capability>
10   </Requires>
11   <Behaviour>
12     SCXML behaviour definition
13   </Behaviour>
14 </Plan>
```

For the sake of brevity, we excluded XML namespace definitions. The plan is defined with the unique identifier `Example`, enabling the plan management to unambiguously identify the plan. The plan does not provide anything to its environment (line 3) and requires only one capability (lines 4 – 10). The capability is accessed using event-based calling conventions (indicated by the `x-mbim-event` targettype in line 5) and consists of an FC with the id `SomeCapability` and the version `1.0` (lines 6 – 8). This information is used to ensure that the identified FC is available to the model instance at the beginning of the execution. In line 7, the plan specifies that event exchange with the FC is to be done using the `monitoring` scope identifier. This value is used to setup the event dispatching mechanisms of the platform to deliver events with the given topic to the plan instance. The behaviour is specified using a SCXML definition enclosed within the `<Behaviour>` and `</Behaviour>` tag pairs (lines 11 – 13). The content within these tags is passed to the SCXML engine without modification.

4.5.1 Architecture and Operation

A high-level view of an MPU's internal structure, the communication between its subsystems as well as the communication with external entities is shown in Figure 4.14. Central to the MPU are the Plans, which specify BMs along with binding information for FCs. The instantiation and handling of plans is managed by the MPU through the use of OSGi service invocations and dispatching of internal events. The MPU assumes the role of the Manager subsystem in the generic interpreter architecture (see Section 4.1.2). The MPU itself is controlled by the MA (see Section 2.3), which we assume to be a human operator. The Control Interface is implemented as a web GUI, employing the Hypertext Transfer Protocol (HTTP) [235] and the Asynchronous JavaScript and XML (AJAX) [77] principle for data transfer and updating of the displayed operational data. Using a web interface is a solution that lets us conveniently experiment with the software. In a larger deployment scenario, this interface could be replaced by something more appropriate, e. g. a Web Service API [286]. The web interface exposes controls for instantiating, starting, stopping and removing plans.

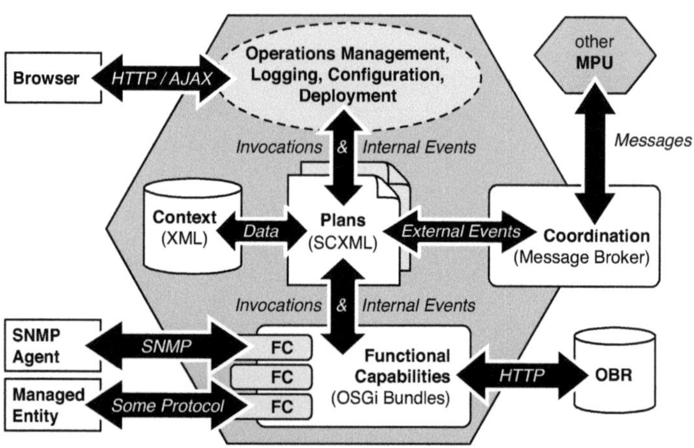

Figure 4.14: Structure of the MPU prototype

Plans are deployed from a BM Repository. We are currently using the local file system, but have also successfully employed a remote XML Document Management Server (XDMS) [236] for storage and retrieval of plan documents.

The generic interpreter architecture's Engine and Event Queue subsystem are implemented by the Apache engine, which conducts a stepwise interpretation of the model according to the SCXML execution semantics (see [289, Appendix B]) and maintains state configurations and context data. The Apache engine provides an extension mechanism for selecting/substituting the employed expression language, the event dispatching infrastructure, the context data binding and for specifying custom action statements, which can be formulated in the native execution platform language. The MPU maintains context data using the DOM format, which makes it easy to persistently store it as XML. The data is bound to the BM and can be accessed during the interpretation process by expressions specified in the plan. We choose to employ the JEXL expression language as it offers a decent performance and is maintained as an Apache commons project as well.

The role of the generic Event Dispatcher is covered by the OSGi Event Admin service [262, Service Compendium, Section 113], which offers a sophisticated mechanism for publishing events using *topic* scopes (see Section 2.2.6). In SCXML the `<send>` tag is employed to dispatch an event using a previously agreed-upon identifier. External communication between MPUs is also event-based, and event messages that are addressed to other MPUs are forwarded to a message broker, which takes care of dispatching the event to the target. For transmitting external events, we are employing the Apache ActiveMQ message broker [218], which is also maintained by the Apache Software Foundation (ASF). We choose this product, as it is released as open-source, mature enough for production purposes and has an active community that supports it.

FCs are maintained as OSGi bundles, which can be invoked using either a method-like call triggered by `<invoke>` or by dispatching events that are addressed to a designated FC using `<send>`. FCs are downloaded from an FC Repository and installed automatically during the dependency resolution process executed when deploying a new plan. This task is significantly alleviated through the usage of the OSGi Bundle Repository (OBR) technology [261], which automates most of the process.

Employed Technologies OSGi defines a standard, but does not prescribe an implementation. Therefore, a number of competing implementations exists. We investigated the use of Knopflerfish [281], Equinox [279] and Felix [216] — settling on Apache Felix, although there should be no problem in running the MPU using any of the other implementations.

The employed Apache SCXML engine is in version 0.9, implementing roughly the feature set specified in the W3C working draft dated May 16th, 2008. The Apache Felix framework is used in version 2.0.5, which implements the OSGi R4.1 standard. The web interface makes use of the Google Web Toolkit [237] in version 2.0 and Apache ActiveMQ was used in version 5.3.2. The versions of other software components is detailed below.

Event Admin Service The event admin service is used for local dispatching of events. It is connected to the SCXML engine and the employed message broker. The used version is 1.2.2.

OBR The bundle repository is either located in the local file system or uses a HTTP server for providing the FC jars. On the MPU side, the Bundle Repository provided by Apache Felix was used in version 1.6.2.

HTTP Service For exposing a web interface, the MPU needs to include an OSGi HTTP service. This is provided by the Pax Web project [259] from the Open Participation Software for Java (OPS4J) community, in version 0.7.2.

Management Interface For managing the MPU, we created a web interface and a textual interface. Additionally, the Apache Felix Web Management Console (3.0.0) and the Apache Felix Shell Service (1.4.2) are started, enabling runtime control of the OSGi implementation itself.

Log Service Logging is build upon version 1.0.0 of the Apache Felix Log Service.

4.5.2 Major Challenges and Key Results

The developed software is stable and offers a range of features required for utilisation of the MPU in a production setting. Using the MPU, we could show that our approach can be applied using an integration of existing, mature products and that the implementation of an MPU based on the OSGi framework is possible and well-suited to the requirements of a CU. The remaining text in this section describes the most challenging problems and solutions encountered while creating the MPU.

SCXML development cycle A major issue concerns the stability of the SCXML specification: it is still changed frequently, with one or more new versions each year. This is a problem in regard to the Apache SCXML implementation, which is not updated in the same cycle. It is sometimes hard to determine if an encountered issue is due to a bug in the software or an incompatibility because of an ambiguous or modified specification document. Although the Apache SCXML engine is still a beta version and we submitted bug reports and functionality patches to the project, this software is the most suitable and mature SCXML execution engine available.

Processing of ε-events The SCXML standard prescribes interpretation semantics using a normative algorithm, specified in a lisp-like notation [289, Appendix B]. The algorithm employs RTC semantics, which dictate that each external event submitted to an interpreter needs to be completely processed before the processing of the next event can occur. In the case of SCXML, this includes the processing of all internal events generated during the processing as well as all (direct and indirect) ε-transitions. This opens up the possibility for life-locks of the interpreter in ε-cycles. If the interpreter enters a ε-cycle, it becomes impossible to process external events, and as external events are defined as the only means to supply information to the interpreter [289, Encapsulation, Appendix B – Principles and Constraints], it is impossible for the interpreter to leave the cycle. This behaviour is explicitly allowed by the standard [289, Termination, Appendix B – Principles and Constraints].

Event Conversion We found that a larger amount of work needed to be invested into engineering the event dispatching routines. Although we employed the ActiveMQ product for external communication, events still need to be converted between three formats: the format of the SCXML implementation, the format of the OSGi Event Admin service and the format used by the JMS, which defines the standard interface used for passing events to the message broker. Conversion of the events does not only apply to a potential payload, but also to the event's topic and addressing scheme (see Section 2.2.6).

Creating and Referencing FCs FCs are intended as a way of packaging functionality to prepare them for invocation by the BMs. As we found out, it is necessary to indicate the used FCs from within the BM, and this is what the plan format is mainly used for. In addition to binding an FC, it might be necessary that the OSGI bundle containing the FC adheres to some constrains. This is due to the way that FC invocations are implemented; invocations from the SCXML engine must be transformed into Java calls that target a method within an OSGi service interface. The SCXML engine uses XML and OSGi bundles employ Java. Thus, not only does the call itself need to be transformed, but also the types and values of the parameters. We tried this approach with a simple invocation format and type system and found that it is possible but complex to implement. We then decided on prescribing a generic event format containing XML payload, which is dispatched to an FC, triggering the invocation of a function. Return values are communicated back in the same manner. This approach is easier to implement, but requires that FC developers are aware of the use of their components and implement the necessary mechanism (registration at the OSGi event admin service under an agreed-upon topic and processing of the received events).

Adaptation of the SCXML BM The current status of the Apache SCXML engine does not fully support an adaptation of the BM at runtime. This is a technical and not a conceptional issue: the interfaces that would allow us to change the runtime format and execution specification are not available after a plan has been started. We inspected the source code of the Apache SCXML engine and found no substantial obstacles for implementing runtime adaptation. Thus, we conclude that an extension of the engine code to support runtime modification of a BM is possible.

4.6 Summary

This chapter contains a description of the four implementations that we created to verify different aspects of our work. At the beginning of the chapter, we introduced a set of fundamental BM features that allowed us to classify the BM feature support provided by each of the interpreters. We also specified a generic interpreter architecture, which helps us to identify common concepts used in our implementation and which enables us to explain the differences between each of the created architectures.

Our earliest implementation is the TMPL engine, which interprets an EFSM to match patterns on a XML data stream. The EFSM is constructed in a lazy fashion at runtime, which demonstrates not only that the general adaptation of BMs at runtime is possible, but also that this approach bears a big potential for performance optimisation. The TMPL engine does not support the full set of fundamental BM features.

The second implementation is the ACE toolkit, which provides a component-based framework for the creation of autonomic systems. ACE behaviour is created through the interpretation of state machines at runtime. The design of this prototype helped us to develop the architecture of our approach and allowed us to study BM interpretation in the context of a group of collaborative entities, leading to interesting results for the specification of behaviour, the support of group communication in CU collectives and the supervision of components with runtime-adaptable behaviours (a topic that is investigated in more depth in Section 5.1). The ACE Toolkit enables novel strategies for creation of BMs, but does not support the full set of fundamental BM features.

The UML State Machine interpreter was the third implementation completed. This implementation is based on the Ecore runtime model format, and we use it to study the interpretation characteristics of the greatest possible range of BM features. Therefore, it implements all of the fundamental BM feature and many additional ones as well. The UML interpreter is not as applicable to real-world scenarios as the ACE toolkit or the MPU implementation, which is why we do not use it for the use case scenarios in Chapter 5. On the other hand, it is the most sophisticated implementation in regard to BM interpretation, and thus, we will use it for performance comparison of our approach in Section 6.3.1.

The last implementation was the MPU, which uses SCXML as the BM format, along with the Apache Felix OSGi framework to provide a sophisticated execution environment for BMs. The SCXML covers all of the fundamental BM features, and the Apache SCXML engine is a popular technology for BM execution. This is why we are interested in the general interpretation performance of the MPU (investigated in Section 6.3.2) and in the applicability of the MPU for real-world use cases (investigated in Section 5.2.2).

5 Use Case Studies

Facts do not cease to exist because they are ignored.
Aldous Huxley

We conduct four use case studies to show the feasibility of a BM interpretation approach in real-world situations and to provide guidance in regard to the estimation of resource constraints. Common to all of them is a network and systems management setting and the use of IP. The first one, *Service Supervision with ACEs*, is employed as a demonstration of the ACE toolkit and published in [57]. The second one, *Management in the Network*, shows the usage of BMs for delegation of management processes from a central management system to the network devices themselves and demonstrates how to technically determine the router load within such a scenario. This use case study is published in [106]. The third one, *Intrinsic Monitoring* investigates an application of our approach to path-based monitoring. It is published in [104]. The fourth use case documents the creation of a BM interpreter on an embedded system platform and is used to study the scalability limits of our approach. This research is published in [107].

5.1 Service Supervision with ACEs

Service supervision is the continuous observation of a system with the goal of determining correct and incorrect behaviour. The idea is to specify constraints on the system behaviour and to match them against the real execution behaviour of the system. This task is made much easier through the use of BMs, as the operational behaviour of a system is available for analysis in a meaningful format. Supervision of a system invariant could then be accomplished by, e. g., matching input and output events or observing the current state configuration.

Within our working group, the foundations for supervision of communicating Extended Finite State Machines (EFSM) [78] have been researched, along with a theory that allows to dynamically abstract from BMs [53]. By utilising dynamic abstraction, it is possible to derive a more abstract BM from (and consistent with) a more specific one. This approach is useful for assessment of complex systems utilising BM interpretation: a more abstract supervision model is generated from the specific BM used for interpretation. The supervision model is transmitted to a supervisor, where it is used in conjunction with runtime operational data to conclude on the correct behaviour of a system.

Supervision can also be extended to include self-healing facilities: by monitoring the operation of BMs, a supervision system can determine not only if another system is working properly, but also undertake means of repairing it. One approach that enables such a functionality is based on the annotation of states with desirability values (see also page 237 f. in Appendix C). In case that a supervision system detects that a BM remains in undesired states, it can try to resolve this problem by planning a transition path that leads to better desired states. System supervision based on annotated BMs has been studied extensively from an engineering perspective in our working group, and the interested reader can find more information in a recent publication [57].

To enable supervision, an interpreter needs to provide the current state configurations of all BM instances to a supervision system. Additionally, if supervision should also be used to handle errors, control facilities need to be provided. These might be as simple as a restart mechanism or more sophisticated, e. g. the ability to directly access the internal event dispatching mechanism. Such control capabilities are built into every ACE (see [54, Section III] and [27, Section 3.6]). Supervision using ACEs and a demonstration of possible applications are also described in detail in our recent publications on the subject [57, 56].

Supervision System Architecture In the ACE toolkit, supervision is considered as a service itself, performed by an collaborating group of ACEs. The supervision of a system is left to a third party that assures cooperating entities of the correct overall system behaviour. Supervision systems are created dynamic and on-demand using the self-organisation capabilities of ACEs, which allows them to form operative clusters, and even do so in the light of potential node failures. This is achieved by the adaptable BM as well as the ACEs ability to migrate between hosts dynamically while continuing to provide a service. To provide services, ACEs use self-organisation principles encoded in their self-models to find and connect to each other and in such a way form collaborating groups that are able to provide services. For the supervision use case, the supervision system creates itself to conform to the supervised system, in a structure that looks similar to the one depicted in Figure 5.1.

The picture shows the general type of ACEs (the hexagonal symbols) which would be involved in a supervision setup but omits their cardinality — in reality there are usually multiple Sensors, Corellators, Effectors and Systems under Supervision (SUS). ACE supervision relies on the interception of messages over two monitoring points (see the description of the Supervision organ in Section 4.3.1). These monitoring points are used by so-called *Checker* objects, of which there are two types: Bus Checker Object (BCO) and Gateway Checker Object (GCO). The scenario employs GCO objects, as only the external communication is monitored. The checker objects are transferred into the supervision organ of the SUS and run locally, handling the events passed through the two monitoring points. The reason for executing local

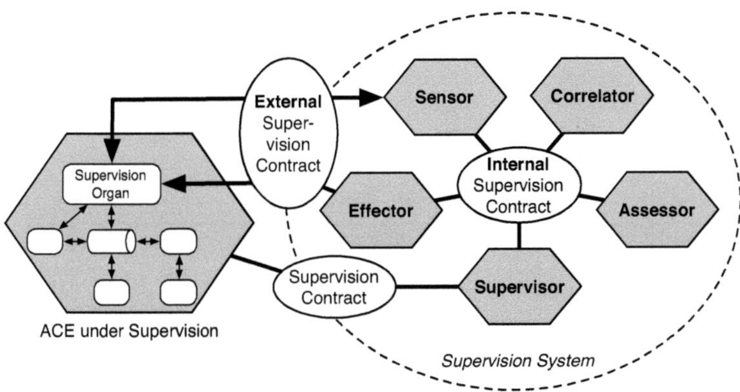

Figure 5.1: Organisation of ACEs for service supervision

functionality is to avoid excessive monitoring traffic being transmitted from the SUS to the supervision system as well as to filter and pre-process monitored data locally, before passing them to the supervision system. The five ACE types [57, Section IV.A 3)] of a supervision system are:

Supervisor is responsible for setting up and configuring the supervision system.

Sensors link the supervision system with the SUS by deploying checker objects into the supervised ACEs and by establishing dedicated communication channels for monitoring. They translate events delivered by the checker objects into the internal message format used by the supervision system and distribute them to other components of the supervision infrastructure.

Correlators are responsible for aggregating monitored data from distributed sources and correlate them with other information in order to extract meaningful indicators of the current condition of the SUS.

Assessor make assumptions on the current (or future) system health based on the output of the Correlators and invoke associated effectors if necessary.

Effectors are responsible to distribute contingency actions to the checker objects of the various ACEs under supervision, where they are used to steer the supervised ACE's execution.

Together, these ACEs form a control loop (from the SUS to the Sensor of the supervision system and back via the Effector), which is a typical feature found in an AS. The drawing also depicts the contracts in place between the ACEs: the Supervisor maintains a supervision contract with the SUS, the Sensor and Effector create an *external* contract with the SUS, which allows them to access the monitoring points and deploy the checker objects. The supervision system ACEs uses a separate, *internal* contract for its communication requirements.

5.1.1 Dynamic Reconfiguration Scenario

We employ the described approach to supervise a video service implemented as a set of distributed ACEs. A more detailed description of the scenario can be found in [57, Section VI]. The motivation for introducing service supervision is to handle failures of ACEs implementing the video client and one of several available video provider ACEs, as depicted in Figure 5.2. The goal of this scenario is to autonomously reconfigure the SUS and the supervision components if the Provider-Client relationship develops a fault.

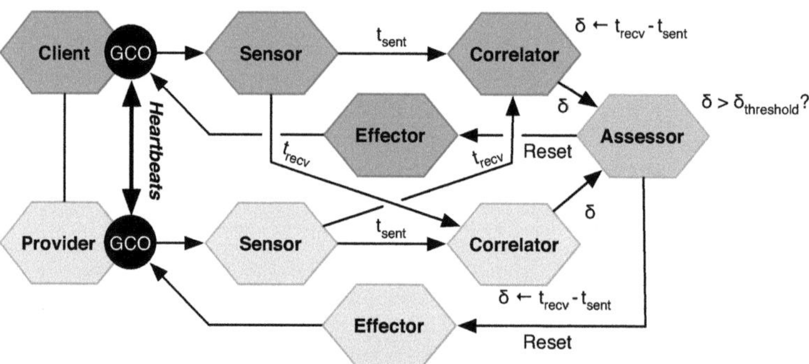

Figure 5.2: ACE-based supervision system for dynamic reconfiguration

The diagram omits the supervision ACE, as it is only relevant for setting up and removing the supervision system. During operation, the supervision system will monitor the state of the contract between the client ACE and the provider ACE. Lifeliness is tested using an exchange of heartbeat signals between two GCOs; hence, if the contract is malfunctioning in one or both directions, this fault can be detected by comparing the difference δ of the timestamps for sending (t_{sent}) or receiving (t_{recv}) a heartbeat signal to a threshold value $\delta_{threshold}$. The timestamps are collected by the Sensor ACEs and forwarded to the Corellator ACEs, which calculate the difference and pass this information on to the Assessor. Once an Assessor ACE determines that a communication delay between client and provider ACE is above a given threshold, it issues a reset command to an Effector ACE, which conducts a correction of the faulty ACE[1].

Employed Self-models In the following section we will give an overview of the self-models for the Supervisor, Correlator, Assessor, Sensor and Effector ACEs. A complete description in ACElandic can be found in Appendix E, while an overview of ACElandic is provided in Appendix C. The self-model of the Supervisor ACE first accepts a supervision contract and subsequently receives configuration information about the SUS (line 14–18). Afterwards, it discovers the necessary ACEs to set up a supervision system (line 20-34), concludes the internal supervision contract (line 36–44) and configures the involved ACEs (line 46–68). On cancellation of the supervision contract, it triggers a cancellation of the internal supervision system contract (line 70–72).

The Corellator ACE's self-models first accept a supervision contract and receive the associated configuration information (line 20–27) before starting. They are then listening to notifications from one of the sensors and store the contained t_{sent}, respective t_{recv}, data in the local context (line 31–40). Alternatively, on receiving a contract cancellation, they exit the inner `forever` loop and are available for contracting as part of another supervision system (line 40–45). Once a notification is received, the FC `corellate` is invoked and the calculated result δ is forwarded to the Assessor ACE.

The Assessor ACE's self-models at first enter a supervision system contract and conduct internal initialisation (line 13–18). Afterwards, they are available to receive notifications from the two Corellators and to store the transmitted δ in the local context (line 21–32); alternatively they receive a contract cancellation and start over (line 33–36). On detecting a transgression of the $\delta_{threshold}$ values, they send a notification to the corresponding Effector (line 39–50).

The Effector ACEs use a self-model that enters two contracts: an external one with the SUS and an internal one with the supervision system (line 20–22). Afterwards, an access to the SUS is established using a specific FC `connect` (line 23) and the Effector waits for an acknowledgment of the setup (line 25). During the regular operation, notifications are received from the Assessor and forwarded to the SUS (line 28–33). Alternatively, the Effector ACE receives a cancellation of the internal supervision contract and starts over.

In the beginning, the a Sensor ACE self-model executes the `config` plan that establishes two contracts: the ACE accepts an internal one, which provides them with the overall system configuration and is used for passing events to the Corellator (line 29–40), and it creates an external one, for monitoring the SUS (line 41–44).

[1]We are working under the assumption that the reason for the communication delay is a crash of a currently interpreted BM instance and that the ACE's Facilitator organ is able to fix this problem by resetting the faulty BM instance to a working state configuration

Afterwards, the Sensor ACE deploys the GCO and waits for confirmation of their deployment (line 45–53). It then spawns a concurrent execution of the `monitor` plan (line 54–55). The `config` plan subsequently waits for cancellation of the internal supervision contract and, in turn, cancels the external supervision contract after the `monitor` plan has finished (line 56–67). The `monitor` plan continuously polls the delay data of incoming and outgoing heartbeat messages and forwards them to the respective Correlators (line 75–87).

The service supervision scenario demonstrates how ACEs can be used to construct a supervision system in an on-demand fashion at runtime. The use case shows how one can monitor the interpretation of BMs at runtime and demonstrates the possibility of repairing a system by resetting a BM instance to a working state configuration. The performance of the dynamic reconfiguration scenario has not been assessed, but we conducted performance measurements with the ACE toolkit itself [27, Section 5].

5.2 Management in the Network

Network and systems management is a complex field that cannot be handled using a single, generic solution, as the infrastructure of an enterprise network may comprise thousands of devices from several vendors, all with slightly varying capabilities, software patch levels and protocol versions. Even if these could be cleanly integrated by following standardised protocols and operating procedures, there are still many problems to face: continuous integration whenever new devices are being introduced in the infrastructure as well as legacy system support, the integration of business goals with the technical infrastructure, or ensuring decent training for the administrative personnel [40]. We mandate the use of BMs for network and systems management, and propose to facilitate AS to tackle these problems.

Motivation for Management in the Network To understand the benefits that AS have over non-autonomic ones, we will take a look at the fundamental characteristics of AS. One characteristic that is repeatedly mentioned is the ability to talk about the behaviour of constituent entities of an AS and to change their behaviour dynamically [188, 136]. Given the assumption that AS are always composed of a collective of interacting entities[2], it is important to know how a system will behave as a whole based on the behaviour of the constituents and how to constrain the overall behaviour of the system to adhere to policies dictated by the system's environment. The idea of capturing behaviour in a way that it can be exchanged, transformed, interpreted and communicated was developed from this insight, which led us to the usage of BMs. BMs allow a network management system to exist as a widely distributed

[2]There is not much sense in regarding a single entity as being an AS; although from a strict point of view this is correct, from a practical point of view, this case is irrelevant.

collective of collaborating components, instead of a central monolithic application. This distribution is made possible through the capturing of management processes in the form of BMs, which are interpreted by a distributed set of CUs.

The *management in the network* use case study is employed to see how this idea works in a real world setting. We postulate that all management processes are captured in BMs, and one of the major ideas behind the employment of BMs for describing management operations is the potential re-use of previously captured expert knowledge. Re-use of knowledge across different administrative roles directly translates to a reduction of training and operational support costs regarding the personnel that executes these tasks. Once a BM is created for solving a routine task, it can then be added to a database or document management system and utilised by other people than the original creator of the model. For example, it would be feasible that BMs are created and maintained by specialised infrastructure experts, solely for other users like support assistants or network administration personnel. Through the use of BMs, operators could exercise control over an infrastructure on a more abstract level. Access to the heterogeneous infrastructure entities is achieved through a homogenous collective of CUs, providing a uniform way of executing management tasks. Re-use of management knowledge becomes feasible.

Managing a homogenous CU collective is easier than directly managing a heterogeneous set of infrastructure elements (routers, switches, servers, firewalls, etc.), each with a potentially different command set and varying management access technology. Even in an environment offering a centralised management system that allows for homogenous access to the devices, an administrator would need to know the specifics of an infrastructure element to manage it appropriately. These specifics can be hidden through the use of BMs that represent an abstraction of a concrete management process in a form that is suitable, both for human understanding, and for execution by a number of CUs. As BMs encapsulate expert knowledge, it is possible for people without this knowledge to not only execute the encapsulated processes, but also to gain an understanding of the internal steps of the processes due to the explicit representation contained within a BM.

Architectural Considerations The *management in the network* use case applies BM interpretation in the context of network and systems management. We researched this subject from a systems integration perspective and published our ideas in two articles [105, 106], using MBIM and *Document Based Integrated Management* as phrases to identify these concepts. The following text is based on these publications. This research also initiated our implementation of an MPU as well as of the associated infrastructure components.

The idea of *management in the network* is to formalise management processes using BMs interpreted by CUs, which are able to translate the processes described in the models to the management protocols understood by infrastructure elements. CUs are conceptually placed between the management plane and the technical infrastructure itself, as shown in Figure 5.3.

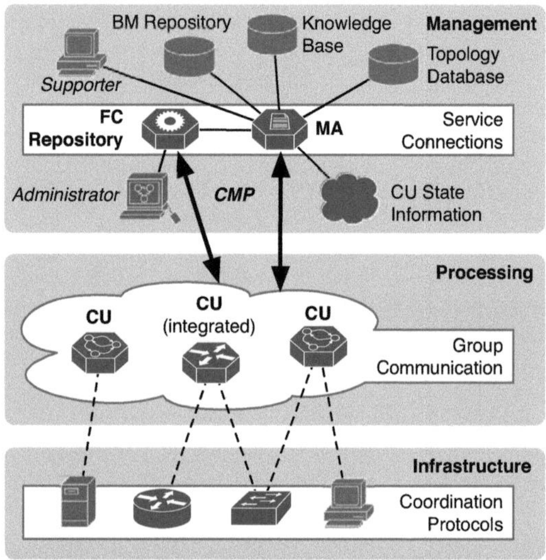

Figure 5.3: "Management in the Network" architecture

For each of the three depicted planes, there are typically specific communication primitives used between the entities on that level[3] and shown as white boxes underlying each of the contained elements. For requirements regarding the different communication protocols, see the discussion on distributed model management in Section 2.3.

All elements that are the actual subject of management are found at the **Infrastructure** level. These do not only encompass network elements, but also include business systems like web portal clusters or directory servers. Internal communication on this plane is typically done through coordination protocols, e. g. routing protocols or application server clustering protocols. Communication with the processing plane could be carried out using existing management protocols like the SNMP, the Network Configuration Protocol (NETCONF) [234] or command line over Secure Shell (SSH) [290], and is depicted using dashed lines in the diagram. MBIM does not add or modify anything at the infrastructure plane.

[3]There are also specific protocols used for inter-plane communication, but we found this to be a suitable criterium for identifying a separation between the conceptual planes.

We choose to place the CUs at the newly introduced **Processing** plane of the network, although it may also be regarded as part of the management plane. The processing plane contains a collective of CUs, optionally integrated with networking hardware, which are able to instantiate and interpret BMs. The interpretation of a BM instance at a CU triggers a number of invocations of FCs (see Section 2.2.5) that result in information exchange with the infrastructure layer via standard management protocols. Within the collective, information is exchanged using group communication facilities. An additional protocol is not needed here, as message content and semantics are determined by the language that is used by the BMs that implement a management task.

Between the management and processing plane, things are different. Information exchange is also based on the group communication primitive, due to its ability to address a set of CUs at once, along with guaranteed reliability aspects. However, this should be realised using a standard interaction protocol, which we term the CU Management Protocol (CMP). The CMP is used for three separate purposes: BM management, FC management and dissemination of CU runtime information. It defines the interaction between CUs and the elements that serve as managers for the collective in the management plane. Thus, a CMP needs be able to handle the semantics of the BMs, FCs and CU concepts.

The **Management** plane contains conventional management systems, including central management information databases as well as additional introduced components, namely the MA, the BM and FC Repositories. The MA is responsible for management of the overall system, including the maintenance of CUs and deployment of BMs in the collective. To accomplish this task, the MA accesses four resources. The first resource is the BM Repository that maintains all BMs that are known to the system. The second one, called the *Knowledge Base*, collects information about troubleshooting processes in the form of previously created Trouble Tickets (TT). The third one, termed the *Topology Database*, contains up-to-date information about the topology of the network. This includes the addresses, names and locations of networked devices and the connections between them. The fourth resource concerns runtime information of the CUs, which includes the currently active BM instances, the active state configurations of these, and the degree of utilisation for each CU. We do not prescribe how such information is collected, but possibilities include e. g. listening to the continuous data flow within the collective or directly polling CUs.

The FC Repository is used to configure, maintain and provide FCs in a network. Provisioning an FC means offering a CU the possibility to download and install software in an executable representation, e. g. a suitable code binary. Enabling the dynamic loading of FCs supports the flexible deployment of models, as missing FCs can be amended at the CU level in response to BM binding requirements.

The MA, FC Repository and other resources are regarded as conceptual elements. For MBIM, it does not matter how a technical implementation would map them to real soft- or hardware, as long as the described functions are available to an operator. Operating personnel itself is modelled using two roles: the Supporter role (someone utilising the system to carry out a management task) and the Admin role (someone who influences the way that the system works by configuring available FCs). Operators directly interact with the MA and FC Repository using human interaction interfaces — any other communication on the management plane would typically be carried out over application-specific service connections.

5.2.1 Performance Troubleshooting Scenario

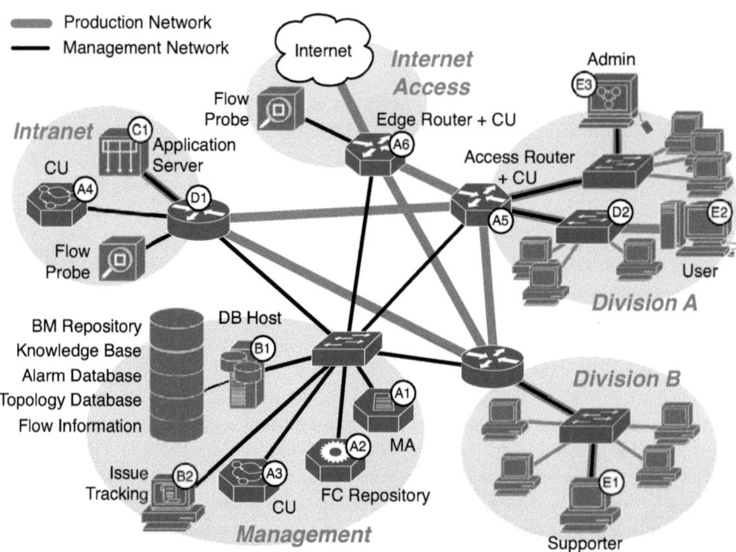

Figure 5.4: Example network topology for the troubleshooting scenario

As a guiding vision for MBIM, we developed a scenario in the realm of performance and fault management. It is based on a hypothetical network of a small enterprise with two divisions. There are three human actors: the Admin – a network administrator, the Supporter – an employee in first level IT support, and the User – an accountant. The scenario is meant to serve as a conceptual framework, allowing us to investigate specific aspects of its implementation within a more complete setting.

Figure 5.4 depicts a simplified view of the examined network topology. Elements that are relevant for the scenario are depicted by a designator indicating their conceptual affiliation. There are two separate networks: a management network (thin black lines) and a production network (thick grey lines). In places where both are on the same physical medium (depicted by a thin black line surrounded by a large grey border), a logical separation with Virtual LAN is used. The complete network consists of five subnets, connected by four routers. There are two fully switched division subnets connected via access routers, an intranet subnet containing the backend servers, a management subnet that contains the administrative systems and a subnet for internet access. Both the internet edge router (A6) as well as the intranet access router (D1) use equipment that allows for capturing of IP flow information. All elements with designators that contain an A are devices that were introduced in the network to support MBIM. Besides the MA and FC Repository (A1 & A2), there are four CUs (A3, A4, A5, A6), two of them integrated with a router. The B group contains other management systems, namely an issue tracking system (B2) and a database host (B1). Besides the Knowledge Base and Topology Database, there is a BM Repository, a database for captured IP flow information and a database that stores alarm notifications from any of the networked devices. Back-end server systems fall into the C category and are found in the intranet subnet. The case study presupposes only an application server (C1). Conventional network equipment has been assigned D designators: The intranet router (D1) and a managed switch in division A (D2). The last category, designated E, is for devices which interface directly with humans. These are the computer of the Supporter in division B (E1), the computer of the User (E2) and the workstation of the Admin (E3).

Anamnesis In the following text, we portray the scenario of a performance troubleshooting process using a narrated dialogue between two roles: the Supporter and the User. The Phone rings at IT support. Supporter answers and talks to the User. The User complains about the network performance: "My access to the accounts is sometimes really slow". Supporter creates a TT and starts to record the incident. The problem is not known to the Supporter and she starts looking up similar issues in the Knowledge Base. She discovers a number of other TTs with similar issues described, pointing to a number of potential root causes.

Root cause hypotheses establishment After reading some of the TT descriptions, the Supporter identifies four reasons that might be causes for the observed behaviour:

1. The application server that executes the accounting software is running under full load. For example, this could be due to a slow processor or a bad configuration of Java VM garbage collection parameters.

2. The network route between the desktop computer of the User and the application server is operating at full capacity. This could be due to, e. g. transmission

of abnormally high data volumes or because of badly dimensioned bandwidth during capacity planning of the network.

3. A device on the route between the desktop computer of the User and the application server is damaged. For example, a cable could have a loose connection or an interface card could have switched off due to high temperature.

4. The desktop computer of the User is operating at its limits, e. g. due to an overeager virus scanner or because the machine is generally not capable of keeping up with the processing requirements.

The User explains that "the problem only happens from time to time and I'm not a computer-savvy guy, anyway". The Supporter decides that all four possibilities are relevant and that they should be monitored to find a solution to the problem.

The Supporter now wants to check all of the four hypotheses. Using nowadays tools, this is a very tough problem for a first-level IT support employee. The Supporter would need to have access to the necessary tools for checking each of the possibilities, plus the expertise on how to use them. Due to the sporadic nature of the problem, it would be unlikely that the User tells the Supporter exactly when the issue is happening. Arranging such feedback is not trivial: helpdesk staff are often not allowed to give out their individual phone extension, or they are busy with another client and unavailable to take the call. The most likely reaction of the Supporter would be to only falsify hypothesis 3 through a manual search in the alarm database and then escalate the TT to second-level support.

Let us now assume that the network facilitates MBIM. In this case, the Supporter has access to a collection of troubleshooting BMs, which she would either find by searching the BM Repository or which would be referenced from an already solved TT in the Knowledge Base.

The Supporter identifies four existing troubleshooting BMs (from now on referenced to as models A, B, C, D – matching to hypotheses 1, 2, 3, 4) in the BM Repository. She uses a graphical tool to add an additional BM (E) to coordinate the four other ones. The four existing BMs and the newly created one are referenced in the TT.

Selected Behaviour Models for Activation The five employed BMs are formulated as UML State Machine diagrams and can be found in Appendix F. They are shortly described here.

Model A contains the logic for a performance audit of a given application server and measures performance values by employing cyclic polling using Java Management Extensions (JMX). It also calculates statistical results using the measured values and classifies them as *red*, *yellow* or *green*.

Model B is used to execute a performance audit on a given network route, measuring the performance values of all network elements on a given route using cyclic polling via SNMP. It also calculates performance statistics and classifies the results, providing an overall view of a route's state.

Model C collects all alarms of a given type, raised during a given time period, on a given route by querying the alarm database for alarms that were send by any network element on that route and in that period of time. It prepares the results by correlating and filtering the alarms.

Model D executes a performance audit of a given client computer by measuring the machine's performance through cyclic polling over SNMP. It will also calculate statistical values and classify the result.

Model E sends a start event to the models A – D once the User is accessing the application server, which it can conclude by analysing IP flow information from the intranet router D1. It is responsible for collecting the results and errors that appeared over the period of a week and informs the Supporter by activation of the TT. All models are automatically removed once they reach a final state in their process logic.

Behaviour Model Deployment Process The Supporter now uses the MA to deploy the model with the network using the step-by-step process as described in Section 2.3. She starts with the selection step by using the five models that will capture the overall troubleshooting activity.

During the mapping process she conducts a static configuration of the BMs by going through a list of open parameters and assigning values to each of them. With some parameters, she keeps the default values, e. g. the time period of the activity is set to one week. Other values come from information in the TT, for example the identification of the User's computer or are disclosed by the User himself, e. g. the identification of the accounting system he uses. They might also stem from her own experience, for example the identification of the credentials for logging into a system. After filling in the missing parameters, the MA automatically completes the step by querying the topology database for unresolved topology parameters like IP addresses or route configurations. For example, the process logic contained in Model B receives the host name of E2 as a value for the source host identifier and the name of C1 as destination host identifier to carry out the route audit; during the mapping step this would be resolved to a sequence of IP addresses that correspond to the route E2 - D2 - A5 - D1 - C1[4].

The mapping step results in an assignment as follows: CU A3 is assigned the coordination model E and the collection of alarms using BM C. A4 will measure

[4]compare with Figure 5.4

the performance of the application server (model A), because this device can easily access the application server via JMX. CU A5 is assigned model D because of the required FCs and the proximity to the User's computer. A6 will process BM B due to a low utilisation of the device.

As it is not necessary for the User to participate in the subsequent activation steps, the Supporter explains the start of the measurement activity, promises to resume contact in a week's time and ends the phone call.

In the following transmission step, each BM is deployed at a CU using CMP. Once the local model is received at a CU, the FC dependencies need to be resolved, eventually resulting in one or more, binary FC downloads from the FC Repository and subsequent installation of any new FCs. Once all necessary FCs are in place, the BMs are instantiated. For the fourth step, activation, a ready event is disseminated to other CUs, allowing for the synchronised start of BM logic evaluation at each of the local model state machines.

Observation and Diagnosis Every time that the User accesses the accounting system, models A, B and D are triggered with a start event from model E. Similarly, a stop event will be sent if the IP flow information between E2 and C1 indicates that the User stopped accessing the server. After one week, the measured performance values for each cycle are combined through the local model E with any alarms queried from the alarm database using BM C. The classified results are stored in the TT and the Supporter is notified by an open TT that is assigned to her support team.

These are the results found in the TT: server utilisation measurements were classified as green, implying that the server was working well all the time. The route audit results are marked with a warning value: the network link between D2 and A5 of the audited route in the division A subnet was over-utilised at two times, on a Monday between 14:01h – 14:23h and on a Friday between 14:05h – 14:18h. This was determined through the unusually high number of TCP re-transmits and packet losses on the link. No relevant alarms were detected in the time-span and the client computer had some utilisation peaks, but these were in a normal range for the device.

The Supporter concludes that a specific audit on the over-utilised link is to be conducted, to further narrow down the problems that exist. The User is informed about the intermediary results. After further analysis of the link in question, for example using intrinsic monitoring, it turns out that all computers in the subnet of division A start to run a backup script at 14:00h each day – this traffic chokes the link completely. The Admin modifies the backup scripts and the problem vanishes. The User is informed, and the TT closed and added to the Knowledge Base. This information is now available to other troubleshooters as directly re-usable knowledge through the appropriate BM models in the BM Repository.

5.2.2 Monitoring Router-Load Using MBIM

The previously described scenario enabled us to form a vision on how BM interpretation can play a role in the context of network and systems management. However, this scenario is too large to be completely implemented with the resources available to us. We therefore concentrated on demonstrating key issues. One of the them concerns the interpretation of a model, which captures monitoring behaviour using SNMP. The employed plan (see Section 4.5) contains a BM akin to model D in Appendix F, but is used for monitoring a router, not a client computer. For interpretation of the monitoring model, we employed the MPU discussed in Section 4.5, integrated within a CISCO 2800 Integrated Services Router (ISR) [224]. This setup is shown in Figure 5.5.

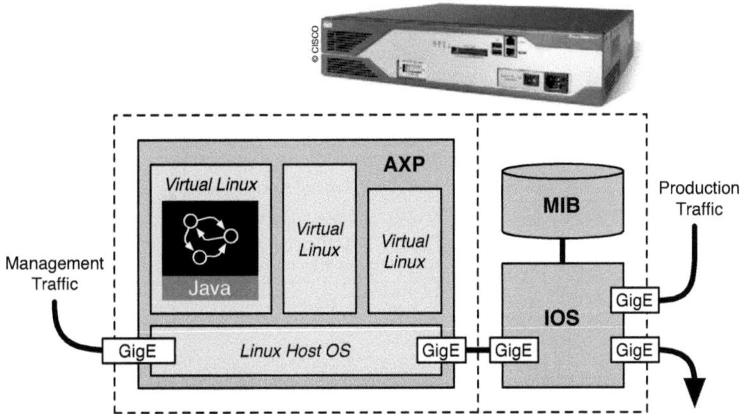

Figure 5.5: Integration of the interpreter with a CISCO 2800 ISR

Cisco names this technology the Application eXtension Platform (AXP) [225]. From a hardware point of view, it consists of a small computer using a form factor compatible with the network-module slot of the 2800 ISR series. This enables it to be directly inserted into the router chassis, receiving power by the router and communicating with the router's OS[5] via a dedicated Gigabit Ethernet (GigE) [241] connection. The AXP machine provides a separate, external GigE interface, which we are using to manage the MPU by means of a web interface. From a software point of view, the AXP platform provides a hardened Linux host OS, which is able to run a number of virtual instances of itself. Each virtual instance serves as a sandbox

[5]The Internetwork Operating System (IOS)

that can be constrained in regard to available resources. The MPU, in turn, executes on top of a Java VM in one of these virtual instances.

The Employed BM To obtain performance data of the current production traffic that is passing through the router's network interfaces, the MPU assumes the role of an SNMP manager. It uses the plan shown on page 253 ff. in Appendix F, while the plan format itself is described in Section 4.5.

The plan definition starts by specification of a unique id and namespace (line 2). Afterwards, the dependencies are listed. The BM requires three FCs to be present (line 7–15). These support the communication using the SNMP protocol, calculate of statistical values and are able to classify the measurement results. Additionally, the dependencies include the declaration of addressing details for an external plan with the identifier `Collector` (line 16–17). The collector plan receives the classification reports created by this plan.

The BM is defined in SCXML (see Appendix B) as a direct child of the `<Behaviour>` element (line 21 –117). The nested SCXML script starts with a declaration of the context (line 26–36), which holds the current measurement values for CPU and RAM utilisation, the calculated average of these utilisation values over the last minute and a classification result. The XML namespaces for these data need to be set or cleared[6], as the elements would wrongfully belong to the SCXML namespace, otherwise. The BM starts in the state `Init` and enters the state `Idle` upon reception of a `ready` event (line 39–41). It then waits for reception of either a `start` or `exit` event (line 44–45). In case of a reception of the `exit` event, the BM continues to state `Exit`, where a `done` event will trigger the termination of the BM (line 111-115). Otherwise, a `start` event will cause the BM to enter the substate `PollCPU` of the compound state `MeasurePerfomanceSNMP`.

The compound state `MeasurePerfomanceSNMP` can only be left using two transitions: on the reception of the `stop` event, the BM will continue in the `Classified` state, or on the reception of the `exit` event, it will go to the `Exit` state (line 50–51). While the BM stays in the compound state, the execution flow is circular: at first, the `PollCPU` state is traversed, then the `PollRAM` state. The BM then arrives at the `CalcStatistics` state and continues to the `Waiting` state, where it stops for a minute before continuing with another cycle by entering the `PollCPU` state again (line 53–90). In both of the `Poll...` states, the BM triggers the sending of a SNMP GetRequest Protocol Data Unit (PDU) to the agent running in the IOS part of the router by invoking a suitable SNMP FC that uses the router's internal GigE connection. This invocation is done using the `Snmp` FC (line 54–59 and line 67–72). The router's SNMP agent queries the relevant MIBs and sends the obtained data back to the MPU by employing a SNMP Response PDU. The SNMP FC receives the response and delivers it back to the BM in a `done.invoke...` event. The result

[6] Done by the `xmlns=""` statement

of this invocation is then stored in the context data for later retrieval (line 61–26 and line 74–75). Another FC invocation, this time of the `StatisticsCalculator` FC, is processed in the state `CalcStatistics`. During the invocation, the complete context is passed to the FC. The FC calculates an average of the recorded values and stores the results in the `Averages` section of the context (line 80–81). Once the average has been calculated, the `Waiting` state is entered, where an internal timeout event is used to restart the cycle after one minute by entering the state `PollCPU` (line 85–90).

Once the performance measurement cycle has stopped, the `Classify` state is entered. In this state, the classification FC is invoked, which calculates a classification result (e. g. *red* for a router under maximum load) and stores it in the context (line 95–96). Afterwards the state `Report` is entered, and a `report` event is send to the external `Collector` plan (line 101–107). The BM then returns to the state `Idle` and waits for another `start` event.

There are a number of alternatives within this scheme that we further investigated. For example, SNMP requests and responses can be directly mapped to events, allowing the model to continue with the execution while a request is being processed. Another option concerns the use of SNMP; there are APIs for the AXP platform provided by Cisco that allow for privileged access to the IOS, facilitating the monitoring or control of the device without the usage of SNMP at all.

To manage operational aspects of the MPU (existing plans, available functional repositories, logging) via a Control Interface, we employ a web GUI that allows us to inspect an MPU's operation, the deployed FCs and the state configuration of the active plans. Following the MBIM vision, the management would be carried out using a dedicated system like the previously discussed MA component, but this has not been concretely demonstrated yet. In our current scenario, an operator directly monitors an MPU's runtime data using a web browser, while the CMP governs the AJAX-based data exchange between an MPU and the HTTP client.

Apart from the MPU, the MBIM components that have been concretely implemented within this scenario are the FC Repository, which is engineered as a web server that provides FCs via the OBR standard, and the BM Repository, which is implemented as an XDMS or a file system. We found that by using the BM interpreted with MPUs on the AXP platform we can drastically reduce management traffic. Additionally, the approach promises unmatched flexibility when introducing new monitoring functions into a network.

5.3 Intrinsic Monitoring

This use case was created in the context of an investigation of novel mechanisms that allow the monitoring of routers along a given path, based on IPv6 [43, Chapter 22] features. It has also been published in [104].

When observing the properties of resources in a telecommunications network along a route and in an on-demand manner, a typical setup like the one seen in Figure 5.6 is often used.

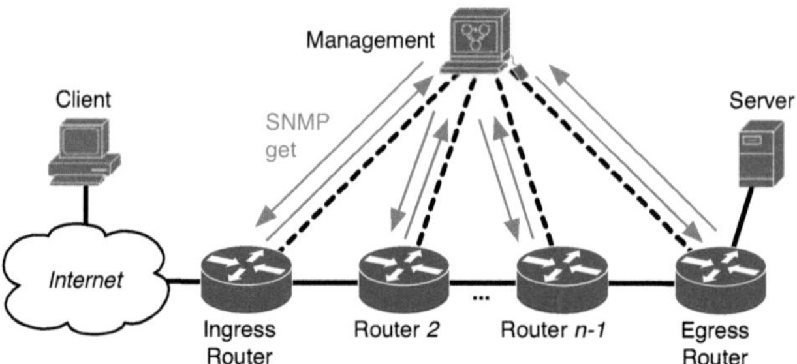

Figure 5.6: Monitoring a route using SNMP polling

Depicted is the path of IPv6 packets that travel from a client to a server machine through the internet. One part of the route lies within a single administrative domain, traffic entering the domain comes trough the Ingress router and leaves through the Egress router. To monitor information along the route inside the domain, a central management system would first need to determine which routers were traversed by a given packet by inspection of routing tables or querying of topology databases and subsequently poll every device using SNMP (or similar mechanism) over its management interface. Using such an approach is straightforward to implement and works with the majority of networking devices. Unfortunately, it exhibits some overhead concerning the amount of SNMP packets that need to be transmitted for each observation. Usually, scalability is also an issue because of the centralised organisation of the monitoring management system.

In contrast, our approach, called *intrinsic monitoring*, introduces a new method to network monitoring that promises a reduction of monitoring and management traffic through an increased autonomy of the network monitoring system.

The idea behind intrinsic monitoring is simple; we embed monitoring data within a suitable conventional packet and forward that packet along the route. Each device on the route updates the embedded information until the last router reports it back to the management system. Figure 5.7 shows that there is a reduction in the number of packets used to obtain the monitoring result. It can also be seen that routers are now behaving more autonomically: Router *2* ... Router *n-1* are not directly communicating with the management system, they operate on their own accord.

Intrinsic monitoring only focusses on a single domain rather than on an internet-wide application. The reason for this is simple: control of network elements in a

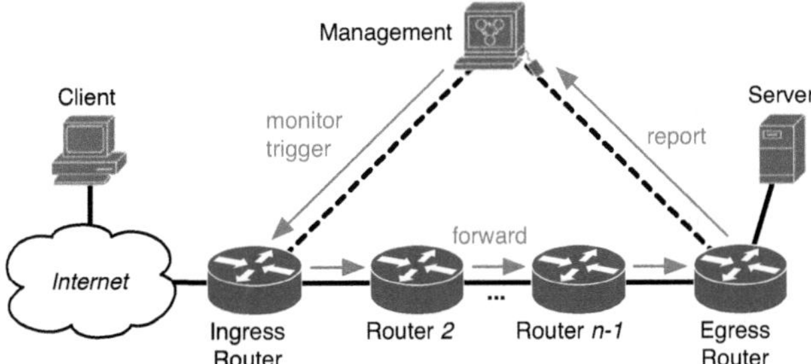

Figure 5.7: Monitoring a route using intrinsic monitoring

single administrative domain is fully in the hand of an operator, giving them the freedom to apply new techniques (even proprietary ones). Using new extension headers would be such a proprietary extension, as none of the currently available devices supports this feature, and packets with unknown extensions trigger an error or are simply discarded. Furthermore, different administrators have different policies and use different mechanisms, even to accomplish the same task. Hence, intrinsic monitoring can only be viable within a single management domain.

For this use case, we employ two mechanisms: IPv6 extension headers [104, Section 4] and BMs. Extension headers enable the embedding of monitoring data in-band to normal IPv6 traffic and thus support a distributed approach to monitoring. BMs are used to formalise the operations that each router can apply on a packet and are interpreted during runtime, thereby orchestrating a device's behaviour. This presupposes that BMs are already deployed at the network devices prior to executing the monitoring task and that they are selectable using an identification number.

5.3.1 Execution of Monitoring Behaviour

Once an Ingress router has identified an IPv6 packet to use for intrinsic monitoring, it adds an intrinsic monitoring header (for details regarding this extension header, see [104, Section 4.1]) and forwards the packet along the path. An intermediary router will pick it up and process the contained monitoring data in the way depicted in Figure 5.8.

The diagram shows the flow of a single IPv6 packet, containing an intrinsic monitoring extension header, through an intrinsic-monitoring aware router. The router detects (e. g. by means of Deep Packet Inspection (DPI)) [142] that the packet contains an intrinsic monitoring extension header. The data carried within the header is then used to select a BM through the **Type** field. The selected BM is then interpreted, resulting in the execution of a number of actions, in this case monitoring

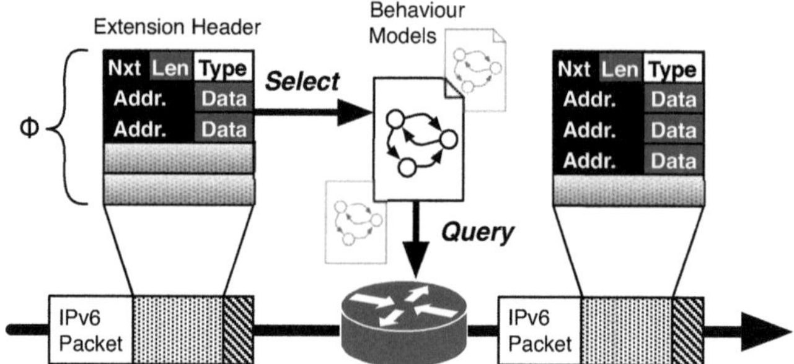

Figure 5.8: Packet forwarding using intrinsic monitoring

queries that retrieves some performance data from the router itself. The extension header contents are updated with the router's address and the obtained value(s), and the packet is forwarded further along the path. In the diagram, the maximum extension header size is indicated as Φ.

Employed BMs There are four example BMs found in Appendix G, which demonstrate the use of intrinsic monitoring for collection of a monitoring data element from each router along a path. BM **D** queries a router for the current value of a monitored data element and subsequently updates the extension header. The model consists of three states connected by ε-transitions. There are two actions used: read_performance_datum(), which queries the router for the current value of the resource attribute via an FC binding, and update_ext_header(), which appends a given value to the header's content. We do not describe in detail how a datum would be obtained at the router but assume that it should generally be possible, i. e. using internal SNMP calls or by directly interfacing with the device's hardware. The returned value is stored in the context data under the identifier u and thereafter used to update the header content. The packet that is being modified can be accessed using the identifier p, which is handed as a parameter to the model.

The BM **A** waits for a trigger from the management system and subsequently selects a packet to embed in the extension header. Finding a suitable packet depends on the packet size: If one would attempt in-band monitoring in a naïve manner and simply attach a new extension header to an existing packet, the packet's size could easily grow larger than the paths Maximum Transmission Unit (MTU) [43, p. 336 ff.], resulting in a packet drop. One solution to get around the problem is by calculating Φ in advance using $\Phi = M \times (16 + D) + 3$ and then choosing a packet that can accommodate Φ bytes of additional data without invalidating the path MTU. The maximum size Φ depends on the number of routers M on the path, the size of data D to acquire on the route and a constant given by the IPv6 extension header layout (we assume 3 bytes). In the worst case, M is the number of hops on the longest, non-circular path within the administrative domain.

Insertion of an intrinsic monitoring extension header is triggered by the management system through transmission of a *trigger* message that activates the first transition of the matching BM **A** at the Ingress router. The router starts to scan every packet for its size, identifies the first suitable one and removes it from the forwarding mechanism using packet filtering. It then utilises the functionality depicted in BM **D** to update the extension header before enqueuing the packet for forwarding and returning to the initial behaviour state.

Intermediary routers have a more trivial task: they need to update any packet arriving with an existing intrinsic monitoring extension header. The BM **B** shows how this is done, again relying on model **D** to query the datum and update the header. This BM is executed by all the intermediary routers on the path.

Lastly, the extension header needs to be removed from the in-band traffic at the Egress router, which is achieved by the BM **C**. After retrieving the packet, the header is updated with the Egress router's datum to complete the data acquisition, and the data is afterwards consolidated in a report format. The report is then sent with a report message to the management system. Subsequently, the intrinsic monitoring header is removed from the packet, and the packet forwarded to its actual destination.

The overall study has not been evaluated completely in a real-world setting, but important aspects have been proven to work. For example, the embedded systems experiment (described in Section 5.4 and in [107]) was conducted in the context of this setting, as we are interested in the feasibility of BM interpretation in resource-constrained platforms, such as routers. Our colleagues L. Shi and A. Davy also researched intrinsic monitoring in more detail [176], including the implications regarding system security [175].

5.4 An Application to Embedded Systems

Our final use case concerns the creation of a BM interpreter for embedded systems and has been published together with P.H. Deussen and H. Coşkun [107].This experiment was conducted to determine the scalability limits of the approach in regard to resource consumption and to demonstrate the feasibility of such an undertaking, while determining if the performance is reasonably adequate for our application purposes.

We decided to use the simplest hardware that could serve as an interpreter platform to mark the possibly *low end* regarding the resource usage of the interpretation approach. The interpreter for this use case was implemented using the C language and an *Arduino* board [220] with an 8 bit ATmega328P microcontroller. The features of the Arduino prototyping platform are listed in Table 5.1.

Feature	Description
Model	Arduino Duemilanove
CPU	ATmega328P Microcontroller
Core Frequency	16 MHz
RAM	2 KB
Non-volatile Memory	32 KB Flash and 1 KB EEPROM[7]
Operating System	—

Table 5.1: Platform used for measuring the embedded interpreter

The platform has been extended with a custom board that allows for input and output events by the means of three buttons, a potentiometer and three lights of different colours. Universal Serial Bus (USB) [283] is used for providing current to power the board, transmitting BMs and more sophisticated output, e. g. of measurement values. Error diagnostics is done via blink sequences of a blue light. The utilised platform is shown in Figure 5.9.

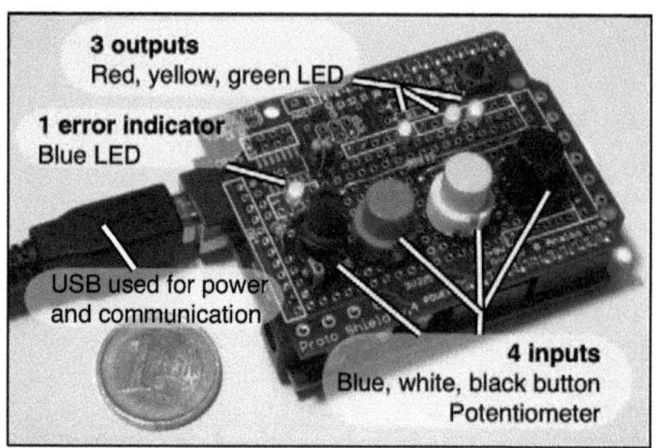

Figure 5.9: Target platform for the embedded system interpreter

Software-wise we are using the simplest design that still enables us to show a working approach. This interpreter has little in common with the generic interpreter architecture, but still includes all of the fundamental BM features, apart from a history mechanism (see Section 4.1).

Architecture and Operation We abstained from defining a presentation or persistent storage format for the utilised BMs and work directly with the in-memory representation Abstract Syntax Tree (AST) [3, Vol. 1, p. 60]. For each model, the

[7]Electrically Erasable Programmable Read Only Memory

complete AST data is allocated as a single chunk of memory, and the AST structure is constructed with single-byte references to this data. Prior to interpretation, an additional *executor* structure is allocated that holds input and output event queues as well as data structures for processing parallel regions and a reference to the initial starting state for execution.

The number of states is restricted to 256 symbols. Each state is represented by a data structure containing fields that allow navigation of the composition hierarchy. For performance reasons, we separate the state data structure into a set of substates, a set of parallel regions and an additional reference to a superstate. In addition, the structure contains a set of references to outgoing edges and a so-called *flag* byte used to indicate state properties, e. g. marking of initial states is implemented as a single bit in the flag byte. Sets are generally implemented as byte arrays with an additional field that holds set size. For aggregated states and states containing parallel regions, it is necessary to identify the start state of contained component(s) and to additionally create data structures that allow for pseudo-concurrent processing of parallel regions.

There can be 256 transitions, which are defined by a data structure with a reference to a destination state, assignment of a triggering event and an output event assignment. Events are numbered from 0 to 255 and identified by their numerical value — 0 marks the special ε-event. The transition structure also contains references to a guard condition predicate and an action mapping. Due to the parallel processing of transitions, it is possible for multiple events to be received during a single step of a model. Events are buffered for input and output in ring-buffers, limited to 10 elements. The context data variables are limited to a maximum of 246 readable and writeable entries per BM and 10 global entries shared between all executing models. The variables are limited to 8 bit integer numbers and there is no other type system. When data values are evaluated within boolean expressions, we follow C conventions for assigning logical values: 0 corresponds to a logical *false*, other values are *true*. The guard condition predicates are specified within the model AST and can be constructed from variable or constant references (notationally depicted using a \$ sign), boolean operators ($!$, $\wedge$, $\vee$) and comparison operators ($=$, $<$, $>$, $\leq$, $\geq$). Evaluation precedence is implicitly given through the AST hierarchy. Actions are implemented as statically bound code. An action binding is a conventional function call with an arbitrary number of input and output parameters, and represents fixed capabilities of a device that are orchestrated using the BM's logic. FC bindings are implemented using a function pointer and an ordered set of variable references. Parameters need to be de-referenced inside of the action function and can be used to read or write the variable value. There are also two predefined actions that can be used for delayed event sending. We created three timers that can be set with a delay value using `set_timer(id,delay)` to deliver the specific events 8, 9 and 10 once the delay time passes. Timers can be cleared using `clear_timer(id)` which suppresses dispatching of the timer event.

Performance of Transition Matching We measured the time that our implementation needs to react to a single input event with a single output event by firing a single transition, and we also determined the latency of the interpreter when processing multiple transitions. For this, we employed 30 different BMs with an increasing number of transitions leaving a single state. Each transition is triggered by a specific event (numbered from 1 to 30) and sends a corresponding output event 101 to 130. Each model is then supplied with exactly one event, activating the transition that is triggered by the event with the highest number. This is done to force the interpreter into exhibiting worst-case behaviour (it needs to check each transition before finding the transition that matches). The results, along with an illustration of the experimental models, are depicted in Fig. 5.10.

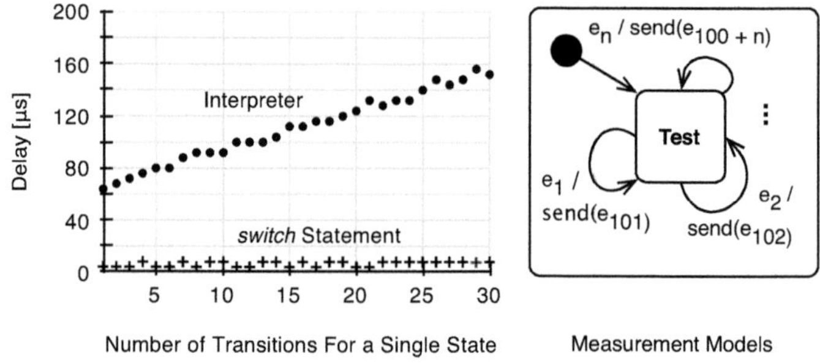

Figure 5.10: Transition matching performance of the embedded interpreter

To put the measurements into perspective, we also measured the time that it takes for a conventional *switch* statement in C to deliver the same result. Latency measurements have been conducted using in-line timestamps with an accuracy of ~4 µs and the latency for a simple transition is ~64 µs, which includes event processing, timer handling, transition selection and firing the transition. It is a factor of ~10 slower than a conventional switch statement, which executes at ~6 µs. Latency increases linearly with each additional transition, ~3 µs for each transition up to 152 µs for 30 transitions. The switch statement has a roughly constant delay, independent of the given event. To determine the performance of dynamic action bindings, we created models that trigger an action using a single transition from a single state and altered the number of parameters (0 to 10) passed to the action. The additionally introduced delay amounts to an average of ~3 µs per additional parameter. For conventional function calls, an additional delay must exist as well, but we were unable to determine it, as the measured runtime latencies fell within the precision range of the employed timing mechanism.

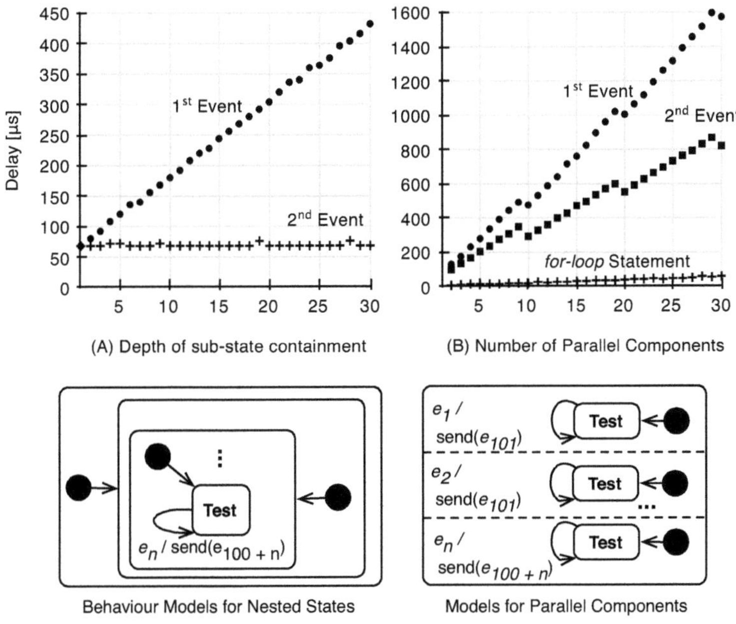

Figure 5.11: Embedded interpreter performance for composition and concurrency

Performance of Processing of Compound States and Parallel Regions The two major features that differentiate statecharts from EFSMs are state composition and the ability to specify parallel regions. To measure the performance of processing composite states, we used a series of models with an increasing number of nested states (from a single state to a compound with a nesting depth of 30), where the most deeply nested state has a transition that matches on a given input event. The parallel region processing was analysed using 30 models, where each model consists of a state with an increasing number of parallel regions, each triggering on the same input event. The results are displayed along with the experimental models in Figure 5.11.

We found it necessary to differentiate between the first input event and subsequent events[8] processed in the same state. This is due to additional functionality executed when entering a composite state or a state that contains parallel regions. Figure 5.11(A) shows an average delay of ~12.5 µs per additional nested state for an event

[8]In the diagram labelled as 2nd Event, representative for all subsequent events

that triggers the entering of the composition hierarchy. Once the compound state has been entered, the delay for processing subsequent events is independent of the nesting level. This is different for parallel regions, as shown in Figure 5.11(B). Entering a state with parallel regions for the first time has an average latency of ~52 µs per parallel region. There is an average overhead of approx. 26 µs per active component for each subsequent event. To compare the latency overhead with conventional constructs, we also show the delay of a standard *for-loop* construct that sequentially processes the input event. In this case, the overhead is at approx. 2 µs per additional iteration.

Expression Evaluation Performance The expression evaluator is implemented as a tree walker that recursively traverses a binary tree of statement tokens (variables, constants and operators). We are using the same expressions as described in the EXPRESSION scenario in Section 6.1.7 to measure the evaluation performance. The measured values are listed in the following Table 5.2, along with the recursion depth of the tree walker.

Expression	Delay	Recursion
$\$0 < 15$	24 µs	2 levels
$(\$0 < 15) \wedge (\$1 = \$2)$	56 µs	3 levels
$((\$0 < 15) \wedge (\$1 = \$2)) \wedge ((30 > \$4) \vee (\$3 = \$5))$	116 µs	4 levels

Table 5.2: Expression evaluation performance of the embedded interpreter

Our approach has a remarkable performance overhead; a hard-coded version of **any** of these expressions in the C language executes in less than 4 µs. The evaluator uses an additional 11 bytes per recursive level used when processing the expression, e. g. the most complex expression uses a total of 44 bytes stack memory during evaluation, as the interpreter (re-)enters the evaluation method four times.

Memory Consumption Heap memory depends on the model structure. Table 5.3 details the memory requirements for various BM features, in bytes.

Element	Size	Additional size requirements
BM	12	
State	12	+ 1 per referenced edge, parallel region, substate
Transition	7	
Parallel region	4	+ 1 per referenced substate
Action binding	4	+ 1 per bound parameter
Expression token	6	
Global context data	10	

Element	Size	Additional size requirements
Local context data	0	As defined by BM
Control Flow	5	

Table 5.3: Memory requirements for embedded interpreter data structures

To analyse stack performance, we exercised the BM shown in Fig. 5.12.

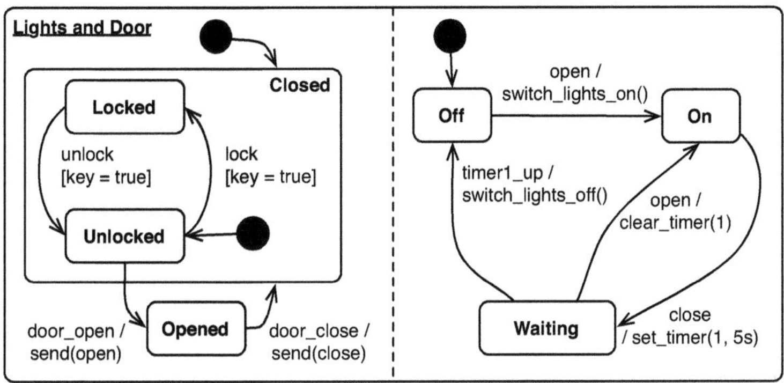

Figure 5.12: Example BM *Lights & Door*

Stack memory measurements were conducted by dumping the stack pointer during runtime. The performance of these routines is non-critical, as such experiments only measured memory consumption, never latency. The employed BM imitates the behaviour of a car door and passenger compartment lights, which we regard as a simple but typical example for applications in the embedded systems field.

We used the following sequence to measure the stack allocation: *key* $\leftarrow$ *false*, *door_open*, *door_close*, *lock*, *door_open*, *door_close*, *key* $\leftarrow$ *true*, *lock*, *door_open*, *key* $\leftarrow$ *false*, *unlock*, *door_open*, *key* $\leftarrow$ *true*, *unlock*, *door_open*, *door_close*, *wait for the lights to turn off*. The interpreter uses 25 bytes of additional stack memory when processing input events and 23 bytes when processing ε events. Evaluation of the guard conditions on the transitions between the **Locked** and **Unlocked** states related to the key variable show up as peaks in the stack usage.

There are strict limitations on the available memory: 2 KB of RAM contain the BM data structures as well as the runtime data needed for its interpretation. Volatile memory can be exhausted easily by moderately complex models, e. g. the performance benchmark's L2 BM (see Section 6.1.1) would already be too large to fit into the platform's available memory. The interpreter itself uses less than 8 KB of Flash memory, leaving 24 KB for definition of FCs.

This use case demonstrates that it is possible to use runtime BM interpretation on a hardware platform with extremely limited resources. This opens up a number of possibilities. Usually, one needs to go through complicated processes for updating software in embedded systems (e. g. conducting firmware upgrades). This does not need to be the case when employing our approach: customisable parts of an application can be modelled using state machines, while highly performant functions are provided by FCs. It might be even easier to adopt our approach in the world of embedded systems, as state machines are widely used to design functionality, and thus, complete BMs already exist.

5.5 Summary

The main goal for creation of the use case studies is to ground our work by applying it within a realistic context. By conducting the service supervision study, we found that our approach can be successfully applied for monitoring a number of services using a collective of CUs that employ interpreted BMs. It has been demonstrated that the interpretation approach, together with a well-defined communication model, is a decent choice for managing the re-configuration of a supervision service. The resource consumption of the employed technology (the Java-based ACE Toolkit) was adequate to execute this scenario on plain personal computer hardware.

Within the *management in the network* use case, we demonstrated the usage of the MPU for deploying and administration of BMs. Required FCs are loaded on demand as part of the model deployment process. The benefits of the interpretation approach were immediately visible during development of the demonstrator for monitoring router loads: the use of statechart-based BMs allowed us to easily communicate, discuss and change the monitoring functions. By using interpretation, it is also possible to adapt the modelled management processes while they are active. For long running processes, this is an advantage over conventional approaches, where system functionality is usually altered by deploying a patch or new version of a component and then rebooting the executing device. Such an approach is more disruptive to the operation of the management system and possibly to the production network than the one proposed. We also showed that it is possible to reduce management overhead by moving management processes closer to the actual devices that should be managed. Take, as an example, the employed Cisco AXP platform, where the BM executes on a machine that shares a single physical chassis with the router hardware, communicating with the device via a dedicated internal interface. The advantages of such an approach are a reduction in management traffic, the removal of load from the management system and a shorter delay for obtaining the monitored values. BM interpretation supports this strategy by enabling the use of models for description of management processes. This allows network and system administrators to create, enact, and modify management processes using a symbology that is more advanced and intuitive than the current state of the art in this field.

The intrinsic monitoring use case study also employs BMs to encode decision processes, which are then interpreted within routers. The idea is to have a flexible tool for describing the monitoring processes and to be able to delegate these processes to devices that are in the network, rather than executing them in a centralised network management system. Apart from several issues that have been brought forward against the idea of embedding monitoring information in an IPv6 extension header (violation of the path MTU, the end-to-end principle, the security mechanisms), a major concern was execution speed. Critics do have a point here. Although we did show that data analysis with a solid throughput can be achieved by using interpretation of automata (see [98] and Section 4.2), it does not make sense to trigger interpreted BMs using packets as events within a router's forwarding mechanism, as an interpreter would need to process packets at line speed. Given that an event equals a packet, that we use a GigE link with a minimal IPv6 packet of 78 bytes[9] and there is no packet loss, an interpreter would need to completely process a packet within 624 nanoseconds. This does not seem to be possible in software, even when executing generated code instead of using interpretation. In contrast, if only some of the packets ought to be processed, a router could filter out packets, before supplying only the relevant ones to the BM interpreter. Relaying of a packet to the interpreter and the subsequent execution of the BM will always incur a processing delay, which might disqualify this approach for certain types of traffic, e. g. data streams with time sensitive information. For all other types of traffic, and especially for an application to management processes in the system and network management domains, employing BM interpreters constitutes an adequate approach.

The embedded systems use case documents in detail that BM interpretation is not a question of resource availability. The concepts can be used over a very wide range of available hardware platforms, from high-performance server-cluster down to the level of single 8-bit microcontrollers.

[9] 40 byte IPv6 header, 26 byte Ethernet frame, 12 byte for the Interframe Gap

6 Performance Benchmark

A hundred objective measurements didn't sum the worth of a garden; only the delight of its users did that. Only the use made it mean something.
Lois McMaster Bujold

Demonstrating the feasibility of BM interpretation for application in the network and systems management domains is a valuable result; however, it is more important to show the performance impact that such an approach incurs. To determine the performance that a specific interpreter implementation delivers, we designed a benchmarking suite that enables the comparison of a set of different implementations, based on standardised performance measurement scenarios. The benchmark suite is not restricted to BM interpreters and can be used with execution approaches that rely on code generation as well.

In this chapter, we will first introduce a novel and comprehensive benchmark suite for determining the performance of BM execution mechanisms. Each of the ten scenarios used in the benchmark will be discussed in detail. Subsequently, we are defining mappings of the fundamental BM features identified in Section 4.1.1 to three concrete measurement platforms. This is necessary because each of our implementations differs in the employed expression languages and supported BM features, and we need to state how these differences relate to the BM features used in the benchmark suite definition. Finally, we use the benchmark to asses the performance of two of our implementations in regard to a reference implementation. Namely, we compare the performance of the UML interpreter and the MPU to static C++ code generated by the Rational Rhapsody tool.

6.1 The Benchmark Suite

The goal of the benchmark suite is to establish a baseline for quantitative judgement on the execution performance of a given implementation. Such an instrument is necessary for classifying the overhead that the interpretation approach introduces when compared with a BM execution strategy that involves code generation and compilation. It is also a useful tool for comparison of different implementations of execution engines.

Requirements The benchmark is specified using the fundamental BM features introduced in Section 4.1.1 and the BMs, which are employed for the individual scenarios, are specified using UML syntax. Should a certain feature not be available for a given implementation[1], then the relevant benchmarking scenario must be considered invalid.

We also need to specify some requirements regarding the context, expression language and available actions. The context needs to support integer variables, denoted by the letters a to f. We utilise three comparison operators for integer numbers: equals '=', lesser '<' and greater '>'. The only required arithmetic operation is addition '+'. Furthermore, we need two boolean operations: the *and* operation '$\wedge$' as well as the *or* operation '$\vee$'. Assignment to a context variable a is depicted using the ':=' symbol. Pairs of braces '(...)' are used for specifying evaluation precedence in expressions. Three specific actions need to be provided through the expression language. The action timestamp() records a timestamp value for subsequent use in analysis. The send(*event*) action takes an event as an argument and supplies the given event to the BM instance. The action call(*fc*,*value*) invokes a functional component. The first parameter *fc* identifies the operation and functional component to call, the second parameter *value* is an integer value supplied to the operation during invocation. The call function provides an integer return value. We use only a single FC, called DIV 10, which returns the input value divided by 10.

The benchmark relies on the measurement of three different kinds of performance indicators: occupied CPU time, allocated memory during runtime and static executable size. Timespans are stated in units of Microseconds (µs) and memory size values will be given in Kilobyte (KB) units. We employ the traditional definition of KB, where one KB is defined as 8192 ($2^{10} \times 8$) bits of data. Any platform used for executing the benchmark must supply functionality that enables the reliable computation of these values. Benchmark results are obtained by sampling CPU time and used memory over time and through a subsequent analysis of the obtained data.

Structure and Objectives The benchmark suite is divided into ten scenarios, each aiming at objectively determining certain performance characteristics, expressed through a set of performance indicators. The ten scenarios are SIZE, ALTERNATIVE, EPSILON, EVENT, GUARD, COMPOUND, EXPRESSION, CONCURRENT, CONFIG and LIFECYCLE. Each of the scenarios is described following a similar structure, comprised of the following sections:

- The scenario name and a general description of the scenario and its goals
- The BM(s) necessary to execute the scenario
- A step-by-step description of the procedure used to conduct the scenario
- A list of metrics (called performance indicators) that represent the results of the scenario execution

[1] E. g. some implementation might not implement a deep history construct.

- Further background information, detailing common stumbling blocks when implementing the scenario and mentioning any further points of interest.

Together, the ten scenarios are designed to provide a complete picture of an execution mechanism's performance. The relation between the benchmark's objectives and the scenarios that accomplish the objective are described in Table 6.1.

Objective	Scenario
Determine impact of the benchmark instrumentation	LIFECYCLE, TSTAMP[2]
Determine the resource consumption (dynamic memory, executable size) of the execution mechanism itself	SIZE, LIFECYCLE
Determine execution mechanism's resource consumption (dynamic memory, executable size) in relation to the employed BM's size	SIZE
Determine execution mechanism's dynamic memory usage during execution	LIFECYCLE
Determine execution mechanism's speed of matching basic transitions triggered by an event. Basic transitions are transitions that do not have a guard condition, are not self-referencing and do not cross nesting levels in the composition hierarchy.	ALTERNATIVE
Determine execution mechanism's speed of matching basic ε-transitions.	EPSILON
Determine execution mechanism's speed of matching transitions that are self-referencing or cross nesting levels in the composition hierarchy	COMPOUND
Determine execution mechanism's speed of selecting a transition among multiple potential ones	EVENT, GUARD
Determine execution mechanism's speed of evaluating guard conditions	EXPRESSION
Determine execution mechanism's speed of sending and receiving events	EXPRESSION
Determine execution mechanism's speed of calling an FC	EXPRESSION
Determine execution mechanism's speed when entering and exiting parallel regions	CONCURRENT
Determine execution mechanism's speed when storing and re-establishing a state configuration	CONCURRENT

[2]Not a scenario, described in Section 6.1.11

Objective	Scenario
Determine execution mechanism's speed when accessing the active state configuration	CONFIG
Determine speed of activating and deactivating a BM with the execution mechanism	LIFECYCLE

Table 6.1: Objectives of the benchmark and the relevant scenarios

The benchmark covers all major features of BM execution mechanisms, making it suitable for determination of the overall performance of our approach and for carrying out comparisons between different interpreter implementations. The focus lies on the detailed measurement of the transition matching performance and the performance overhead introduced by the compound states and parallel region constructs. A general evaluation of guard conditions is conducted, as well as a determination of FC calling and event sending overhead. Besides the execution characteristics, the performance of management operations, such as activation of a BM and the speed for accessing the active state configuration, is determined. The benchmark also determines the performance and resource overhead of the execution mechanism itself (without any activated BMs) as well as the impact of the measurement instrumentation on the results. We will now continue by describing each of the ten scenarios that make up the benchmark suite.

6.1.1 SIZE Scenario

The SIZE scenario determines the relation of the execution system's memory consumption in relation to the size of the BM. Five BMs are deployed with the execution system and the memory consumption of the system is determined for each model.

Employed Behaviour Models The five BMs are termed the *L0*, *L1*, *L2*, *L3* and *L4* models, referring to the level of nested states that they contain. Each of them contains an exponentially larger number of states (and transitions) than the previous one, according to the following formula for calculation of the number of states n_{states}.

$$n_{states} := \sum_{k=0}^{L} 10^k$$

The value of L determines the nesting level of the states (0..4). For model L0 the number of states is 1, for L1 it is 11 and for L4 it is 11111. As larger numbers of states are hard to depict graphically, we only give textual instructions to construct the BMs. The idea is simple: start with an initial transition leading to a state labelled Root — this is L0. For L1 add ten children to the root state, each one reachable by a single transition firing on the reception of an event e01 to e10. Name the child states State0 to State9. Every subsequent level is constructed by appending ten children to each leaf state using the same transition structure and appending a number from 0 to 9 to the parent's state name, i. e. State00, State000, et cetera. Figure 6.1 shows the complete L2 BM that is in the process of being extended to L3.

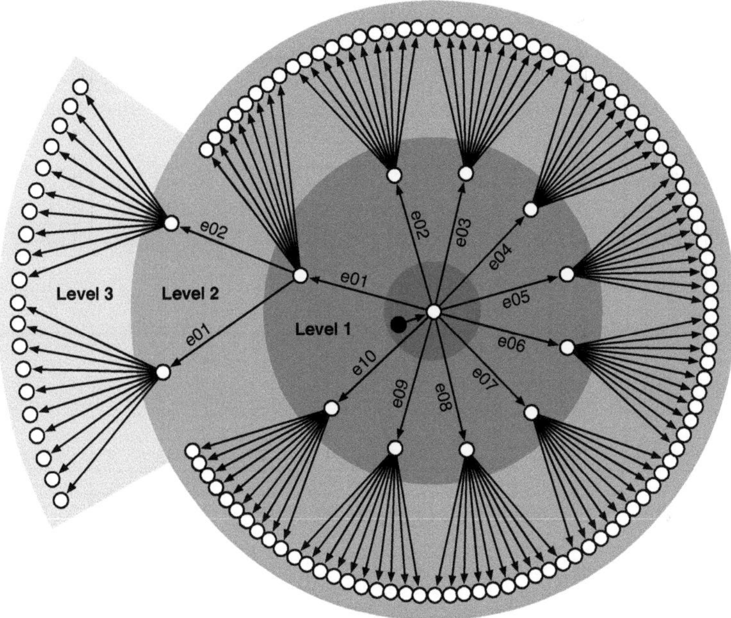

Figure 6.1: Constructing benchmark models for the SIZE scenario

Benchmarking Procedure For the first measurement, the execution runtime is started without a deployed BM and the consumed runtime memory, as well as the binary executable size of the execution engine, is recorded. For benchmarking the BMs L0 to L4, each BM is individually deployed at the execution system and the memory, as well as the executable size of the implementation, is recorded. Consumed runtime memory is recorded after the engine finished the startup process and for each of the measurements a freshly started execution runtime has to be used. The BMs are only instantiated but never executed. Each of the runtime memory measurements is to be carried out 50 times and the final result is the arithmetic mean[3] of all 50 measurement runs — this is done to remove variations in the measured values due to effects of any memory management mechanisms.

Outcome The obtained values refer to size measurements. A measurement run collects six values for runtime memory and one or six values for the executable size (an interpreter's executable does not change in size, whereas the size of a generated runtime system does). Table 6.2 lists the performance indicators of the SIZE scenario. Derived performance indicators (indicators that are calculated from other ones) are set in *italic* type.

Indicator	Meaning
SIZE.MEMORY.INIT	The average consumed memory after system start, without any deployed BM
SIZE.MEMORY.L0	The average consumed memory after deploying the L0 model
SIZE.MEMORY.L1	The average consumed memory after deploying the L1 model
SIZE.MEMORY.L2	The average consumed memory after deploying the L2 model
SIZE.MEMORY.L3	The average consumed memory after deploying the L3 model
SIZE.MEMORY.L4	The average consumed memory after deploying the L4 model
SIZE.MEMORY.GROW	(SIZE.MEMORY.L4 - SIZE.MEMORY.INIT) / 11111
SIZE.EXECUTABLE.INIT	The executable size without any included BM
SIZE.EXECUTABLE.L0	The executable size including the L0 model
SIZE.EXECUTABLE.L1	The executable size including the L1 model
SIZE.EXECUTABLE.L2	The executable size including the L2 model
SIZE.EXECUTABLE.L3	The executable size including the L3 model
SIZE.EXECUTABLE.L4	The executable size including the L4 model
SIZE.EXECUTABLE	A convenience name for the previous SIZE.EXECUTABLE indicators, in case that all have the same value (for example when the same executable is used)
SIZE.EXECUTABLE.GROW	(SIZE.EXECUTABLE.L4 - SIZE.EXECUTABLE.INIT) / 11111

Table 6.2: Performance indicators of the SIZE scenario

[3] From now on simply referred to as the *average*.

Further Information The motivation for SIZE is to judge upon the amount of memory that is utilised by the **static** structures of a BM, in relation to the model size. The **dynamic** aspects of BM execution are examined within the subsequent scenarios.

Relying only on states and transitions is adequate for this purpose, as these types constitute the majority of elements used when modelling behaviour. Furthermore, most other BM features have similar storage requirements as these structures. Also, we found that using a small number of exponentially larger models allows us to more quickly observe the static storage characteristics of the runtime (in comparison to using a larger number of models that grow linearily in size).

Creating the L3 and L4 BMs might be a challenge. While L2 could still be created by manually modifying a graphical representation, this is not feasible for the larger models. We found that it works well to follow a programmatic approach, either using direct modification of the in-memory format of the model (possible with Ecore) or by creating a suitable persistent storage representation (e. g. by textually creating a XMI or SCXML representation). We would also like to point out that the creation of larger models does take some time and might collide with the constraints imposed by an employed tool chain.

6.1.2 ALTERNATIVE Scenario

This scenario determines the timespan that the execution runtime needs to fire a simple transition (a transition that is triggered by an event and has an associated action but no guard condition). A single, self-referential transition will be activated 99 times in a row and the time between each processing step of the transition is recorded.

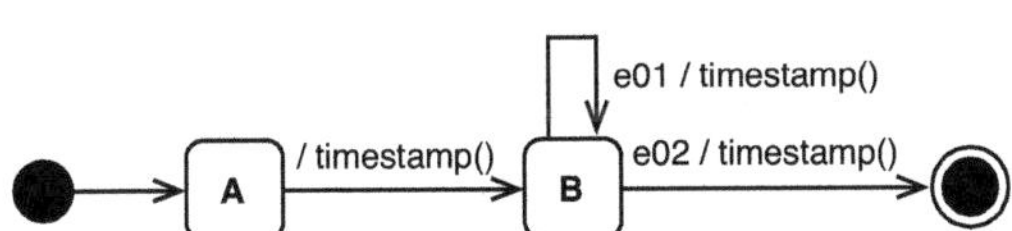

Figure 6.2: BM for the ALTERNATIVE scenario

Employed Behaviour Model Figure 6.2 depicts the BM used to carry out the measurement. The control flow initially starts in state **A**, where an ε-transition is taken to state **B** and the transition time is recorded. **B** contains an alternative: a reception of e01 returns to state **B** via a self-referential transition while recording the time and a reception of e02 records the time and ends the measurement.

Benchmarking Procedure After the BM is deployed and started, the execution system is supplied with 99 e01 events, followed by a single e02 event. Sending of the events should be done as fast as possible. After the events have been supplied, the measurement environment needs to wait until the model has terminated, before continuing with an analysis of the compiled values.

Outcome The BM execution will yield 101 time stamps, which are used to calculate the duration of the 100 intervals between the successive time stamps. Using these intervals the following three performance indicators are determined.

Indicator	Meaning
ALTERNATIVE.MIN	The shortest recorded interval duration between two successive timestamp values
ALTERNATIVE.AVG	The average interval duration between two successive timestamp values
ALTERNATIVE.MAX	The longest recorded interval duration between two successive timestamp values

Table 6.3: Performance indicators of the ALTERNATIVE scenario

Further Information The ALTERNATIVE scenario conducts a basic measurement for determining the duration of a simple transition trigger. On some platforms, a clear difference can be observed between the duration of the first interval and all other interval durations. Inclusion of this value is intended, as the benchmark does not aim at determination of the fastest possible execution speed but rather the realistic performance characteristics of an execution runtime.

6.1.3 EPSILON Scenario

The EPSILON scenario determines the performance of ε-transition processing. A sequence of states is connected through ε-transitions and this "chain" is repeatedly processed, while measuring the elapsed time from chain processing start to end.

Employed Behaviour Model The BM used to measure ε-transition processing performance is depicted in Figure 6.3. The BM begins in state **Pre** and enters the transition chain on reception of an e01 event. The ε-transition chain connects the states from **A** to **E** and the first and last ε-transition records a timestamp value. In state **E** at the end of sequence, the control flow has two alternative paths: a reception of e01 returns to the beginning of the transition chain for the next measurement, and the reception of e02 ends the measurement process.

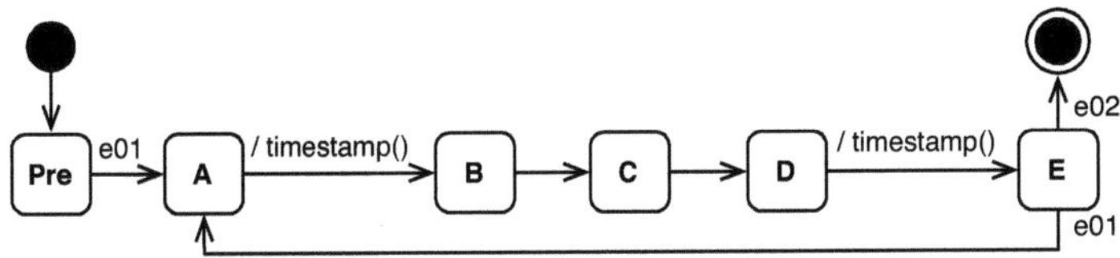

Figure 6.3: BM for the EPSILON scenario

Benchmarking Procedure After startup, the model is supplied with 100 e01 events, followed by a single e02 event. Subsequently, the benchmarking infrastructure needs to wait until the BM finishes execution before continuing with data analysis.

Outcome Exercising the BM in this manner will result in a list of 100 timestamp pairs (overall, a total of 200 single timestamp values). For each pair, the duration between the start and end times is determined by subtracting the earlier timestamp value from the later one. Based on these calculated values, the following three performance indicators are determined.

Indicator	Meaning
EPSILON.MIN	The shortest duration between calculated values, divided by three
EPSILON.AVG	The average duration for all calculated values, divided by three
EPSILON.MAX	The longest normalised duration between calculated values, divided by three

Table 6.4: Performance indicators of the EPSILON scenario

Further Information The processing of ε-transitions is often implemented differently (e. g. by internal completion events) than the processing of transitions that are triggered by regular events. It is interesting to determine the runtime performance and compare it with the performance of regular transition processing. The normalisation of the obtained duration times using division by three enables this comparison.

Figuratively described: the earlier timestamp is recorded after the first "half" of the first transition is processed, the next two transitions are processed completely and the later timestamp value is taken after the first "half" of the last transition is processed — the measured duration should be roughly similar to a processing of three complete ε-transitions, which is the reason for the division by three.

6.1.4 EVENT Scenario

In this scenario, five different events **e01** to **e05** are used to identify the transition matching performance in regard to event reception. The goal is to determine the performance indicators independently of the order of transitions as defined in the BM execution format.

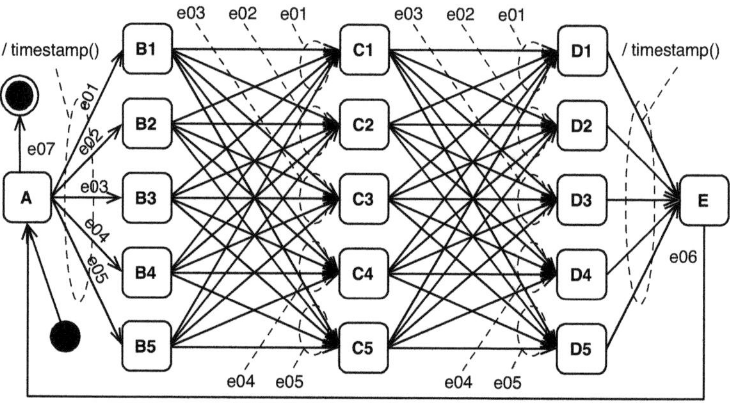

Figure 6.4: BM for the EVENT scenario

Employed Behaviour Model The utilised BM is shown in Figure 6.4. Although the model might look complicated, the composition is simple: a control flow always starts at state **A** and continues along a path through states $\mathbf{B}_x$, $\mathbf{C}_y$, $\mathbf{D}_z$, finally arriving at state **E**. The values of x, y and z are determined by received corresponding events e_x, e_y and e_z. They can range from 1 (triggered by e01) to 5 (triggered by e05). At state **E**, a reception of e06 returns the flow to the beginning of the BM in state **A**, where the behaviour can also be ended through the reception of an e07 event.

Benchmarking Procedure The benchmark scenario is executed by going through all possible paths in the model using events for all permutations of x, y and z (which we refer to as a *complete run*). For example, a sequence of e01, e04, e03, e06 will lead to the following path of entered states: **A**, **B1**, **C4**, **D3**, **E** and **A**. There are 125 possible paths ($5 \times 5 \times 5$). A complete run is repeated 125 times, each time starting with a different permutation but going through all of the possible events. Algorithm 4 shows the procedure for executing this measurement.

Algorithm 4 Benchmarking procedure for EVENT scenario

1: **for** $o = 0$ to 124 **do**
2:   Start Execution of BM
3:   **for** $p = 0$ to 124 **do**
4:     $x \leftarrow ((p + o)/25) \mod 5 + 1$
5:     $y \leftarrow ((p + o)/5) \mod 5 + 1$
6:     $z \leftarrow (p + o) \mod 5 + 1$
7:     Send e_x, then e_y, then e_z, then e_6
8:   **end for**
9:   Send e_7
10:   Wait for Termination
11: **end for**

There are two loops: the outer one (lines 1 to 11) determines the permutation offset (indicated by the variable o) and executes the overall measurement. The inner loop (lines 3 to 8) executes a complete run of all path permutations (indicated by the variable p) by calculating and sending the appropriate sequences of e_x, e_y and e_z and e06 events. After each complete run the measurement is terminated using an e07 event.

Outcome Running the described procedure results in 15625 timestamp pairs, each pair determining the duration that the execution runtime used to process each one of the paths within each complete run. Based on these durations, the following performance indicators are determined.

Indicator	Meaning
EVENT.MIN	The shortest duration found in any timestamp pair
EVENT.AVG	The average duration of all timestamp pairs
EVENT.MAX	The longest duration found in any timestamp pair

Table 6.5: Performance indicators of the EVENT scenario

Further Information Any employed model element needs to be represented within data structures of the runtime execution format. As all outgoing transitions of a state are potentially matched with each incoming event, the exact nature of the access performance characteristics of these data structures, as well as the order in which the transitions are contained within them, can have an impact on the performance of the overall transition matching process.

To expunge the effects of storage order, all possible orders of transitions are executed. As results for a complete run might also vary over time, this measurement is conducted several times and, for each of these repetitions, the starting permutation is altered. The reason for this is that on some platforms, earlier measurement runs are always slower than later ones, presumably due to internal runtime optimisations of the execution platform (e. g. caching). If the measurement were rerun in a naïve manner (always starting with 1,1,1; then 1,1,2; etc.) these effects would add up, which is what we would like to prevent.

6.1.5 GUARD Scenario

The GUARD scenario identifies the transition matching performance for transitions that carry guard conditions. Only a single event is used, which is handled according to the value of context data variables.

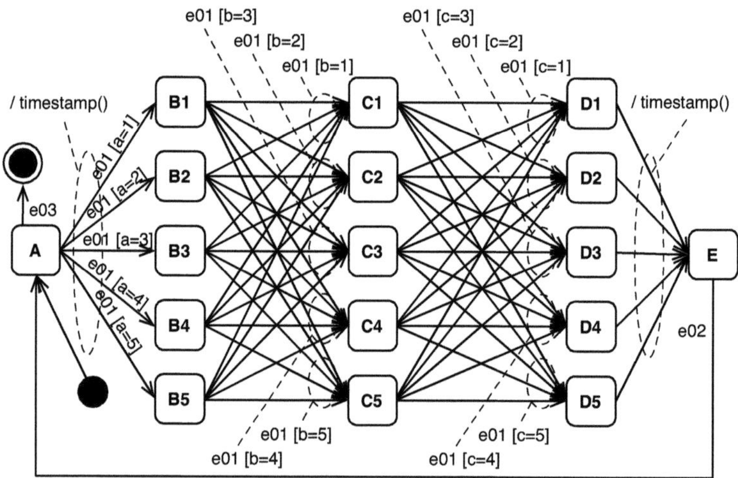

Figure 6.5: BM for the GUARD scenario

Employed Behaviour Model The relevant BM for this scenario is depicted in Figure 6.5. It is very similar to the model used for the EVENT scenario. The difference is that, instead of using the events e01 to e07, the model only employs three events: e01, e02 and e03. Only the single event e01 is used in conjunction with varying guard conditions to establish a path along the states **A**, $\mathbf{B}_x$, $\mathbf{C}_y$, $\mathbf{D}_z$ and **E**. The value of context data variables define the selection of x (variable a), y (variable

b) and z (variable c). Measurement runs can be repeated using **e02** and end when the execution runtime receives an **e03** event in state **A**.

Benchmarking Procedure The procedure for exercising the BM is also quite similar to the EVENT benchmarking scenario. Algorithm 5 shows the necessary procedure to trigger the measurement execution. Note the differences in lines 4 – 8: the calculated permutation values are assigned to the context data variables, instead of being used to directly select an event. Only the event **e01** is used to select the transition path. Line 8 is important, as it is necessary for the measurement infrastructure to wait until the execution runtime actually processes the events for a single run. Apart from these differences, the procedure is similar to the one described in Section 6.1.4.

Algorithm 5 Benchmarking procedure for GUARD scenario

1: **for** $o = 0$ to 124 **do**
2:    Start Execution of BM
3:    **for** $p = 0$ to 124 **do**
4:       $a \leftarrow ((p + o)/25) \mod 5 + 1$
5:       $b \leftarrow ((p + o)/5) \mod 5 + 1$
6:       $c \leftarrow (p + o) \mod 5 + 1$
7:       Send $3 \times e_1$, followed by e_2
8:       Wait until model is in state **E**
9:    **end for**
10:    Send e_3
11:    Wait for Termination
12: **end for**

Outcome Running the procedure given above results in 15625 timestamp pairs, which contain the duration that the execution runtime used for processing each run. Based on these durations, the following performance indicators are determined.

Indicator	Meaning
GUARD.MIN	The shortest duration found in any timestamp pair
GUARD.AVG	The average duration of all timestamp pairs
GUARD.MAX	The longest duration found in any timestamp pair

Table 6.6: Performance indicators of the GUARD scenario

Further Information The motivation for the EVENT scenario is similar to the one behind the GUARD scenario — matching guard conditions is one of the most important operations when executing BMs. Potentially a single condition might be evaluated many times over, e. g. when a BM changes its state from **A** to **B5**, it is likely that five guard conditions from $a = 1$ to $a = 5$ will be evaluated. Again, this depends on the storage order of transitions in the execution format data structures, which is why all possible paths are measured.

Waiting for a runtime engine to process all sent events is necessary, as it has to be guaranteed that the context is in a certain state when the guard condition statement is evaluated. Imagine that the inner loop runs without this statement; due to the multitasking capabilities of the underlying operating system, the loop could have executed several times before the runtime engine thread starts fetching the external events from the incoming queue. When subsequently evaluating the guard condition statements, the values of x, y and z would be wrong. This problem does not exist in the EVENT scenario; thus, Algorithm 4 does not contain such a command.

6.1.6 COMPOUND Scenario

The COMPOUND scenario measures the execution performance of transitions that cross nesting levels in the composition hierarchy. A number of self-referential transitions that leave and enter various levels of the composition hierarchy are triggered using suitable event sequences.

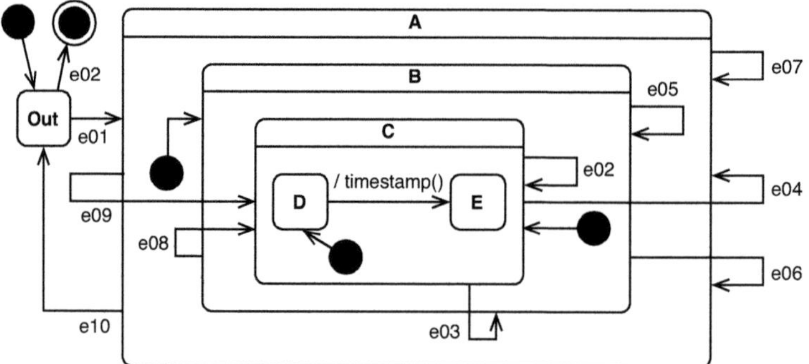

Figure 6.6: BM for the COMPOUND scenario

Employed Behaviour Model Figure 6.6 shows the utilised BM. The model comprises a number of nested states on four levels (top level, contained within **A**, contained within **B**, contained within **C**). There are 10 events in use; note that e01 and e10 are solely used for managing recurring runs and do not participate in the measurement functionality. Once the model starts in the **Out** state, a reception of e01 induces the entering of the initial states **A**, **B**, **C** and **D**. The next step is carried out automatically via an ε-transition and records a timestamp while changing to state **E**. Once the BM resides in **E**, it will return to this state on reception of any of the events e02 to e09 and record a timestamp on doing so. Each of these events triggers a single transition with different source and target states. A measurement run might be ended by sending e10, prompting the model to enter the **Out** state. Another measurement run could then be initiated using the event e01, while the event e02 would terminate the BM.

Benchmarking Procedure The COMPOUND scenario BM is exercised using sequences of events, so-called patterns. Patterns specify the order of the eight events e02 (referred to as "2") to e09 (referred to as "9"). Each complete measurement run consists of an execution of all of the 72 patterns listed in Table 6.7.

1	2, 3, 4, 5, 6, 8, 7, 9	**2**	2, 4, 3, 5, 6, 8, 7, 9	**3**	3, 2, 4, 5, 6, 8, 7, 9
4	3, 4, 2, 5, 6, 8, 7, 9	**5**	4, 2, 3, 5, 6, 8, 7, 9	**6**	4, 3, 2, 5, 6, 8, 7, 9
7	2, 3, 4, 5, 8, 6, 7, 9	**8**	2, 4, 3, 5, 8, 6, 7, 9	**9**	3, 2, 4, 5, 8, 6, 7, 9
10	3, 4, 2, 5, 8, 6, 7, 9	**11**	4, 2, 3, 5, 8, 6, 7, 9	**12**	4, 3, 2, 5, 8, 6, 7, 9
13	2, 3, 4, 6, 5, 8, 7, 9	**14**	2, 4, 3, 6, 5, 8, 7, 9	**15**	3, 2, 4, 6, 5, 8, 7, 9
16	3, 4, 2, 6, 5, 8, 7, 9	**17**	4, 2, 3, 6, 5, 8, 7, 9	**18**	4, 3, 2, 6, 5, 8, 7, 9
19	2, 3, 4, 6, 8, 5, 7, 9	**20**	2, 4, 3, 6, 8, 5, 7, 9	**21**	3, 2, 4, 6, 8, 5, 7, 9
22	3, 4, 2, 6, 8, 5, 7, 9	**23**	4, 2, 3, 6, 8, 5, 7, 9	**24**	4, 3, 2, 6, 8, 5, 7, 9
25	2, 3, 4, 8, 5, 6, 7, 9	**26**	2, 4, 3, 8, 5, 6, 7, 9	**27**	3, 2, 4, 8, 5, 6, 7, 9
28	3, 4, 2, 8, 5, 6, 7, 9	**29**	4, 2, 3, 8, 5, 6, 7, 9	**30**	4, 3, 2, 8, 5, 6, 7, 9
31	2, 3, 4, 8, 6, 5, 7, 9	**32**	2, 4, 3, 8, 6, 5, 7, 9	**33**	3, 2, 4, 8, 6, 5, 7, 9
34	3, 4, 2, 8, 6, 5, 7, 9	**35**	4, 2, 3, 8, 6, 5, 7, 9	**36**	4, 3, 2, 8, 6, 5, 7, 9
37	2, 3, 4, 5, 6, 8, 9, 7	**38**	2, 4, 3, 5, 6, 8, 9, 7	**39**	3, 2, 4, 5, 6, 8, 9, 7
40	3, 4, 2, 5, 6, 8, 9, 7	**41**	4, 2, 3, 5, 6, 8, 9, 7	**42**	4, 3, 2, 5, 6, 8, 9, 7
43	2, 3, 4, 5, 8, 6, 9, 7	**44**	2, 4, 3, 5, 8, 6, 9, 7	**45**	3, 2, 4, 5, 8, 6, 9, 7
46	3, 4, 2, 5, 8, 6, 9, 7	**47**	4, 2, 3, 5, 8, 6, 9, 7	**48**	4, 3, 2, 5, 8, 6, 9, 7
49	2, 3, 4, 6, 5, 8, 9, 7	**50**	2, 4, 3, 6, 5, 8, 9, 7	**51**	3, 2, 4, 6, 5, 8, 9, 7
52	3, 4, 2, 6, 5, 8, 9, 7	**53**	4, 2, 3, 6, 5, 8, 9, 7	**54**	4, 3, 2, 6, 5, 8, 9, 7
55	2, 3, 4, 6, 8, 5, 9, 7	**56**	2, 4, 3, 6, 8, 5, 9, 7	**57**	3, 2, 4, 6, 8, 5, 9, 7
58	3, 4, 2, 6, 8, 5, 9, 7	**59**	4, 2, 3, 6, 8, 5, 9, 7	**60**	4, 3, 2, 6, 8, 5, 9, 7
61	2, 3, 4, 8, 5, 6, 9, 7	**62**	2, 4, 3, 8, 5, 6, 9, 7	**63**	3, 2, 4, 8, 5, 6, 9, 7
64	3, 4, 2, 8, 5, 6, 9, 7	**65**	4, 2, 3, 8, 5, 6, 9, 7	**66**	4, 3, 2, 8, 5, 6, 9, 7
67	2, 3, 4, 8, 6, 5, 9, 7	**68**	2, 4, 3, 8, 6, 5, 9, 7	**69**	3, 2, 4, 8, 6, 5, 9, 7
70	3, 4, 2, 8, 6, 5, 9, 7	**71**	4, 2, 3, 8, 6, 5, 9, 7	**72**	4, 3, 2, 8, 6, 5, 9, 7

Table 6.7: Event patterns used for the COMPOUND scenario

After executing a pattern, the compound state will be left and a new pattern is selected. The procedure is then repeated with the new pattern until all patterns have been executed, which constitutes a complete measurement run. Complete measurement runs are executed several times as described in Algorithm 6, which shows the procedure for controlling the overall measurement execution.

Algorithm 6 Benchmarking procedure for COMPOUND scenario

```
for o = 0 to 71 do
  Start Execution of BM
  for p = 0 to 71 do
    Send e_1
    x ← (o + p) mod 72 + 1
    for all y in Pattern No. x do
      Send e_y
    end for
    Send e_10
  end for
  Send e_2
  Wait for Termination
end for
```

Outcome Each pattern execution yields nine timestamps. From these timestamps, the durations of the eight intervals between consecutive measurement values are determined and assigned to the corresponding event that was used to trigger them, i. e. for pattern 23, the first interval is assigned to event e04, whereas the last interval is assigned to e09. A complete measurement run therefore results in 72 values assigned to each of the events e02 to e09. As there are 72 complete runs in the complete scenario, this leads to a total of 5184 timestamp values assigned per event. From these values, the 27 performance indicators listed in Table 6.8 are calculated.

Indicator	Meaning
COMPOUND.E0*X*.MIN	The shortest duration measured for e0*X*, where *X* can range from 2 to 9. There are eight indicators of this kind.
COMPOUND.E0*X*.AVG	The average duration measured for e0*X*, where *X* can range from 2 to 9. There are eight indicators of this kind.
COMPOUND.E0*X*.MAX	The longest duration measured for e0*X*, where *X* can range from 2 to 9. There are eight indicators of this kind.

Indicator	Meaning
COMPOUND.MIN	The shortest value measured for any duration.
COMPOUND.AVG	The average value for all 41472 ($72 \times 72 \times 8$) durations.
COMPOUND.MAX	The longest value measured for any duration.

Table 6.8: Performance indicators of the COMPOUND scenario

Further Information The order in which we measure the transitions is always from the innermost nesting level to the outermost one, e. g. the outgoing transitions of **C** first, then the outgoing transitions of **B**, then the ones of **A**. The 72 patterns are designed to cancel out the effects that the outgoing transition storage order has on the performance. Therefore, it is not necessary to go through all possible permutations of events (256 variants), but to only measure the variants for utilised transitions outgoing from a single state, e. g. for state **B** these are the transitions triggered by event e05, e06 and e08. All possible permutations of the order of these need to be measured in conjunction with the possible variants for transitions of other states; there are six further variants for state **C** and two variants for state **A**, which explains the overall $3! \times 3! \times 2! = 72$ patterns used.

The determined duration for each event is a combination of the time used for the processing of the transition from the source state to the target state, the time used for the implicitly exited states and the time used for entering the initial states. The processing times for these three aspects are different for each of the transitions and the scenario is constructed in a way that aims at determining an overall balanced proportion.

6.1.7 EXPRESSION Scenario

This scenario determines the performance of transitions that conduct expression evaluations as part of their guard or action statements. Considered categories for action statements are: integer arithmetic, event handling, FC calling and the evaluation of boolean expressions with context variables.

Employed Behaviour Model The BM used for the EXPRESSION scenario forms a chain of states and transitions that execute a certain action at each step, while recording timestamps between steps. The model is depicted in Figure 6.7. The BM starts in state **A** and follows the chain on reception of event e01 to state **B**, while assigning a value of zero to the variable a. An ε-transition leaves state **B**, while recording the first timestamp value. Arriving in state **C**, the model waits for a number of e01 events that initiate an incrementation of the value of a with every received event. Once a has a value of 100, the state is left, a second timestamp

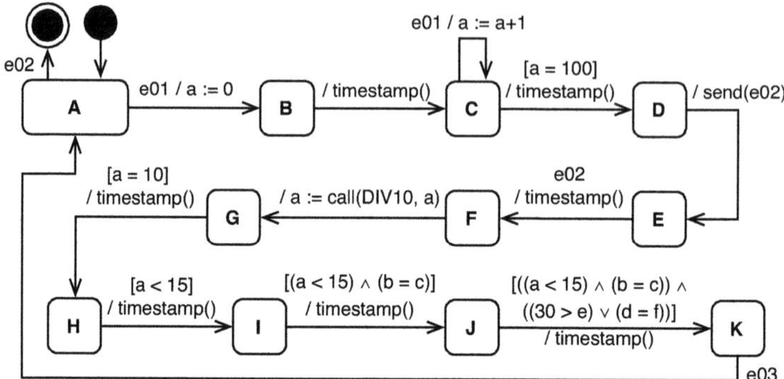

Figure 6.7: BM for the EXPRESSION scenario

is recorded and state **D** is entered. Again, the BM automatically leaves the state via an ε-transition shortly after entering it, triggering the sending of event e02 and entering state **E**. This state is left on reception of the previously send event e02, a third timestamp value is recorded, and the next state is entered. State **F** is left by processing an ε-transition, that includes the synchronous invocation of an FC and storage of the obtained result in variable a. State **G** is entered and left if variable a contains the correct value. A timestamp value is recorded before the model changes its state to **H**. The transitions to the following three states (**I**, **J** and **K**) each provoke the evaluation of increasingly more complex guard conditions while recording the fifth, sixth and seventh timestamp values. When the control flow finally reaches state **K**, a reception of event e03 leads it back to state **A**. The scenario is terminated when receiving event e02 in state **A**.

Benchmarking Procedure Firstly, all employed variables, apart from a, are initialised in the following manner: b := 15, c := 15, d := 23, e := 46, f := 23. Subsequently, a measurement run is conducted by sending 101 e01 events, followed by an e03 event. This procedure is repeated 150 times before terminating the measurement by sending a e02 event in state **A**.

Outcome Each measurement run yields 7 timestamps. Based on consecutive timestamps, a sequence of six duration values is calculated. These durations represent the processing time that it took to carry out a certain action, and we refer to the corresponding six actions with the following phrases:

COUNT Counting

EVENT Sending and receiving and event

CALL Synchronously calling an FC and storing the result

GUARD1 Evaluation of guard condition 1

GUARD2 Evaluation of guard condition 2

GUARD3 Evaluation of guard condition 3

Based on the 900 (150 × 6) collected duration values, the 18 performance indicators listed in Table 6.9 are calculated.

Indicator	Meaning
EXPRESSION.COUNT.MIN	The shortest duration of the counting action
EXPRESSION.COUNT.AVG	The average duration of the counting action
EXPRESSION.COUNT.MAX	The longest duration of the counting action
EXPRESSION.EVENT.MIN	The shortest duration for sending and receiving an event
EXPRESSION.EVENT.AVG	The average duration for sending and receiving an event
EXPRESSION.EVENT.MAX	The longest duration for sending and receiving an event
EXPRESSION.CALL.MIN	The shortest duration for calling the 'DIV10' FC
EXPRESSION.CALL.AVG	The average duration for calling a 'DIV10' FC
EXPRESSION.CALL.MAX	The longest duration for calling a 'DIV10' FC
EXPRESSION.GUARD1.MIN	The shortest duration for evaluation of condition 1
EXPRESSION.GUARD1.AVG	The average duration for evaluation of condition 1
EXPRESSION.GUARD1.MAX	The longest duration for evaluation of condition 1
EXPRESSION.GUARD2.MIN	The shortest duration for evaluation of condition 2
EXPRESSION.GUARD2.AVG	The average duration for evaluation of condition 2
EXPRESSION.GUARD2.MAX	The longest duration for evaluation of condition 2
EXPRESSION.GUARD3.MIN	The shortest duration for evaluation of condition 3

Indicator	Meaning
EXPRESSION.GUARD3.AVG	The average duration for evaluation of condition 3
EXPRESSION.GUARD3.MAX	The longest duration for evaluation of condition 3
EXPRESSION.GUARD.MIN	The minimum of EXPRESSION.GUARD1.-MIN, EXPRESSION.GUARD2.MIN, EXPRESSION.GUARD3.MIN
EXPRESSION.GUARD.AVG	(EXPRESSION.GUARD1.AVG + EXPRESSION.GUARD2.AVG + EXPRESSION.-GUARD3.AVG) / 3
EXPRESSION.GUARD.MAX	The maximum of EXPRESSION.GUARD1.-MAX, EXPRESSION.GUARD2.MAX, EXPRESSION.GUARD3.MAX

Table 6.9: Performance indicators of the EXPRESSION scenario

Further Information Languages used for specification of actions can vary greatly in regard to the richness of features and the execution performance. Giving a general and exhaustive performance benchmark for such languages is not the aim of this scenario, nor this thesis. However, judging the performance impact of certain types of actions has to be a necessary part for a BM runtime benchmark. We decided that by determination of the performance of a set of typical actions we can at least help to provide a representative, high-level understanding of the performance characteristics of the employed expression languages. Regarding the guard conditions GUARD1, GUARD2 and GUARD3, it should be noted, that along with their bound values, these are constructed in a way that a left-associative expression evaluator with the usual operator precedence rules will need to process all components before being able to come to a conclusion.

6.1.8 CONCURRENT Scenario

This scenario determines the execution performance for BM constructs that manipulate the number of concurrent control flows. It determines the performance characteristics for entering, executing and exiting parallel regions as well as providing an analysis of the history mechanism.

Employed Behaviour Model Figure 6.8 depicts the BM used for measuring performance indicators related to concurrent control flows. Although the model consists of a number of states, the basic structure is simple; on reception of event `e01`, a

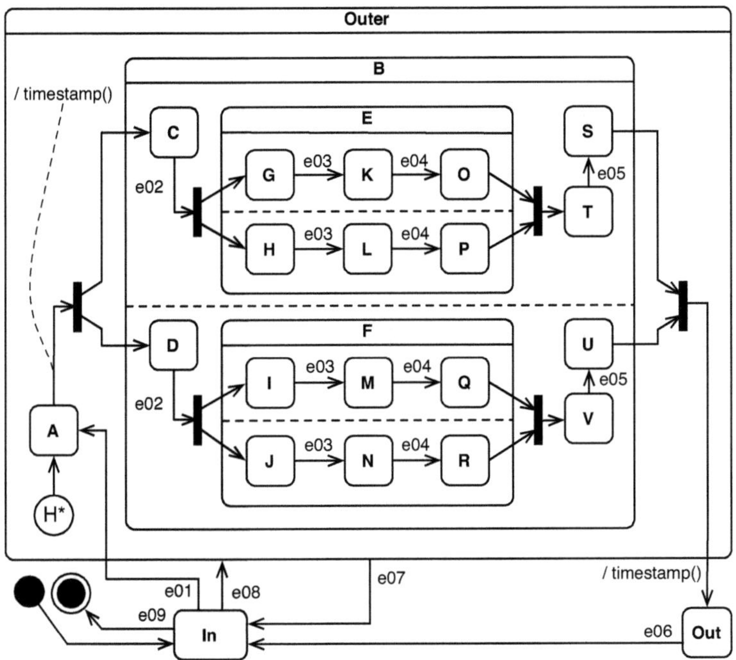

Figure 6.8: BM for the CONCURRENT scenario

control flow is forked into two concurrent ones on entry of state **B**. On the reception of event e02, this fork is repeated for each of the control flows on entry of state **E** and **F**, leading to four concurrent control flows on the lowest nesting level of the composition hierarchy. These control flows then progress along a sequence of states, induced through the events e03 and e04. As soon as two control flows reach the states **O** and **P**, they are joined, and the model enters state **T**. The same thing happens to the two control flows that enter states **Q** and **R**; they are joined and enter state **V**. This procedure is repeated with the two remaining control flows on reception of event e05, and only one control flows remains.

Apart from the structures responsible for concurrency, there are additional features that help to conduct the measurements. The states **In** and **Out** are used to trigger runs of the fork/join functionality contained in state **Outer**. The model starts in state **In**, from where it will also terminate on reception of event e09. There are only two timestamps taken: one directly before the first fork and one just after the last join node. Two additional events e07 and e08 are used for measuring the performance of the deep history feature.

Benchmarking Procedure The model always starts in state **In**. Executing a complete measurement run consists of triggering a sequence of events, depending on the type of measurement; for non-history measurements, a sequence of e01, e02, e03, e04, e05, e06 will exercise the functionality, take two timestamps and return to state **In**. For history measurements, a sequence of e01, e02, e03, e07, e08, e04, e05, e06 will also have the model change to state **In** and record two timestamps, but includes the time needed for the runtime to execute the operations necessary for recording and restoring state configurations.

The overall measurement procedure consists of going through 100 complete runs, where on odd repetitions[4], the non-history sequence is used and on even ones the sequence that activates the history mechanism is used. At the end of the procedure, event e09 is used to terminate the measurement.

Outcome The measurement procedure yields 50 timestamp pairs for *normal* runs and 50 timestamp pairs for runs that employ the history feature. The timestamp pairs are used to determine the duration for processing the fork/join functionality. Based on these durations, the performance indicators listed in Table 6.10 are calculated.

Indicator	Meaning
CONCURRENT.MIN	The shortest duration found in any *normal* timestamp pair
CONCURRENT.AVG	The average duration of all *normal* timestamp pairs
CONCURRENT.MAX	The longest duration found in any *normal* timestamp pair
HISTORY.MIN	The shortest duration found in any *history* timestamp pair
HISTORY.AVG	The average duration of all *history* timestamp pairs
HISTORY.MAX	The longest duration found in any *history* timestamp pair

Table 6.10: Performance indicators of the CONCURRENT scenario

Further Information The reason for the introduction of additional states beyond the described ones in Section 6.1.8 is twofold. They have been introduced due to

[4]Starting at 1 and counting to 100

constraints in the UML standards, e. g. the state **T** was introduced to be able to wait for e05 before continuing with joining the control flows. The UML standard forbids using only a single join element for this purpose: "Transitions outgoing pseudostates may not have a trigger (except for those coming out of the initial pseudostate)." [255, p.573] and "The transitions entering a join vertex cannot have guards or triggers." [255, p.542]. In addition, they enable better control over the model when conducting the measurement process.

The idea to alternate between a measurement with history usage and one without history usage, is due to our observation that on some platforms measurement runs might provide quite different result values, for example depending on the number of iterations that were conducted beforehand. We found that a simple solution for maintaining comparability between runs with and without history is to interleave them.

We picked this model for integration of history measurements due to its structural complexity. The model uses both concurrency as well as compound states, making it necessary for the deep history mechanism to restore control flows as well as state configurations with more than one nesting level.

6.1.9 CONFIG Scenario

This scenario is used to determine the time that it takes for an execution engine to retrieve an active state configuration.

Employed Behaviour Model We use the previously presented model of the CONCURRENT scenario, discussed in Section 6.1.8, but employ a different benchmarking procedure.

Benchmarking Procedure After starting the model, it is prompted to enter the states **K**, **L**, **M** and **N** by supplying the runtime with the event sequence e01, e02 and e03. The measurement infrastructure then needs to assure that the BM actually entered these states (e. g. by waiting for a timespan long enough to let the execution runtime process all events from the input queue). The execution runtime is then requested to provide the active state configuration, which should be the one shown in Figure 6.9. A timestamp is taken directly before and directly after completion of this request. Timestamps taken as part of the BM itself are ignored.

After the active state configuration has been retrieved, the BM is prepared for the next measurement run by sending the event sequence e04, e05 and e06. The measurement process is repeated 50 times and terminated by sending a single e09 event.

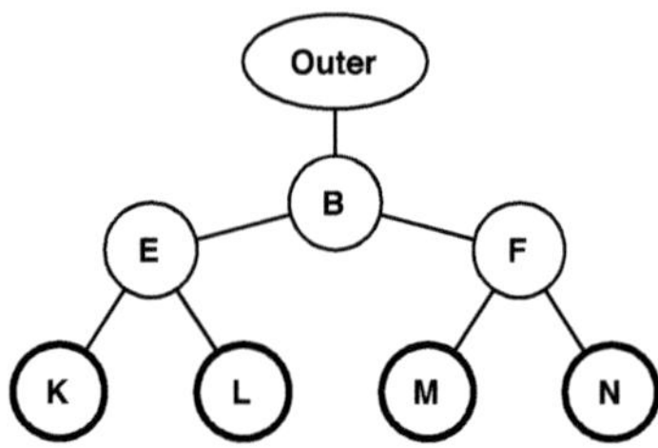

Figure 6.9: Active state configuration expected in the CONFIG scenario

Outcome On completion of the measurement process, 50 timestamp pairs will have been collected. For each timestamp pair, the duration between the values is determined, and the following performance indicators are calculated.

Indicator	Meaning
CONFIGURATION.MIN	The shortest duration for retrieving the active state configuration
CONFIGURATION.AVG	The average duration of all collected timespans
CONFIGURATION.MAX	The longest duration for retrieving the active state configuration

Table 6.11: Performance indicators of the CONFIG scenario

Further Information Retrieving the active state configuration is a unique feature when using BMs instead of conventionally coded application logic. As a BM forms an abstraction of the real system behaviour, it usually provides additional semantics, e. g. through state names, the composition hierarchy or the specification of parallel regions. This information can be accessed by retrieving the active state configuration, which makes it a useful feature for determining and tracing system operation.

6.1.10 LIFECYCLE Scenario

This scenario measures the runtime performance for behaviour deployment and removal. A BM is deployed, started and removed on termination, while recording dynamic memory consumption and process duration.

Employed Behaviour Model Figure 6.10 shows the BM. The model is very simple: On deployment and start of the BM state **A** is entered and immediately left via an ε-transition, while recording a timestamp. The model then terminates.

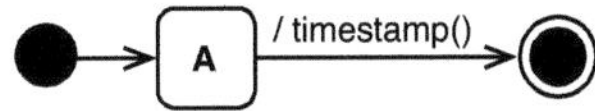

Figure 6.10: BM for the LIFECYCLE scenario

Benchmarking Procedure The benchmarking procedure is simple as well; all that is required is starting an execution runtime system. The given BM is instantiated, started, and the instance is removed after termination. This process is repeated 50 times with the same execution runtime instance. Before the BM is instantiated, a timestamp value is recorded. Also, directly after the instance is removed, a timestamp value is taken. This results in three timestamps collected for each of the 50 measurement runs. The consumed dynamic runtime memory is recorded at various points during this process:

BEGIN Taken at the very beginning of the measurement processes, before the execution runtime system is created.

INIT Once the execution runtime system has been created and before it is started.

START When the execution runtime system has been started but before the BM is being instantiated.

OPERATION After a BM has been instantiated, started, terminated and the instance removed. There will be 50 values of this type, one for each measurement run.

END After the execution runtime system has terminated at the end of the measurement runs.

Outcome Two durations are calculated from the three timestamps recorded for each measurement run; the first duration (ENTER) is the duration from the first timestamp to the second timestamp, and the second duration is the overall (OVERALL) timespan between the first and the third timestamp. Table 6.12 lists all of the thirteen performance indicators calculated from these 150 duration values and 54 recorded memory sizes.

Indicator	Meaning
LIFECYCLE.MEMORY.BEGIN	The consumed dynamic memory at the beginning of the process
LIFECYCLE.MEMORY.INIT	The consumed dynamic memory after the execution runtime has been created

Indicator	Meaning
LIFECYCLE.MEMORY.START	The consumed dynamic memory after the execution runtime has been started
LIFECYCLE.MEMORY.MIN	The least consumed dynamic memory during measurement of the execution runtime operations (uses the **OPERATION** timstamps)
LIFECYCLE.MEMORY.AVG	The average consumed dynamic memory during measurement of the execution runtime operations (uses the **OPERATION** timstamps)
LIFECYCLE.MEMORY.MAX	The most consumed dynamic memory during measurement of the execution runtime operations (uses the **OPERATION** timstamps)
LIFECYCLE.MEMORY.END	The consumed dynamic memory at the end of the process
LIFECYCLE.ENTER.MIN	The shortest timespan calculated for instantiating and starting the model
LIFECYCLE.ENTER.AVG	The average timespan calculated for instantiating and starting the model
LIFECYCLE.ENTER.MAX	The longest timespan calculated for instantiating and starting the model
LIFECYCLE.OVERALL.MIN	The shortest timespan calculated for instantiating, starting, stopping and removing the model
LIFECYCLE.OVERALL.AVG	The average timespan calculated for instantiating, starting, stopping and removing the model
LIFECYCLE.OVERALL.MAX	The longest timespan calculated for instantiating, starting, stopping and removing the model

Table 6.12: Performance indicators of the LIFECYCLE scenario

Further Information Originally the used BM was merely an initial pseudostate that directly led to a final state, while recording a timestamp. This was later modified, as the chosen SCXML mapping for specifying initial states (as an attribute of the parent element) does not allow for actions on initial transitions.

6.1.11 The General Benchmark Process

Measuring the performance of a piece of software can be a sophisticated task on most of the recent hardware platforms; it is wise to check (and re-check) measurement results when implementing the benchmark. There are many factors that can influence the gathered values. For example, measuring the so-called wall-time[5] is usually a bad idea as most of the current hardware platforms execute many processes at the same time — it is necessary to ensure that performance measurements only collect data relevant to the BM execution process(es). It should also be noted that performance measurements are highly dependent on the hardware used for running the benchmark and comparisons of measurement results are only meaningful when conducted on the same platform. The benchmarking suite is designed to be platform independent, but we can give some helpful hints on the measurement process for the platforms we implemented the benchmark on.

Taking Timestamps When measuring elapsed time, it is best to rely on functions, which enable calculating the time that a process (or thread) spent executing on a processor. For the Java platform, such timespans can be measured on a per-thread basis by utilising the `getThreadCpuTime` method of the `java.lang.management.ThreadMXBean` class, which is available since version 1.5. On Portable Operating System Interface (POSIX) compliant platforms [181, p. 26 ff.], an option is to employ the `getrusage` system call, which is able to retrieve CPU usage per process. From the returned `rusage` structure, one adds the `ru_utime` and `ru_stime` fields and converts to µs.

Algorithm 7 Determination of timer resolution

$a \leftarrow$ Current Time
$b \leftarrow$ Current Time
while $a = b$ **do**
  $b \leftarrow$ Current Time
end while
print $b - a$

When taking timestamps, it is necessary to be aware of the resolution of the timer. Although some platforms offer timing values expressed in nanosecond units, the employed timing hardware will usually have a resolution with a far larger granularity. Algorithm 7 implements a simple way to determine the timing resolution. It is important to be aware of the limits of timestamp recording instrumentation in order to ensure a correct interpretation of the benchmark results. One piece of required information is the timer resolution, another one concerns the impact of the employed measurement instrumentation.

[5] Time that one can measure using a clock hanging on the wall

Determination of timestamp overhead We require that the following method is used when determining the performance overhead for recording a timestamp value. A measurement process repeatedly records 101 timestamp values, as fast as possible. From these values, use the 100 durations between the successive timestamp values to calculate the performance indicators shown in Table 6.13. When interpreting the timestamping overhead in relation to some benchmark scenario, it is useful to know the approximate impact that timestamping has on each measurement run.

Indicator	Meaning
TIMESTAMP.MIN	The shortest duration for recording a timestamp
TIMESTAMP.AVG	The average duration for recording a timestamp
TIMESTAMP.MAX	The longest duration for recording a timestamp

Table 6.13: Performance indicators in regard to timestamping overhead

The following Table 6.14 contains this information. We treat the collection of a duration value by using timestamping pairs as having the impact of a single recorded timestamp, due to the following reason: the recorded duration includes the time used for recording the first timestamp, exiting from the timestamping function, carrying out some processing, entering the second timestamping function and recording the second timestamp. It does not contain the time used for entering the first timestamp function, nor the time needed to exit the second one, thus forming two times "half" a timestamp. This approach is not overly accurate, but gives us at least an approximate of the impact, without going to extreme lengths (e. g. determination of the exact timing of user space/kernel interactions).

Scenario	Approximate overhead
ALTERNATIVE	One timestamp per run (single, send event)
EPSILON	One timestamp per run (single, send event)
EVENT	One timestamp per run (processing of complete path)
GUARD	One timestamp per run (processing of complete path)
COMPOUND	One timestamp per obtained duration, 576 timestamps per measurement run (processing of all patterns)
EXPRESSION	One timestamp per obtained duration, six timestamps per measurement run (completed state sequence)
GUARD	One timestamp per measurement run (from **In** to **Out**)
CONFIG	One timestamp per obtained retrieval duration
LIFECYCLE	One timestamp per ENTER duration, two timestamps per OVERALL duration

Table 6.14: Approximate timestamping overhead per scenario and measurement run

Recording Dynamic Memory Consumption On the Java platform, we add the values obtained from the `getNonHeapMemoryUsage` and `getHeapMemoryUsage` methods of the `java.lang.management.MemoryMXBean` class to calculate the overall consumed memory. For the C++ runtime, we again employed the `getrusage` system call, using the `ru_maxrss` field of the `rusage` struct and converting the obtained value to KB.

On the Java platform, obtained memory values can be erratic, due to the employed garbage collection scheme. It might be possible to suppress these fluctuations by triggering garbage collection runs between measurements using the `System.gc()` call. The benchmark is constructed in a way that memory measurements should not interfere with performance measurements; therefore, we neglect determining the performance impact associated with recording memory. The same is true for indicators relating to executable size.

Measuring Executable Size This can usually be done with OS-supplied tools. For the Java platform, the size of the virtual machine executable should be used. When dealing with compiled languages, one has to control more closely which features are compiled and linked into the final executable; a compiled executable should only contain symbols for the current target architecture. This must not be taken for granted. For example, the GNU Compiler Collection (GCC) configuration supplied with the current development tools [219] for Mac OS X creates a combined executable for three different processor architectures (32bit Intel, 64bit Intel, 32bit PowerPC) per default. Executable size is also influenced by the way that libraries are linked with the final binary: either statically or dynamically. As there might be a wide spectrum of options, we stipulate only that all dependencies are clearly stated when documenting the measured executable size as part of the benchmark.

Correct execution of measurement runs As already mentioned in Section 6.1.5, there are situations were the concurrent execution of measurement infrastructure and execution runtime might need to be synchronised to make sure that measurement runs are processed completely. This can be achieved by employing platform-dependent primitives like Mutual Exclusion (Mutex) and conditional variables. A measurement infrastructure is not allowed to use active waiting, and the measurement thread(s) needs to be dormant while waiting on the completion of the execution runtime thread(s). It can easily be observed if execution runtime and measurement infrastructure are out of sync, as the number of captured timestamps will be less than the required amount at the end of a scenario's measurement process.

A Note Regarding the Java Platform Due to runtime optimisation processes like JIT or caching within a Java VM (e.g. the Sun HotSpot VM [260]) subsequent measurement runs can vary drastically in speed. The inclusion of such phenomena in the benchmark results is not intended; therefore, the benchmark should be executed several times and only measurement values from the last execution need to be considered. The only exceptions are the runtime memory measurements, where the values have to be determined during the first run.

6.1.12 Comparing the Results

Executing the complete benchmark yields 100 measured or derived performance indicators. To allow for a quick comparison of results for different platforms, we introduce the calculations for two overview values based on comparison of the benchmark values with values obtained from the generated C++ version of the benchmark. For this, a ratio between a given performance indicator P_{given} and the corresponding value P_{C++} (taken from the results of a C++ benchmark run on the same platform) is calculated using $\frac{P_{given}}{P_{C++}}$. If a ratio cannot be calculated, e. g. due to a C++ performance indicator of 0, the concerned value is omitted from the final calculation. This fact has to be stated clearly with the final benchmark results. Based on these ratios, two overview indicators can be calculated.

SPEED Using the geometric mean of the ratios for these performance indicators:

- ALTERNATIVE.AVG
- EPSILON.AVG
- EVENT.AVG
- GUARD.AVG
- COMPOUND.AVG
- EXPRESSION.COUNT.AVG
- EXPRESSION.EVENT.AVG
- EXPRESSION.CALL.AVG
- EXPRESSION.GUARD.AVG
- CONCURRENT.AVG
- HISTORY.AVG
- CONFIGURATION.AVG

MEMORY Using the geometric mean of the ratios for these indicators:

- SIZE.MEMORY.INIT
- SIZE.MEMORY.L0
- SIZE.MEMORY.L1
- SIZE.MEMORY.L2
- SIZE.MEMORY.L3

- SIZE.MEMORY.L4
- LIFECYCLE.MEMORY.AVG

For both indicators, lower values represent better results. This approach for calculating overview indicators was inspired by the calculation of metrics with the Standard Performance Evaluation Corporation (SPEC) CPU2006 benchmark suite [269]. While the overview values provide easy access for comparing different platforms, it is recommended to examine the complete set of indicators in more detail, rather than just using the overview values.

6.2 Execution Platform Mappings

The definition of the benchmark allows us to conduct a platform independent performance assessment. As our implementations use specific technologies and support different expression languages and BM features, we have to first define mappings of the BM features used in the benchmark (see Section 4.1.1) to a target platform. We define three mappings. The first mapping specifies benchmarking details for the BM interpreter implementation using UML State Machines and Ecore (see Section 4.4). The second mapping refers to the MPU implementation in Java and OSGi (see Section 4.5). The third mapping is used for a reference benchmark implementation using generated C++ with the Rational Rhapsody tool (see Section 3.2.3).

6.2.1 Mapping to the UML Adaptive Systems Profile and Ecore

A mapping of the UML interpreter implementation is straightforward, as we already use a UML notation for describing the BMs that make up the benchmark. MVEL is employed as an expression language [275]. Table 6.15 contains the mapping for the set fundamental BM features to features employed in the specific UML interpreter implementation. For binding of context data and FCs, we are relying on the ContextImport stereotype defined in the UML ASP profile (see Section 4.4 on the implementation of the UML interpreter).

Feature	**Description of Mapping**
States	Are mapped to instances of the *State* class. Initial states are *Pseudostate* instances with the *kind* attribute set to *initial*, final states are represented by instances of the *FinalState* class.
Compound States	Supported through hierarchies of nested *Region* class instances. Navigable over the *container* and *state* transitions of the *State* and *Region* classes.

Feature	Description of Mapping
Transitions	Instances of the *Transition* class. Access to the ECA labels is provided via the *trigger*, *guard* and *effect* associations.
Events	Represented as instances of the *SignalEvent* class.
Conditions	Guard conditions are expressed in MVEL syntax using instances of the *OpaqueBehavior* class with the attributes *language* set to *java* and the attribute *body* set to the corresponding MVEL source code. Operators have a similar semantics, but a different syntax: $=$ is mapped to $==$ in MVEL, $\wedge$ to &&, $\vee$ to || and $:=$ to $=$. The other operators use equivalent symbols, and parenthesis can be used in the usual way.
Context	Variables are mapped to public accessible integer fields of a provided *SessionData* Java class, referenced using a *ContextImport* stereotype and created using instances of the *InstanceSpecification* class. Data access is handled via MVEL code. Constants are mapped to Java literals.
Actions	Actions directly map to Java method invocations using MVEL. Action expressions utilise instances of the *OpaqueExpression* class with the attributes *language* set to *java* and the attribute *body* set to the corresponding MVEL source code. The timestamp() action should be implemented as part of the interpreter functionality — this enables the collection of timestamp measurements with a low overhead. The send(...) and call(...) actions are provided as methods of specific Java classes, bound to the model via *ContextImport* and *InstanceSpecification* classes.
Parallelism	Supported using multiple *Region* class instances as well as instances of the *Fork* and *Join* classes.
History	Represented as an instance of the *Pseudostate* class with the *kind* attribute set to *deepHistory*.

Table 6.15: Mapping of benchmark features to the UML ASP, Ecore and MVEL

6.2.2 Mapping to State Chart XML and JEXL

SCXML is used for the implementation of the MPU (see Section 4.5) and also employed in the *Management in the Network* use case described in Section 5.2. Most of the fundamental BM features have a direct counterpart in SCXML; for the missing features (fork/join), an identical functionality can be specified by using transitions that directly lead to (or leave from) an orthogonal state. JEXL is used for the specification of expressions [217]. This particular combination of interpretation engine and choice of expression language is the default configuration used by the

Apache Commons SCXML project [215]. Table 6.16 contains the mapping of SCXML and JEXL features to the fundamental BM features used in the benchmark.

Feature	**Description of Mapping**
States	Represented by the `<state>` tag. Final states are represented by `<final>` tags. There are two ways for representing an initial state: either through the `<initial>` element or by specifying the `initial` attribute for a `<state>` element. The benchmark mapping requires the attribute use.
Compound States	Enabled by the nesting of `<state>` tags. A `<state>` element can have an arbitrary number of child `<state>` elements, which are considered substates.
Transitions	Represented by the `<transition>` tag with the attributes `event` and `cond` for specifying an event trigger using a string identifier and a guard condition by means of a JEXL expression. An optional action is represented using executable child content contained under the `<transition>` tag.
Events	Specified as immutable data structures and handled by a unique string identifier.
Conditions	Formulated in JEXL and used in various places as condition, location or value expressions. All operators that are used in the benchmark exist in JEXL. The following syntax has to be used: equals 'eq', lesser 'lt' and greater 'gt'. Addition uses the '+' operator. The boolean operators also use cleartext 'and' and 'or'. Assignment uses the '=' symbol and parenthesis can be employed in the usual way.
Context	The context is stored in `<data>` entries as part of a `<datamodel>` element. Constants are represented as JEXL integer literals.
Actions	The **timestamp()** action has to be implemented as part of the interpreter (e. g. via the *CustomAction* class as explained on page 226 in Appendix B). The **send(...)** function is provided through the `<raise>` element, as the event is supposed to be used in the internal session only. The **call(...)** action needs to be implemented using a `<invoke>` element. As `<invoke>` can only be used within a state, the action will not be executed as part of a transition but considered as a child of the exited source state (this is only relevant in a single situation and refers to the state **F** of Figure 6.7 on page 166). The `<invoke>` statement needs to contain a single `<param>` for passing an integer value. The state will be left on a transition that fires on the corresponding 'invoke.done' event, after updating a data entry with the result of the invocation.

Feature	Description of Mapping
Parallelism	Is supported through the use of the `<parallel>` element that represents a state, where all substate children are considered disjoint parallel regions. Once all parallel regions finished execution an engine will raise a *done.state.**id*** completion event, where ***id*** refers to the id of the `<parallel>` element. This event needs to be used as a trigger on an outgoing transition from the `<parallel>` element to imitate the semantics of a join construct. Control flow forking happens implicitly when entering a `<parallel>` state via an incoming transition. Parallelism will introduce a new superstate per parallel region - these states need to carry the identifier of the enclosing `<parallel>` element, with an appended sequence number[6]. The newly introduced states must carry an `initial` attribute providing the initial state of the control flow.
History	Corresponds to a `<history>` element with an existing attribute `type` set to '`deep`'.

Table 6.16: Mapping of benchmark features to the SCXML and JEXL

6.2.3 Mapping to UML and Generated C++

By assessing the performance of generated code for the benchmark suite, we are able to define a baseline performance. We suppose that any BM interpreter will be slower than the performance of generated static C++ code. This does not take into account the potential optimisations that are possible when facilitating the similarities between a number of BMs using an interpretation approach (see the description of the TMPL engine in Section 4.2).

For benchmark creation, we are using IBM's Rational Rhapsody [239], which is a graphical tool for generating C++ code from UML diagrams. Each of the Benchmark scenarios is represented as an individual UML Class with its behaviour defined by a statechart. The classes are then automatically transformed to C++ code, which is compiled and subsequently measured. Each scenario yields the header and implementation file for exactly one C++ class, which encodes all states and transitions of the BM. When generating the benchmark from Rhapsody, no additional instrumentation code (e. g. tracing) is to be embedded with the created C++ source. Table 6.17 contains a mapping of the fundamental BM features used in the benchmark to Rhapsody primitives.

[6]E.g. if the `<parallel>` state has the id *B*, two parallel sub components will carry the state ids *B1* and *B2*.

Feature	Description of Mapping
States	States are created graphically using the *State* tool and are represented using enumerations within the resulting C++ class, which also provides methods for determining the active states. Final and initial states are mapped similarily.
Compound States	Compound states are supported in the usual UML notation (see Appendix A). The code generator creates a single event dispatching method per compound state.
Transitions	Specified in UML notation and represented implicitly as part of the code that determines state changes. Transition labels are specified using the syntax described on page 219 or by using configuration forms that allow to specify trigger events, guard conditions and actions separately.
Events	Events are specified as textual identifiers and represented as C++ classes, one per event. Each event that is dispatched from outside of the provided Rhapsody runtime needs to be created by the developer but is destroyed automatically by the runtime.
Conditions	Statements are formulated using C++ and automatically integrated within the generated classes. The operational semantics of C++ are similar, but the syntax is different for some of the symbols: $=$ is mapped to $==$, $\wedge$ to &&, $\vee$ to || and $:=$ to $=$. The other operators use equivalent symbols and parenthesis can be used in the usual way.
Context	Specified using a separate *SessionData* class with publicly accessible attributes. Scenario classes that make use of context data are specified using a unilateral composition association with the *SessionData* class, enabling them to access these attributes using C++ dot notation[7].
Actions	The timestamp() action is implemented as a method of an additional *Interpreter* class and also accessed through referencing an association. The send(...) function is provided by the *OMReactive* class, which is the base class of all generated BMs. Accessing FCs via the call(...) action is implemented as a function call on a *FunctionalComponent* class.
Parallelism	Supported through orthogonal states and specified using dashed *And* lines as well as fork/join constructs.
History	Is specified using the provided graphical tools.

Table 6.17: Mapping of benchmark features to a generated C++ runtime

[7] e. g. `dat.a` in case that the context class association end is labelled 'dat' with an attribute 'a'.

6.3 Quantitative Assessment of the Approach

The evaluation of our approach has been carried out using two methods. Using the first first method we conducted a qualitative assessment, facilitating the use case studies described in Chapter 5. With the second method we conducted a quantitative assessment of the two prototype implementations using the performance benchmark, along with a documentation of the baseline performance for the benchmark, and the results are documented in the following text. The collected data for the benchmark measurements is documented in Appendix D.

6.3.1 Performance of the UML Interpreter

We implemented and executed the benchmark suite using the UML interpreter. For driving the benchmarking process, we used version 4 of the JUnit framework [267] to execute the individual measurement scenarios. The determination of memory, timing and binary size values has been implemented according to the considerations in Section 6.1.11. Execution of the benchmark was done on a laptop computer supplied with power from the grid over the duration of the measurements. The machine had the following features:

Feature	Description
Computer Model	Apple MacBook Pro
CPU	Intel Core 2 Duo Processor, 2 Cores with 2.5 GHz
L2-Cache	6 MB
RAM	4 GB
Bus Frequency	800 GHz
Operating System	Mac OS X 10.6.3
Java VM	Sun Java HotSpot 64-Bit Server VM
Java Runtime Environment	Sun Java SE, version 1.6.0_17

Table 6.18: Platform used for benchmarking interpreter implementations

The complete result data of the UML interpreter benchmark measurements can be found in Appendix D, in a combined table with data from other benchmark measurements. A timer resolution of approximate 1 µs was determined, and the employed timestamping method incurred an average delay of 3.64 µs. We will not discuss every performance indicator in detail but only point out some of the more interesting performance characteristics in the following text.

Transition matching The average delay for matching self-referencing transitions is ~40 µs (ALTERNATIVE.AVG), while the average delay for matching ε-transitions is faster with a value of ~25 µs (EPSILON.AVG). The EVENT scenario tests the performance for matching single, non-self-referencing transitions from a number of outgoing ones. Figure 6.11 shows the shortest, average and longest delay values for all 125 subsequent measurements.

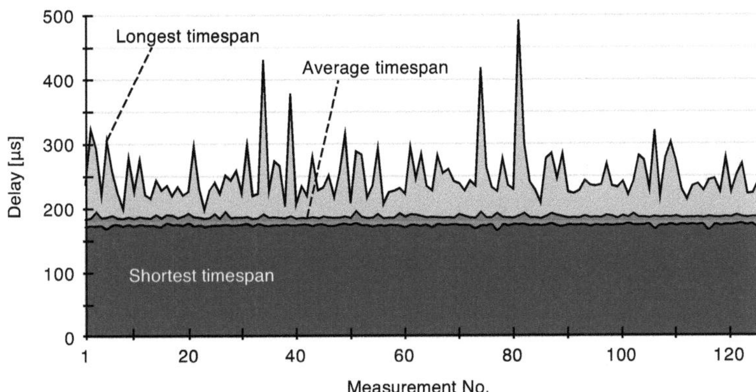

Figure 6.11: UML interpreter performance for matching multiple transitions

The individual, discrete values have been connected by lines to better indicate the trend. As can be seen from the performance indicators, as well as the given figures, the minimal and average values have a low variance[8] (both of the two series have values that vary only within a range of ~13 µs), while the maximal values are much more erratic (varying within a ~294 µs range). We suspect that these spikes are caused by effects on VM and OS level. Although the variance of the worst case values is high, this has little impact on the average matching delay for events, which is closer to the minimal matching delay, as longer delay times are observed only sporadically. Results for the GUARD scenario measurements are similar, with an additional delay of ~14 µs (on average) when compared with the results from the EVENT scenario.

When plotting the average measured matching timespans for the GUARD scenario on a per path basis (the path number corresponds to the variable p of Algorithm 5, incremented by one), it is possible to directly see the effect that the model data structure has on the transition matching delay. Figure 6.12 shows the matching delays of the 125 different paths.

[8]We are giving the variance in value ranges. We believe that this is more descriptive than quoting

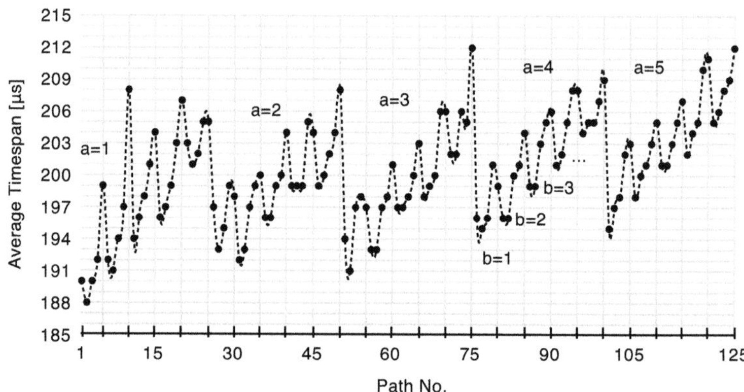

Figure 6.12: UML interpreter guard condition evaluation performance (per path)

For understanding the data, one needs to remember the composition of the different paths. Along all of the paths, the interpreter needs to consecutively evaluate three context data variables: a, b and c. For the first 25 paths, a is fixed to a value of 1, for the next 25 paths to the value 2, et cetera. For each of these 5×25 paths, the variable b is set to 1 for the first five paths, to 2 for the second five paths and so on. The variable c is continuously altered with every path. The data values corresponding to this schema have been measured, and we can conclude that the internal data structure stores outgoing transitions in the order in which they were defined (in our case this order is consistent with the context data variable values used in the guard conditions), and the matching algorithm processes them in the same order. This implies, e. g., that a transition annotated with [a=1] is tested first and that a transition with [a=5] is tested last. In the worst case (path 125) the interpreter needs to evaluate 15 guard conditions, as one condition after the other needs to be tested until a match is found. Coming back to the data plot in Figure 6.12: the measurement values have been connected by a dotted line, forming a curve with five large jags — these correspond to the values of a. Each of the jags is again made up of five smaller spikes, reflecting the influence of the b values. Lastly, each of the smaller spikes is made up of five data values, related to the c values.

Processing self-referencing transitions that traverse nesting levels within the composition hierarchy of the COMPOUND scenario is slower than the processing of

a statistical variance value.

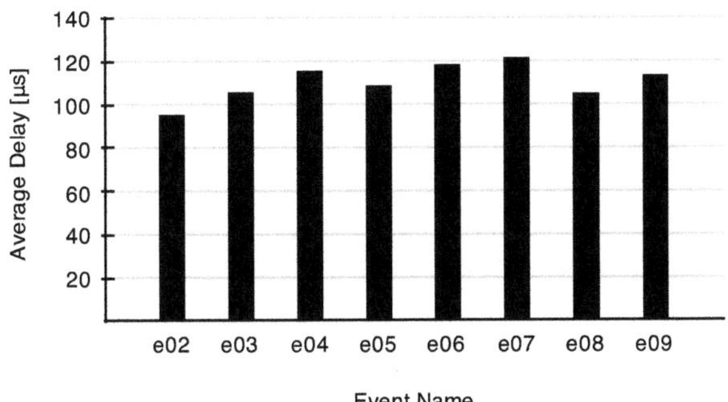

Figure 6.13: Performance of the UML interpreter in the COMPOUND scenario

simple transitions. This performance reduction depends on the number of exited and entered states, with an average factor between ~2.5 (COMPOUND.E02.AVG = 95.06 µs) and ~3 (COMPOUND.E07.AVG = 121.45 µs). Figure 6.13 shows the average delays incurred by processing an event within the scenario.

The primary factor that influences the processing time difference is the number of nesting levels that need to be considered during firing of a transition (which can be either 1, 2 or 3). The second factor is the ratio between states that are explicitly given by a transition and the ones that need to be determined implicitly. E. g., processing the e04 and e07 transitions in Figure 6.6 produces the same behaviour, but the e07 transition is processed slower — the exited states **C** and **B** have to be discovered implicitly, while the source state **C** is explicitly given for the e04 transition.

Expression Evaluation The measurement values taken during execution of the EXPRESSION scenario have one thing in common: the first conducted measurement always yields the longest processing time of all measurements. The worst case is found for the expression that calls an FC: EXPRESSION.CALL.MAX is ~1259 µs, whereas EXPRESSION.CALL.AVG is ~66 µs, a difference of approximately a factor of 19. We found that these exceptional values are caused by one-time initialisation processes within the MVEL library. After initialisation, the expressions are evaluated with a lower variance: FC call execution time varies in the range of ~15 µs, event sending varies within ~20 µs and condition evaluation within a ~30 µs range. The evaluation of guard conditions tends to be moderately slower for more complex conditions, as demonstrated by the values for EXPRESSION.GUARD1.AVG = 30.67 µs, EXPRESSION.GUARD2.AVG = 34.20 µs and EXPRESSION.GUARD3.AVG = 36.51 µs.

Concurrency Interpreter performance when handling concurrent control flows is depicted in Figure 6.14. There have been two dashed lines fitted to the diagram, showing the trend of the measured values.

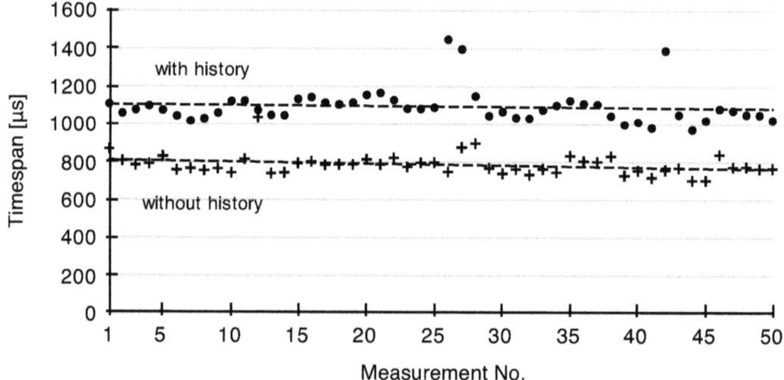

Figure 6.14: Performance of the UML interpreter for the CONCURRENT scenario

The timespan values form a steady sequence with the averages CONCURRENT.-AVG = 785.96 µs and HISTORY.AVG = 1094.72 µs with only a few visible spikes. The difference between the scenario execution with history information and the execution without history, is on average ∼ 308 µs.

Configuration & Lifecycle Management Issues The interpreter performance for both instantiating and starting, as well as stopping and removing models, is steady. Values for starting (the time it takes for the model to reach the timestamp action) have been measured between 972 µs – 1275 µs, while the stopping and removing processes vary within a timespan of 186 µs – 252 µs. The average start time is LIFECYCLE.ENTER.AVG = 1073.52 µs, while the overall time is LIFECYCLE.OVERALL.AVG = 1226.40 µs. Generally, it can be said that BM start and deployment takes ∼ 1 ms and that stopping and removing a BM takes only a fraction ($\sim \frac{1}{7}$) of that time. This is due to the more complex processes needed when creating an initial BM instance.

Retrieval of configuration values was measured to occur within a timeframe of CONFIGURATION.MIN = 14.00 µs and CONFIGURATION.MAX = 144.00 µs, with an average value of CONFIGURATION.AVG = 47.72 µs. The collected values show variation, but 90% fall below 65 µs.

Figure 6.15 shows the consumed memory at key points during the process. Depicted values are separated into heap and non-heap (static and stack) memory. After the interpreter has been initialised, the allocated memory is roughly constant (around

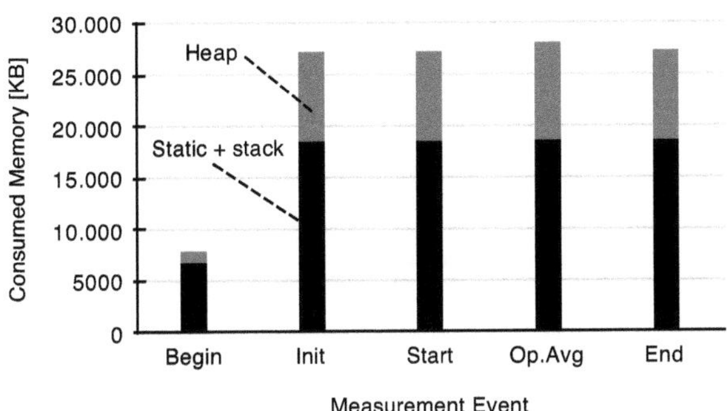

Figure 6.15: Consumed memory by the UML interpreter in the LIFECYCLE scenario

27–28 MB), although we measured some spikes during the operation where consumed memory goes up to a value of LIFECYCLE.MEMORY.MAX = 38519.00 KB.

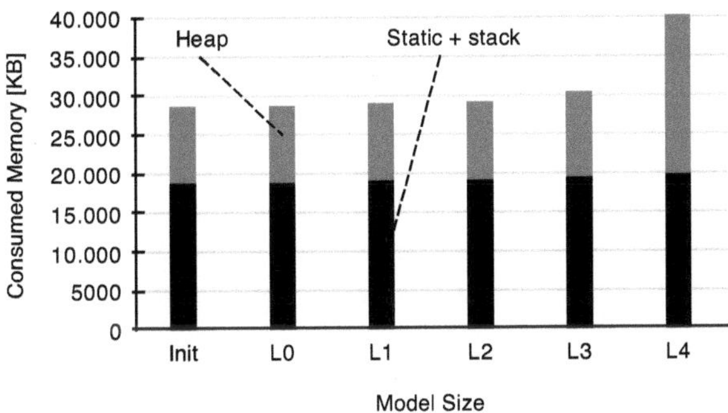

Figure 6.16: Consumed memory by the UML interpreter in the SIZE scenario

The influence of model size is neglected in the LIFECYCLE scenario but can be observed from measurements conducted in the SIZE scenario. A similar diagram is shown in Figure 6.16, depicting the values of consumed memory in relation to the differently sized models L0 to L4. Again, the diagram shows measured values separated into heap and non-heap values, but this time only the heap value substantially increases with growing model size. The overall amount is ~ 1 KB per additional state in the BMs for the SIZE scenario (SIZE.MEMORY.GROW = 1.04 KB / State). Note that the difference in size between each of the employed models is exponential, thus, **L4** is significantly larger than the other ones. In general, memory consumption does not seem to be a relevant factor for desktop or server applications for BM interpretation, unless the interpreter is executed with a large number of models or with extremely large ones. For other platforms, this is quite different (see Section 5.4).

6.3.2 Performance of the Model Processing Unit

The MPU was also subjected to measurements according to the benchmark suite, on the same platform as used for benchmarking the UML interpreter (see Table 6.18 on page 184). The average timestamping overhead was determined at less than 1 µs, and the accuracy of the timer is the same as for the UML interpreter. The benchmark was carried out using JUnit 3.8 test classes, which were executed via the JUnit OSGi bundle provided by the Apache Felix project. Logging was configured at a minimal verbosity (errors only), and the web interface was disabled. The measured values can be found in Appendix D.

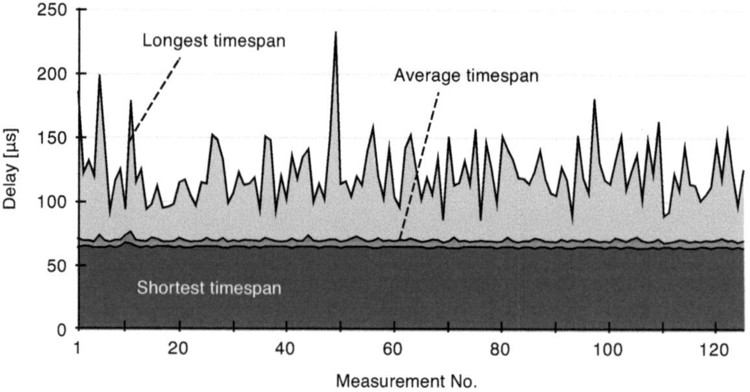

Figure 6.17: MPU performance for matching multiple transitions

Transition Matching The average ε-transition delay is EPSILON.AVG = 14.24 µs, while the matching of simple self-referencing transitions is considerably slower at an average of ALTERNATIVE.AVG = 53.20 µs. This is not surprising, as ε-events are handled quite differently to the completion events used in the UML interpreter. For simple transitions, the MPU is ~12 µs slower than the one for UML. Variance of simple transitions is low, with 95% of all values within a range of ~5 µs; for ε-transitions this is still good — more than 90% of the measured values lie within a similar interval.

Figure 6.17 shows the performance of the MPU in the EVENT scenario. The measurement results have a similar distribution as the ones shown in Figure 6.11 (with an average of EVENT.AVG = 70.06 µs close to the optimum EVENT.MIN = 64.00 µs) but with an execution speed that is on average ~2.5 times faster than the one determined for the UML engine. This is different in the GUARD scenario, where the MPU uses an average of GUARD.AVG = 191.96 µs for processing of a complete path in the BM. A delay that is 10 µs less than the one of the UML equivalent. Differences

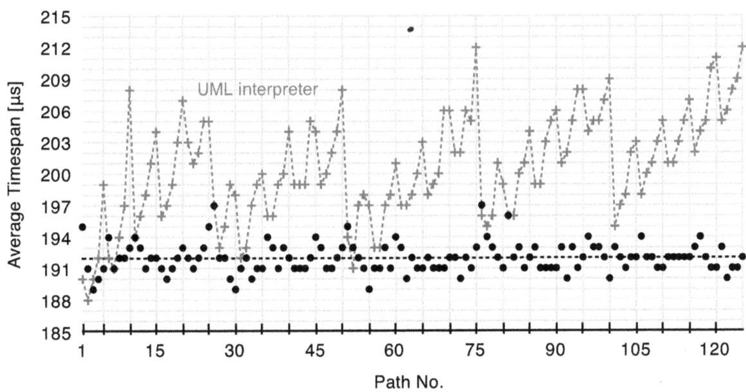

Figure 6.18: MPU guard condition evaluation performance (per path)

in the implementation of transition matching data structures and algorithms become obvious when looking at the average measured matching timespans per path in Figure 6.18. The diagram also shows the values of the corresponding UML engine measurements (Figure 6.12) for comparison purposes, and a dashed trend line has been added to the plotted data, showing that the values are evenly distributed within a ±5 µs interval around the average delay GUARD.AVG. While the UML interpreter exhibits a clear pattern that depends on the transition matching sequence, the MPU has no such characteristics. As all possible patterns are tested, it is very likely[9] that the SCXML implementation will necessarily have to test all of the given conditions at some stage — thus the depicted measurement results might seem puzzling. The explanation is simple: the measured time spans indicate the time needed to check the conditions for all of the five transitions leading out of a state. The MPU employs an algorithm that first constructs a set of transitions that trigger for a given event and then filters this set by evaluating each of the guard conditions. Although this approach has a larger overhead than the one chosen for the UML engine, the average time of the MPU is still a bit faster for the GUARD scenario model.

The processing delays of self-referencing transitions, measured using the MPU within the COMPOUND scenario, exhibit similar characteristics with regard to the event types as the ones depicted for the UML interpreter in Figure 6.13. Regarding the average speed of execution, the SCXML implementation is ~ 50 µs faster (COMPOUND.AVG = 60.91 µs) than the UML interpreter (110.28 µs). Values for the average processing times are steady, falling within a range of 3 µs when compared between each of the individual patterns. The overall variance of values is in the range of COMPOUND.MIN = 52.00 µs and COMPOUND.MAX = 197.00 µs. Regarding the best-case execution times, the UML engine still has an advantage of ~ 30 µs. The worst-case values exhibit similar characteristics for both interpreters: the ratio $\frac{MAX}{AVG}$ is roughly the same within each of the transition measurement scenarios (e. g. in the COMPOUND scenario, it is ~ 2.96 for the UML interpreter and ~ 3.23 for the MPU).

Expression Evaluation Performance of the MPU for evaluation of expression is worse than that of the UML interpreter. While it is still on par for the sending of events (EXPRESSION.EVENT.AVG = 68.99 µs, the UML interpreter needs an average of 69.94 µs), the counting loop takes twice as long at EXPRESSION.COUNT.AVG = 6918.77 µs. This difference increases when evaluating more complex expressions: EXPRESSION.GUARD1.AVG = 44.92 µs (takes ~ 1.5 times longer than the UML engine), EXPRESSION.GUARD2.AVG = 64.08 µs (~ 1.9 times longer), EXPRESSION.GUARD3.AVG = 93.23 µs (~ 2.6 times longer). The calling of an FC has the worst average execution time at EXPRESSION.CALL.AVG = 479.21 µs, which is more than 7 times longer than the execution time of the UML interpreter.

The observed delays for evaluating guard conditions are due to the speed of the employed JEXL engine, which evaluates statements based on an AST representation of a given statement, presumably with no pre-compilation taking place within the library code. These conclusions are also supported by comparative measurements conducted by M. Brock et al. [276]. Regarding the FC call, which is implemented in SCXML using an `<invoke>` tag, it is clear that this is a more complicated operation than the simple invocation of a Java method, as there are additional events used

[9]Unless the data structure is subjected to runtime re-ordering processes.

for communicating the return value back to the calling BM, explaining the observed overhead.

Concurrency Parallel regions within the CONCURRENT scenario are executed more than twice as fast by the MPU, as by the UML interpreter, at CONCURRENT.AVG = 358.76 µs. This is also true when conducting the scenario using the additional history step: HISTORY.AVG = 480.12 µs, whereas 1094.72 µs have been measured on average for the UML engine.

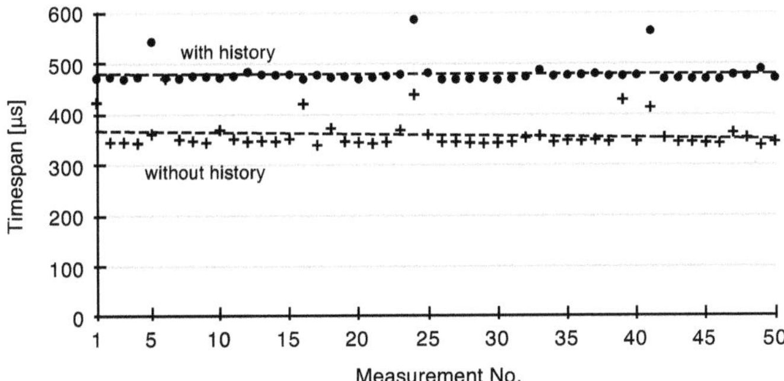

Figure 6.19: Performance of the MPU for the CONCURRENT scenario

Figure 6.19 shows the values for both the history and the normal measurement scenario. Apart from the offset caused by the faster execution, the plot looks similar to the one created for the UML interpreter (see Figure 6.14). As can be seen from the plotted values, there are a number of outliers (3 of 50 values for the normal scenario and 6 out of 50 for the history scenario), but generally the values cluster closely around the respective average values.

Configuration & Lifecycle Management Issues The retrieval of the active state configuration is fast, as these values are readily available during the interpreter's operation. The determined values are between CONFIGURATION.MIN = 12.00 µs and CONFIGURATION.MAX = 31.00 µs with an average of 16.04 µs. In 90% of the measured trials the time was less than 20 µs.

While the times for stopping and removing a model from the interpreter are similar (on average ~150 µs with the UML engine vs. ~200 µs for the MPU), there is a big difference when instantiating and starting a BM. The MPU needs on average ~12 times more time for this task (LIFECYCLE.ENTER.AVG = 13697.42 µs). In contrast with the UML interpreter, which is merely a research prototype, the MPU has been designed with a more sophisticated — and realistic — architecture in mind. This additional complexity of the infrastructure is the cause for the measured time differences. Although the differences are remarkable, this should not constitute an issue for real-world applications, as even the worst case deployment time of ~16 ms is fast enough for all purposes that we can possibly think of.

Memory consumption during execution of the LIFECYCLE scenario is on average LIFECYCLE.MEMORY.AVG = 35862.14 KB, and usage varies only slightly within a range of ~180 KB. With a value of 35832.00 KB, even the initial LIFECYCLE.MEMORY.BEGIN indicator has a similar size. This is different when compared with the UML interpreter (see Figure 6.15). Again, these discrepancies are due to the different architectures; in the MPU, the interpreter's bytecode is already available at the very beginning of the benchmark execution, while it is loaded dynamically for the UML engine benchmark.

The consumed memory within the SIZE scenario is shown in Figure 6.20.

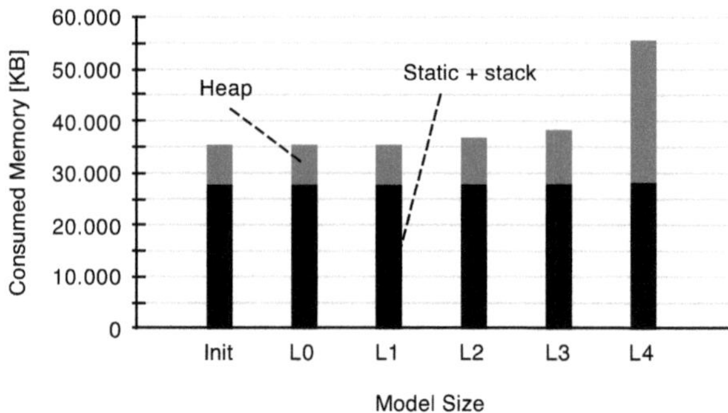

Figure 6.20: Consumed memory by the MPU in the SIZE scenario

The overall picture is similar to the one depicted in Figure 6.16 for the UML interpreter; the memory region that contains static + stack data remains approximately the same, while the heap memory values grow exponentially with each deployed BM. Memory increase per state is at SIZE.MEMORY.GROW = 1.81 KB, which is more than the ~1 KB used by the EMF format in the UML engine. With the L4 BM deployed, the MPU consumes an overall SIZE.MEMORY.L4 = 55509.00 KB of memory. The SIZE.EXECUTABLE value is the same as for the UML version, amounting to 100.67 KB, which is the size of the employed Java VM executable.

6.3.3 Determination of Baseline Performance

To enable a better comparison between the results obtained from benchmarking different interpreter implementations, a baseline performance is determined. We decided to create an executor based on static models that yields the best possible execution performance on a given platform. This is achieved by employing code generation to create C++ classes for all of the benchmark's behaviour models.

For this purpose, we are using version 7.5 of the Rational Rhapsody tool from IBM on Microsoft Windows 7. We created BMs for the various scenarios of the benchmark, either manually within the tool's editor or through generation of suitable XMI files that were imported in the application (for the larger SIZE scenario models L2, L3 and L4). Each scenario of the benchmark was represented by a single class with an attached statechart, defining the behaviour. Context data, timestamping functionality, FCs and routines for configuration retrieval were added using separate classes, which are referenced by the scenario classes. The tool was subsequently instructed to generate C++ code in a configuration that did not add additional instrumentation code for tracing or simulation. The chosen target platform was Linux, as OS X is not supported by Rhapsody. This also forced us to carry out a minor patch[10] on the runtime framework used by the generated code.

The operation of the code generator is straightforward; each class in the Rhapsody benchmark model is compiled into an individual C++ class. Event processing is implemented by one or more methods that utilise *switch* statements with declared event symbols. Actions bindings are simple method calls, and expression evaluation is also done using untranslated C++ statements. Additionally, there are some methods used in initialisation of the BM and a couple of boolean, inline accessors that support the determination of an instances particular state configuration. States are encoded using integer values.

Taking the generated source code, we then added logic to conduct the measurements and compiled it using the GCC, version 4.2 on OS X 10.6.3. The following parameters were used to compile the source: `-mdynamic-no-pic -arch x86_64 -fvisibility-inlines-hidden -mmacosx-version-min=10.6 -x c++ -Os -fvisibility=hidden`. The resulting binary contained only a single set of instructions for execution on a 64 bit X86 platform. Both timestamps, as well as memory measurements, have been implemented using the `getrusage` system call, as proposed in Section 6.1.11.

For execution of the benchmark, the same platform used to benchmark the previous interpreters was employed (see Table 6.18 on page 184). Due to optimisations on the static code, the executable exhibits only a constant runtime complexity, where the other interpreters have a linear complexity. For example, this can be observed in the EVENT scenario. Also, the evaluation of expressions is heavily optimised by the compiler and well integrated with the execution code, so that the introduced

[10] Modification of an identifier related to pthreads semaphore handling

delay often becomes too small to be measurable. The timer resolution has been determined at ~1 µs, and the average delay incurred by the timestamping mechanism is TIMESTAMP.AVG = 2.13 µs. The complete measurement results can be found in Appendix D.

Transition Matching The average time for matching ε-transitions is ~2.25 µs, while the matching of simple transitions takes more than five times longer: ALTERNATIVE.AVG has been determined at 12.2 µs.

Although the performance used for processing paths in the GUARD scenario follows similar rules as already discussed in relation to the UML interpreter on page 186 ff., the resulting measurement values follow a different distribution, as depicted in Figure 6.21.

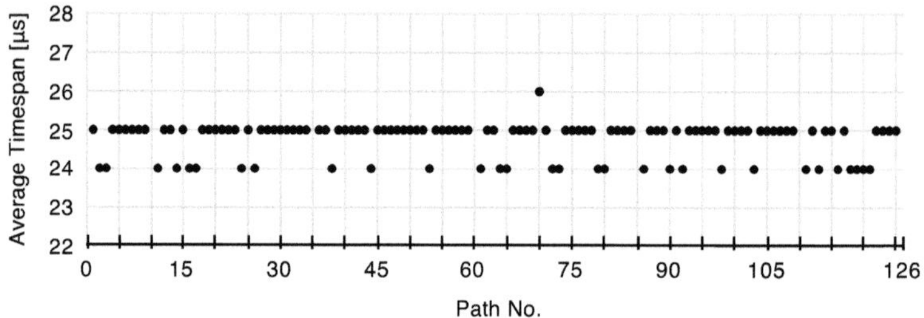

Figure 6.21: Performance of generated code for matching guard conditions

Interpretation of the guard conditions is implemented as nested if-then-else statements, so each condition is evaluated separately. It appears that the speed for evaluation is so fast that this has no real impact; most of the values (more than 95%) fall into an interval between 24 – 26 µs. There are five outliers (the paths where b=2 and c=5, not shown in the diagram) that finish much quicker in ~14 µs. This might be be attributed to caching phenomena of the execution hardware.

Regarding the EVENT scenario, the average time for matching transitions on a single path using only event triggers was measured to be ~23.5 µs (EVENT.AVG), but there were a small number of measurement runs that completed much quicker (taking around 1 or 2 µs for the complete run). Figure 6.22 shows the trends for all of the measurements. It can be observed that the average matching time exhibits only little variance (the values are always between 22 and 25 µs), whereas the worst case times might go up to EVENT.MAX = 128 µs.

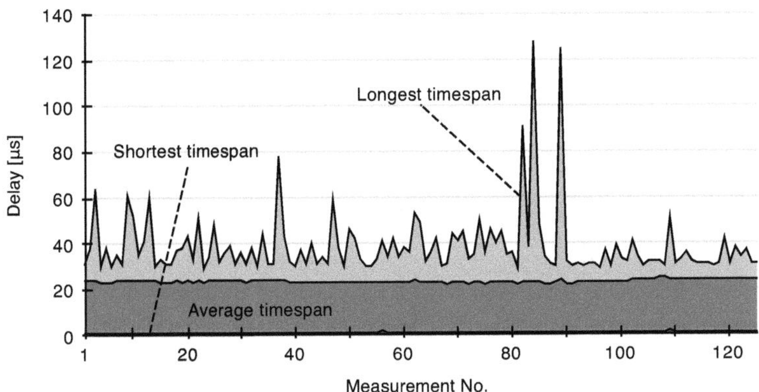

Figure 6.22: Performance of generated code for matching multiple transitions

The values resulting from execution of the COMPOUND scenario are more uniform than the ones taken for the UML interpreter, and the execution of a single pattern takes on average less than 9 µs. Due to the high number of collected timestamps, there is also a higher number of outliers contained in the result set, making for some large worst-case values, e. g. COMPOUND.E06.MAX=2172 µs.

Expression Evaluation The performance for evaluating expressions is steady over the set of collected measurements. EXPRESSION.COUNT.AVG is calculated at ~65 µs but the values contain an outlier (EXPRESSION.COUNT.MAX=5924 µs). Without this outlier, the average would be determined at ~35 µs. All values for the other performance indicators have only a small variance, and the averages are as follows; sending events has an average delay of ~3 µs (EXPRESSION.EVENT.AVG), and the calling of a method (EXPRESSION.CALL.AVG) as well as the evaluation of any of the three guard conditions (EXPRESSION.GUARD1.AVG, EXPRESSION.GUARD2.AVG, EXPRESSION.GUARD3.AVG) all have a similar average of ~1 µs. This demonstrates the big difference that exists between the timespan used for evaluating expressions using an interpretative approach and the time needed when evaluating native code.

Concurrency Performance of the generated code for the CONCURRENT scenario is faster than for the interpreted approach. Figure 6.23 shows the relevant measurement data with added, linear trends as dashed lines.

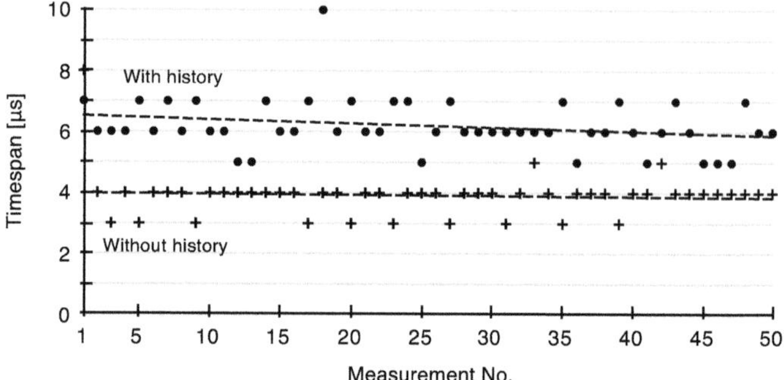

Figure 6.23: Performance of generated code for the CONCURRENT scenario

On average, it takes CONCURRENT.AVG = 3.92 µs to process the complete scenario without using history. With the use of history measurements, this value is at HISTORY.AVG = 6.20 µs. Variance for both of these values is low, with a minimal value of 3 µs (CONCURRENT.MIN) and a maximum timespan of 10 µs (HISTORY.MAX).

Configuration & Lifecycle Management By default, Rhapsody generates no methods for retrieval of the active state configuration. Instead, there are macros provided that can be used to determine if a single state is active. We added code that executed each of the state macros of the CONCURRENT scenario class to determine the active states. The state configuration was then returned as a string containing the active state ids. On average, this code used ~8 µs to complete. The performance indicators CONFIGURATION.MIN and CONFIGURATION.MAX were calculated to be 4 µs and 14 µs, respectively.

The lifecycle management performance of the generated code depends essentially on four things: the instantiation of a *Lifecycle* object, which contains the BM; calling of the provided `startBehaviour` method; waiting for the BM to finish; and deleting the instance. There is no such phase as *deployment*, as the BM is already deployed, in the form of statically bound code. Figure 6.24 shows that measurements are executed relatively fast and that the execution timespan values show little variation. The average time that the executor needed to reach the timestamp statement was LIFECYCLE.ENTER.AVG = 6.04 µs and a single run of the complete scenario was executed on average in LIFECYCLE.OVERALL.AVG = 19.06 µs. Contrary to, e. g., the UML interpreter, the time needed for exiting the model is longer than the time required to initialise it.

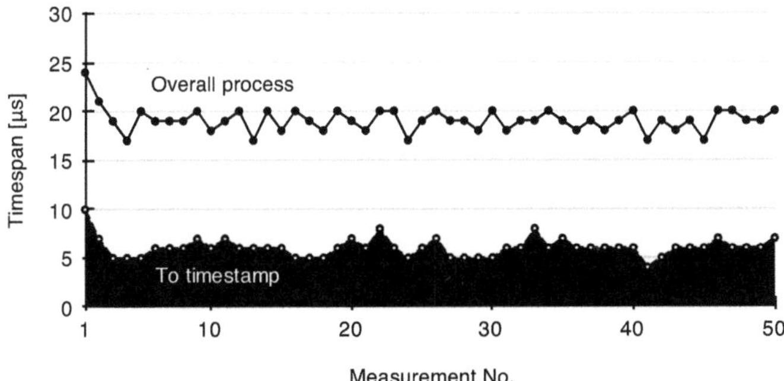

Figure 6.24: Baseline performance for the LIFECYCLE scenario

Memory measurements show that only a small amount of overall memory is consumed during operation (LIFECYCLE.MEMORY.END $<$ 600 KB) and the consumed memory grows continuously, from executor start to measurement end. Figure 6.25 shows the memory consumption at selected measurement points during execution. Due to the nature of the `getrusage` system call, only a single value can be determined, and there is no differentiation between heap and static+stack memory.

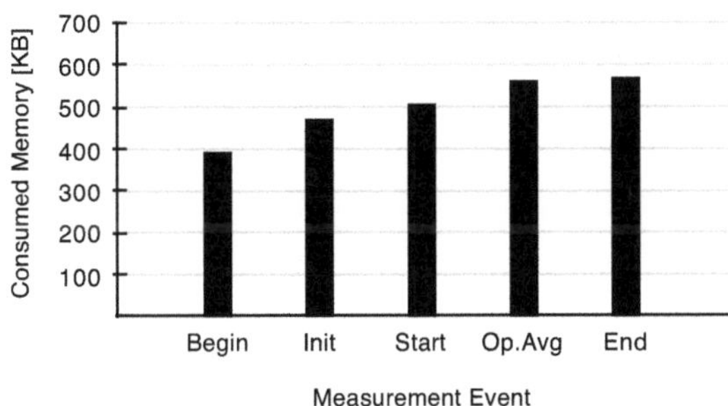

Figure 6.25: Consumed memory of generated code in the LIFECYCLE scenario

The additional memory consumed during the the LIFECYCLE scenario after executor start amounts to $\sim$180 KB and the consumed memory seems to only exhibit small variations. For example, the consumed memory did not grow continuously, but varied within $\sim$12 KB during operation, as seen in the differences of the

SIZE.MEMORY.L0 to SIZE.MEMORY.L4 values. Therefore, the executable size of the BMs is more interesting than the amount of consumed runtime memory. Figure 6.26 shows the values for the different models employed in the SIZE scenario.

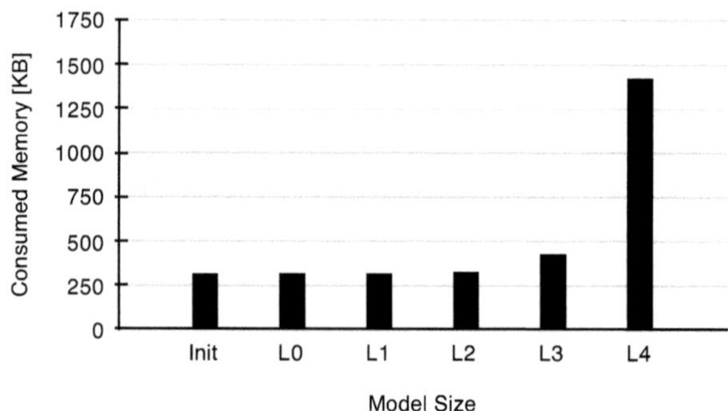

Figure 6.26: Binary executable size of generated code for the SIZE scenario

The executable binaries show a growth in size of SIZE.EXECUTABLE.GROW = 0.1 KB per state. The largest executable binary (the one that executes the L4 BM) has an overall size at SIZE.EXECUTABLE.L4 = 1423.20 KB and the BM code is responsible for more than 75% of the executable size.

6.4 Summary

This chapter contained the specification of a performance benchmark suite for measuring BM execution. Ten benchmark scenarios have been specified that are based on the fundamental set of BM features introduced in Section 4.1.1, and an execution of the benchmark yields 100 performance indicators that can be used to to asses the performance of a given execution platform. As the benchmark is platform-independent, one needs a mapping to a concrete execution platform for conducting an execution of the benchmark. We specified mappings to three different platforms: the UML ASP with Ecore and MVEL; SCXML and JEXL; and UML with C++ statements for code generation with the Rhapsody tool. We then documented the results of an execution of the benchmark for three implementations: the UML interpreter, the MPU and a reference implementation using generated code.

We found that, although the UML interpreter and the MPU are implemented very differently, they have similar overall results in the benchmark. For the UML interpreter, the overall execution speed is ~20 times slower as the baseline performance at SPEED = 22.30, while the MPU has a similar value of 20.33. The overall memory consumption was determined at MEMORY = 64.09 for the UML interpreter and at 81.07 for the MPU. Depending on the scenario, the interpretation processes are on average between 3 – 460 times slower and consume between 50 – 120 times more memory than the baseline implementation. We expected that the interpreter performance is not as good as the one of the baseline code, which is true. Nonetheless, a factor of 20 is not critical for the application purposes described in Chapter 5, and we found that both of the implementations have a more than adequate performance for our purposes. As such general values can convey only a very limited impression, we want to examine the differences in more detail.

The average performance of matching transitions is good for both implementations, with a slowdown factor of less than 10. For an interpreter, this is a decent result. Exceptions to this observation are found in two cases for the UML interpreter: the handling of ε-transitions, as well as the processing of transitions that cross levels in the composition hierarchy, are processed slower with an average factor of ~ 12 each. This is due to the usage of an additional completion event for ε-transitions and the need to determine the C_{active} and C_{target} state configurations when traversing the composition hierarchy (see Section 2.2.3).

Even though we employed the two fastest Java libraries available for expression evaluation, the speed is still an average ~ 30 (compiled MVEL in the UML interpreter) to ~ 60 (interpreted JEXL in the MPU) times slower than native code. The largest observed difference is the invocation of an FC using the MPU, which is on average 460 times slower. The reason is found in the employed architecture, which is relaying the invocation via an event middleware, a feature that is very helpful when implementing FCs as components that can be changed at runtime (OSGi bundles in our case). An FC invocation can be executed much quicker when facilitating the binding mechanism of the underlying programming language. As expression evaluation is used over and over when processing guard conditions, an improvement of this aspect is of crucial importance. This can be done through the use of precompilation, which effectively doubles the speed of expression evaluation for the considered scenarios.

The largest discrepancy between the baseline code and the interpreters concerns the speed of the concurrency mechanism: the average slowdown factor incurred is ~ 90 for the MPU and ~ 200 for the UML interpreter. This is due to the fact that interpreters are required to dynamically maintain control flow information, whereas a code generation process is able to encode this information within the static switch statements that govern state transitions. Although the values suggest quite a shortcoming, explicitly maintaining control flows can potentially have a positive effect by enabling the facilitation of hardware features that support concurrent execution (e. g. multiple processor cores) and by supporting optimisations at runtime.

Retrieving the active state configuration is a fast operation, being only 2 – 10 times slower than the corresponding operation in baseline code. As the state configuration needs to be explicitly maintained for the interpretation processes, it is merely a matter of providing the data to the requester, rather than obtaining it.

Model instantiation has a distinct time penalty, e. g. the MPU is $\sim$2260 times slower as the generated code. We do not deem this value particularly meaningful, as the generated code does not explicitly construct an in-memory representation of the model. Furthermore, the worst-case model instantiation time was measured at $\sim$16 ms, which seems to be sufficient for any application, as BM instantiation is usually not deemed a time-critical process. For the same reason, the LIFECYCLE.OVERALL.AVG performance indicator was also not included in calculation of the overall SPEED value.

Both of the interpreters have been implemented as memory-intensive Java applications; thus, the obtained MEMORY benchmark indicators are quite large. Although these indicators are relevant for judging resource consumption of a certain implementation, we found that they are non-critical and stay well within the resource constraints of current computing systems. Supporting this, the embedded systems experiment also demonstrates that memory is not per se an issue with the approach. We were able to interpret meaningful BMs within 2 KB of RAM, and as Table 5.3 shows, the minimal memory requirements for the various BM constructs can be very moderate.

It is interesting to note that performance values for the embedded systems experiment are in the same magnitude of speed as the ones for the interpreter implementations, even though the embedded system experiment uses only an 16 MHz 8 bit processor, while the UML interpreter and the MPU utilised a 64 bit dual-core processor running at 2.5 GHz.

A final note on the performance concerns the impact of the BM's structure on the interpretation speed. The differences between the various indicators in the benchmark measurements indicate that some constructs in the model structure can be interpreted faster than others. For example, when traversing a transition within a deeply nested composition hierarchy, the interpreter potentially needs to check all outgoing transitions from all parent states of the source state, which can be a costly operation. By employing model runtime and persistency formats that maintain the sequence of outgoing transitions, a BM designer could coerce the interpreter to check transitions in a particular order. Depending on the intended use of the BM, this could have a large impact on the execution performance. Another example concerns guard conditions: as guards on all outgoing transitions might potentially be evaluated for every incoming event, the formulation of these statements can have a huge influence on the performance. Thus, we can say that execution performance also depends on the experience of the model designer and the abilities of the utilised tools.

7 Conclusion

To say of what is, that it is,
or of what is not, that it is not,
is true.

Aristotle

To come to a conclusion on the overall approach, we first summarise the work conducted within this thesis.

Chapter 1 explains our motivation for undertaking the research. An introduction to the AS Engineering field is provided, and we stated the problem that we aimed to solve as well as describing our underlying research hypothesis. The employed methodology is explained and the scientific contributions of the thesis are highlighted.

Chapter 2 creates the foundation that the thesis rests on. We identified, described and discussed the concepts used for modelling runtime behaviour starting from simple states and transitions to the more complex ones, like model composition or control flow concurrency. Building upon these BM concepts the text subsequently introduced a terminology for various model formats and artefacts used in the interpretation process. We then continue to describe BM interpretation in detail and investigated a variety of key topics including BM instantiation, internal and external event processing, behaviour parallelism, the binding of expression languages and the invocation of FCs. There are a numbers of engineering solutions presented in this section (including the specification of algorithms and concrete mechanisms), which we consider central contributions of our work. The chapter ends with a discussion on the management of BMs. In the text, we provide a distributed system architecture for BM management together with a discussion on implementation alternatives.

Chapter 3 investigated the relation of our work to existing research undertakings. The text contains a discussion of the history of state-transition systems, followed by an overview of important publications regarding the execution and transformation of state-machine based BMs. We also looked at alternatives to state-transition systems for behaviour modelling and provided an overview of popular tools used in the context. The text then continues with a state-of-the-art description of dynamic system adaptation and communication mechanism. The reason is to give the reader a background to comprehend how and why major aspects of runtime interpretation of BMs relate to concepts used in AS Engineering. The discussion of the related work also contains an investigation of the network and systems management domains, as the use case studies are conducted within these target domains. The chapter closes with a discussion on the current state-of-the-art for performance benchmarking, which is an interesting topic in relation to the benchmark suite introduced in chapter 6.

Chapter 4 continues by demonstrating the feasibility of our approach using proof-of-concept implementations. We described four implementations of the concept, where each implementation was conducted with a different goal in mind. To enable a comparison of these implementations, we also described a set of fundamental BM features and proposed a generic software architecture for a BM interpreter, at the beginning of the chapter. We then described each of the implementations: the TMPL Engine, which has been created for matching patterns on XML data streams and which demonstrates the potential for runtime optimisation by means of BM adaptation. The ACE Toolkit for creating AS based on interpreted self-models, which allowed us to explore the necessary event transmission mechanisms and the FC concept as well as the creation of BMs by means of high-level language specification. The UML Interpreter, which implements the full set of Behavioral State Machine features of the UML 2.2 standard, providing us not only with an interpreter that utilises the most important BM formalism, but also with a comprehensive expertise on the interpretation of a large number of BM features. The last described implementation, the MPU, puts our concepts into practice by using only mature libraries and technologies. The motivation is to create a prototype that best fulfils the real-world requirements of the network and systems management domains.

Chapter 5 documents four use case studies, that asses the practical usefulness of the implementations. The first use case study demonstrated an application of the ACE toolkit to the problem of self-organised service supervision. The second use case facilitated a collective of MPUs to demonstrate a novel approach for managing systems and networks. This study is motivated by a narrated troubleshooting scenario, and we demonstrate the monitoring of the utilisation of a router by means of BM interpretation. In the third use case study, we are exploring the possibility of using BM interpretation within network entities to drastically reduce management traffic in IPv6 networks. The fourth use case researches the scalability limits of our approach in regard to resource utilisation.

Chapter 6 completes our examination of the runtime interpretation of BMs by providing a benchmark suite that allows us to quantify the performance of a given interpretation mechanism. Such a tool is necessary to compare our approach to the current best-practice of using code generation for the execution of BMs. The benchmark is platform independent and defined using ten scenarios. To execute the benchmark on a concrete measurement platform, one needs a platform mapping and we provide mappings to the UML ASP and MVEL, SCXML and JEXL, and to Rhapsody generated C++. This chapter closes with a quantitative assessment of the UML interpreter, the MPU and the generated reference implementation.

Chapter 7 provides a critical discussion of our research results, based on the elaborated use cases and performance assessment provided by the benchmark measurements. In the first section, we are giving a summary on the overall course of the research contained in the previous chapters. Afterwards, we are reflecting on the feasibility of the approach by contrasting our initial research hypothesis with the established results based on our experience with the implementations, use case studies and benchmark applications. The third section details the major challenges that are encountered when using BM interpretation and captures our lessons learned from solving these. The fourth section describes the relevance of our work for the wider research community and assesses the impact of the results. In the final section, we are describing future work and further, more advanced applications of the approach.

7.1 Feasibility of the Approach

The conducted implementations, along with the use case studies and the performance assessments, clearly support our research hypothesis formulated in Section 1.1.2. The interpretation of BMs at runtime is a viable approach with an adequate performance for all of the examined use case studies.

We were able to systematically determine the performance penalty incurred by such an approach. The results of the performance analysis confirm our assumptions; the performance of the interpretation approach is ~ 3 to ~ 460 times slower than generated code, depending on the utilised features of the BM and the employed technology for the runtime system. The average speed for the benchmark is ~ 20 times slower and the average consumed memory is between ~ 60 and ~ 80 times larger. For an interpreted language, such an overhead is considered normal, e. g. compare with Romer et al. [163] who determine the overheads of a variety of general-purpose interpreted languages at a similar magnitude. As a general rule of thumb, it can be said that adding a level of interpretation slows down the execution time of a program by at least a factor of ten [82]. This is the cost to pay for the advanced runtime adaptation features provided by an interpretative approach.

When comparing the MPU and the UML interpreter, it is surprising that both have a similar overall performance with differences only in some details. Regarding memory consumption, the UML interpreter uses $\sim \frac{1}{5}$ less memory than the MPU. The matching overhead of the MPU is less than the one needed by the UML interpreter, making it up to ~ 2.5 times faster when selecting transitions in the EVENT scenario.

The MPU also tops the UML interpreter when it comes to processing parallel regions. In the CONCURRENT scenario it is more than twice as fast, and the retrieval of the active state configuration is on average $\sim$2.7 times faster. But there are functions were the UML interpreter is faster, for example, on average the UML interpreter is twice as fast as the MPU when evaluating expressions, which explains the similar outcome of both execution mechanisms in the GUARD scenario. The biggest difference is measured when invoking an FC, where the UML interpreter is $\sim$7 times faster than the MPU. As the mechanisms for FC invocation and expression evaluation are exchangeable with the Apache SCXML library that is used in the MPU, one could potentially improve these values.

The embedded systems experiment shows that it is possible to implement an interpreter that works with a very small amount of memory. This is an interesting result as interpreters are usually considered as non-suitable for resource-limited platforms. We also found that the Java-based interpreter prototypes consume more memory than generated C++ code. This is not surprising. To put the measured memory consumption of the UML interpreter and the MPU into perspective: the maximum of allocated dynamic memory for a very large BM (SIZE.MEMORY.L4), including all of the necessary runtime system functions, stayed in all cases below 60 MB. For Java applications 60 MB of allocated memory is not much.

Regarding the use case studies, we found that even though the BM interpretation is slower than generated code, our approach is applicable in all of the use cases. The measured performance data also suggests that the performance of runtime BM interpretation should be adequate for the majority of situations. An exception to this are applications that rely on the processing of high-throughput or delay-sensitive data. In this case, the overhead or introduced delay might render the interpretation approach less applicable. How much a system would benefit from the adoption of the approach needs to be decided on a case-by-case basis, by weighing between the positive features of dynamic system adaptation and the performance loss due to the maintenance of a more complex runtime system.

7.2 Encountered Challenges and Lessons Learned

The major challenges that were encountered during our work on the thesis are discussed in the following subsections. This section explains the reasons behind our design decisions and discusses some of the alternatives. It also contains a general assessment of devised solutions in a wider context. The section is structured in three parts: the first one discusses issues connected to the interpretation of BMs, the second part deals with the integration of BM interpretation and a target execution platform (e. g. the Java VM) and the third part deals with issues that arise in the context of the performance benchmark.

7.2.1 BM Interpretation

Although there is a substantial body of work on the execution of BMs, we found that the hitherto applied approaches either employ code generation or are used for simulation purposes. The problem with the code generation approach is that the BM is assumed to be static. BM interpretation aims at executing models that are adaptable at runtime; thus, this basic assumption is violated. As a result, most of the employed processes and optimisations used for executing BMs cannot be applied in our context. When applying execution of BMs for simulation purposes, it is common to use either code generation (with the restrictions given above) or to implement execution processes that explicitly model time, which is hardly suitable for runtime execution. Due to their explicit notion of time, simulation processes can ignore runtime requirements, choosing more elegant ways for processing of the dynamic aspects of BMs (e. g. based on set theory). This also limits the transferability of established research, forcing us to design our own execution mechanisms that better fit to the requirements of adaptable runtime execution. The following text highlights the key challenges that this thesis deals with, along with the lessons learned from solving them.

UML In regard to interpretation processes, one of the most important and on most challenging parts of our work was the implementation of an interpreter for all of the UML State Machine constructs. One of the biggest problems with the UML 2.2 specification of Behavioral State Machines is that, although the authors aim for a clear description of the semantics, the current standard document is often imprecise or even plain wrong. This problem has also been recognised by others and solutions, such as the xUML profile, have been proposed. Despite the disadvantages of the original UML standard, we implemented the UML interpreter using the specified features set. The motivation for this was not only to implement a large number of different features, but also to create an implementation for the currently most important standard for the description of BMs.

A downside on using the feature-rich UML State Machines is that implemented features are not independent of each other; the inflicted runtime overhead of a mechanism needed to process a certain feature will often contribute to the overall processing overhead, even if the feature is not used within a model. As an example, take the use of deferred events. Although a model might not defer a single event, it is still necessary to maintain individual message queues as well as evaluating a state's "deferrableTrigger" set in conjunction with each received event. This generally means that the more features there are in a BM formalism, the slower the interpretation process will be. Additionally, each feature might have a side effect on other ones, making a working implementation a difficult effort.

The most challenging part when implementing UML State Machine interpretation lies in the correct processing of the transition matching and the firing functionality.

Transitions are far more complex constructs in UML than the plain state-connecting edges known from automata or graph theory. First of all, transitions are segmented, allowing them to connect multiple source states with multiple destination states. The determination of an active transition might involve an evaluation of all transition segments, including the pseudostates between them. Secondly, there are different kinds of transitions, which might influence the set of entered and exited states when firing the transition. Thirdly, transitions may cross the composition hierarchy or leave/enter parallel regions, which requires employing sophisticated mechanisms for correct determination of the entered and exited states. Fourthly, only parts of a transition might be given explicitly while others might need to be inferred implicitly, i. e. parallel regions that are entered by default or substates entered via a history mechanism. It was difficult to design a mechanism that could deal with all of these features.

Activity and ε-events As a state machine interpreter is a reactive system, it should not consume any processing time when there are no external events to process. This can be accomplished by blocking a designated executor thread until a new external event arrives, which is usually done with an appropriate concurrent data structure. This mechanism works well, but fails when allowing the use of ε-events, as these are characterised by the absence of an external event, an additional mechanism needs to be put in place. A solution is to completely process all ε-transitions within a single RTC step, although this might lead to uninterruptible life-locks (as in the case of SCXML). Alternatively, one can employ an active polling approach where the executor thread is never allowed to sleep, but this leads to an exhaustion of all available CPU resources on a CU. This problem can be solved using completion events, as proposed by the UML; such events are sent once state entry is completed and allow to define transitions that fire without receiving an external event, while enabling the executor thread to sleep.

Preprocessing Behaviour Models The execution speed of a BM can be improved by employing preprocessing, and code generation can be regarded as the most extreme example of this approach. When applying this technique to BM interpretation, it is necessary for an interpreter to make sure that changes done in the in-memory storage format are propagated to the execution specification. An example for employing preprocessing to speed up execution, is the usage of MVEL for expression evaluation. As a consequence, we need to recompile expression statements when they are being changed in the in-memory format. We suspect that preprocessing can also be applied beneficially to other features, e. g. we are currently scanning the content of an entered state for history pseudostates every time we enter the state. This information could be determined at BM instantiation time and cached for use by the interpreter. The downside of this strategy is the increased adaptation complexity; the more preprocessed information exists, the more complicated and tedious the adaptation processes need to be, to assure the consistency between in-memory storage and execution specification.

7.2.2 Platform Integration

When using BM interpretation to execute management tasks, a model interpreter is of no use by itself, as it needs to be integrated with the environment in regard to the employed programming language, information model and communication infrastructure.

Evaluation of Expressions The most important aspect for interpretation performance is arguably the relation between the underlying platform that executes the interpreter and the BM formalism that the interpreter processes. This is shown most clearly in the way that the evaluation of (conditional and action) expressions are implemented in the interpreter, and there are three general directions that can be followed. The first option is to directly state expressions in the syntax of the native programming language. They are opaque to the interpreter and passed down unmodified to the underlying platform. This is the fastest option and the one where the model interpreter has the least control over the specification and processing of the expressions. This approach is not always possible, as it depends on the underlying runtime platform to provide sufficient facilities for dynamically binding the given expressions. The second option is to use an external library that provides expression evaluation capabilities, along with bindings to the underlying platform. Expressions are still opaque to the interpreter, but there is more control over the evaluation process and the interpreter can be executed in isolation from the evaluation logic. The third option is to use transparent expressions, by integrating an expression language into the BM formalism. In this case, the expressions are evaluated by the interpreter itself, e. g. through the traversal of an AST structure. This is the slowest option, but provides the most amount of control over the way that expressions are specified and evaluated.

All three of these options have been prototyped, either as part of one of the interpreters or in one of the experiments. All of them are feasible, and a design decision needs to be made based on the concrete operational requirements in a given setting.

Context Data We found that it is beneficial to have context access for all but the simplest BMs and that it is helpful to structure the context, e. g. by enabling locally scoped session data and globally scoped environment data or by using OO principles. Similar to the previously discussed decisions on the choice of an expression language, we do not prescribe a context format. This issue must be treated as a design decision that depends on the setting that an interpreter is supposed to work in. As a general rule of thumb, it is sensible to employ a data model that is already in use in the domain that the approach is applied to. The data model has to be compatible with the BM formats and needs to be compatible with the employed expression language. For example, in our case the choice of JEXL for the MPU was also motivated by the fact that it integrates XPath statements into the language, which allows to work elegantly with the XML context employed by SCXML. For the UML interpreter, we defined the context using UML class diagrams, mapping them to Java classes for evaluation by MVEL. For the embedded systems experiment we used a byte array as the context.

Internal and External Communication BM interpreters are completely event-driven; they are triggered by events and use events to communicate with the environment. Thus, the event handling mechanisms play a key role in our approach. The implementation of a local *broadcast* mechanism is straightforward and usually builds upon message queues. These data structures serve as the interface between the environment that raises events in an asynchronous fashion and the interpreter, which processes events in a synchronous fashion. Although message queues are well understood, they can be tricky to implement due to their inherently concurrent nature.

For external communication, things are a bit more complicated. The *broadcast* model does not scale, which necessitates the use of addressing, preferably by employing group communication (the use of static addresses is not a good idea, as they easily break when network topology changes). Group communication can provide the means for building collectives of cooperating CUs, which is also possible using contract-based communication primitives. A crucial requirement for any communication infrastructure is the support for reliable messages. BMs are not good at dealing with missing events — they get stuck at some state and block further operations. If BMs have to deal with unreliable events, it must be explicitly encoded in the model's logic, e. g. with timed guard statements or by creating alternative transitions. This introduces additional overhead in the BM and forces a BM designer to explicitly model the potential failure cases.

One of the most important issues regarding the communication mechanism is the format of the event's content. As long as an event is only used within a single BM, the format can be decided by the model's creator, but as soon as the event is sent to another entity, the event needs to follow an agreed-upon format, which is interpretable by the receiving entity.

The Application Domain When applying the benchmark to the application domains, we needed to realise that network and systems management are well established fields. This community is very traditional; new approaches are received with a large amount of skepticism, as backwards compatibility is an important concern. Communicating the benefits of our approach is a difficult undertaking, as it deviates from existing standards, tools and practices. This is understandable, as members of the community are involved with ensuring the operability of legacy systems that need to run smoothly alongside more modern technology. We therefore looked for means to clearly demonstrate how BM interpretation can be integrated with existing systems. This is one of the main reasons for employing the Cisco AXP platform in the router-load monitoring use case as well as the motivation for the usage of SNMP as a primary demonstration of the FC functionality. We hope that such a course of action will help support the introduction of our approach to this conservative community.

Behaviour Model Design During discussions with researchers in the field, we realised that creating a BM to capture the processes involved when managing a network seems to be a large conceptual step for people that are not familiar with MDA principles. Not only do we have to communicate the concepts and processes involved, but we must also provide tools that support the creation of models in the context of network and systems management. We investigated this direction with the ACElandic language; by creating BMs that adhere to the ASP using graphical UML editors; by using XML editors to create SCXML models for the MPU and self-models for the ACE toolkit; and through programmatic creation of models using a direct manipulation of the in-memory format. Based on this experience, we found that the worst option is to edit XML files by hand. This is cumbersome and not helpful, as the syntax is not made to be edited manually. All the other options are viable, with the graphical editor likely the most intuitive and ACElandic the most powerful, although the generated models provide little semantical value due to the generated naming. Editing models using a programmatic API is also an option that is not only feasible but also surprisingly easy[1] to use.

7.2.3 The Benchmark

The embedded systems interpreter was evaluated before we created the UML interpreter and before the benchmark was devised. Although adequate for its purpose, there are some aspects missing in the measurement process used for the embedded system interpreter analysis, e. g. the evaluation of transitions that cross nesting boundaries in the composition hierarchy or the determination of the ε-transition matching time. After implementing the UML interpreter, key factors responsible for execution performance were sufficiently clarified in order to create a more meaningful benchmark. For example, refer to the BMs shown in Figure 5.10. It is not necessary to consider 30 different BMs with a constantly increasing number of outgoing

[1]For someone with programming experience, that is.

transitions for a single state if the speed of the lookup in the transition storage structure has a linear runtime complexity. Furthermore, by using self-referential transitions in the BMs, the measurement results contain both the effects of the effort of self-referential transition matching and the speed of the transition data structure lookup mechanism. Only during the investigation on the correct determination of entered and exited states did it become clear that self-referencing transition matching might exhibit a different runtime behaviour than the matching of transitions that are not self-referencing.

Employed Behaviour Models We are confident that the benchmark covers all main aspects that are important for determining the execution performance, although the employed BMs are *artificial*, in the sense that they do not reflect the structure of BMs used in real-world scenarios. BMs can take very different forms, depending on the application domain. As the benchmark aims at a general applicability, an integration of such domain-specific models does not seem to be a good idea. We could have restricted the benchmark to our application domain, but would then face a different problem; currently, there are no BMs that capture best practices for network or systems management processes.

Another challenge in the creation of good measurement BMs was the necessary fine-tuning of the benchmarking scenarios with respect to the technological mappings. We had to ensure that the benchmark works similarly on three different platforms (The UML Interpreter, the MPU and Rhapsody C++), which was especially demanding in case of the COMPOUND and CONCURRENT scenarios. Although not directly visible anymore, this polishing work is reflected in the scenario's BMs and the benchmarking procedures.

Measuring the Java Platform Contrary to the measurements that employed the embedded system prototype, we found that performance data obtained from measurements on the Java platform can vary within a large margin (easily two orders of magnitude). The embedded systems prototype is a computer running a single task and capable of producing the same result for every measurement iteration. This is not true for the platform used for the benchmarking process, which runs many processes in parallel, yielding non-deterministic results. Additionally, the Java platform introduces a number of runtime effects, notably due to garbage collection and JIT compilation. These issues can be alleviated by restricting measurements of resources to certain process or threads (e. g. ignoring the garbage collection thread) as well as by conducting a number of measurements and averaging the obtained values. Another technique is to execute the BM for a number of times before taking the measurements. We deem this procedure valid, as it is assumed that BMs would be executed many times during their lifetime, and the goal is to determine an amortised runtime performance, not the effects when initially introducing a model.

7.3 Relevance of the Results

Our research is mainly motivated by the requirements of AS engineering, namely the need for runtime adaptation of system behaviour in response to changes in a system's environment. In addition to enabling changes at runtime, the use of BM interpretation has a lot more advantages as recently pointed out by J. den Haan et. al [50]. BM interpretation enables a much faster turnaround time for applying system changes, as it does not require conducting code generation or build steps. This also increases the ease of deployment, because the same artefact used for designing a behaviour can also be used for deployment at the runtime system. Similar to a VM, an interpreter supports the portability of applications by de-coupling the concrete execution hardware from the application logic contained in the BM. Using interpreted BMs not only supports functional scalability, but also helps with scalability of resource utilisation, as one can create more processing capability by simply utilising additional CU instances for interpreting a given BM, and where required, adapting employed BMs to account for the newly created instances. Our approach also enables the easy migration and persistency of running BMs by maintaining a separation of BM State and execution logic (for example, this is possible with the ACE toolkit, see [34, Appendix 2.1]). Furthermore, BM interpretation enhances the security of a platform, as the BM usually cannot access resources (e. g. the file system) on a CU directly, but only through the FCs provided by the interpreter. The interpreter forms an abstraction layer on top of the execution system, essentially providing a Platform-as-a-Service (PaaS) infrastructure. Another interesting idea is the possibility of debugging BMs at runtime by using breakpoints at model level. To this list of features, we can add the support of a more understandable monitoring of application behaviour, which can be achieved by inspecting the active state configuration of BM instances. With appropriately designed models, the active state configuration of a BM instance can easily provide valuable runtime information for system management (e. g. a system being in a *fallback* state or in a state *waiting for end of calculation*). We also demonstrated the potential that lies in the optimisation of BMs by facilitating runtime information, e. g. as demonstrated by the *cartesian product optimisation* provided by the TMPL engine discussed in Section 4.2.2.

In terms of the impact of our research within the scientific community, we see our work as consisting of the contributions mentioned in Section 1.3. This includes the identification and verification of a number of concepts for the interpretation of BMs as documented in Chapter 2. These concepts can serve as guidelines for engineers when applying an interpretation approach. By verifying the concepts using four prototypical implementations (see Section 4), we not only demonstrate that the approach is suitable for a wide spectrum of technologies and purposes, but also provide concrete architectural blueprints that can be used. The practical relevance of our work is documented through four use case studies in Chapter 5. Together, these studies form a framework for an application of BM interpretation in the network and systems management domains that is of interest to network engineers, operators and administrators. Although the use case studies are limited to certain domains, we suspect that BM interpretation can successfully be used in a lot of other domains as well.

An important result of our work is the performance benchmark suite introduced in Chapter 6. As there were no previously existing benchmarks that are suitable for assessing the performance of BM execution (see Section 3.5), we have created a novel one, based on the experience gained from concept study and implementation work. This benchmark is available in an executable version from the author upon request. It takes the form of a number of generated C++ classes, together with a corresponding Rational Rhapsody project file. Our final contribution to the scientific community lies in the study of the interpretation performance of three different implementations. The results from these measurements prove that BM interpretation is a feasible approach with an adequate performance for the examined use cases. The performance values itself are also interesting and support the taking of decisions in the design phase of a system that could potentially avail of BM interpretation techniques.

7.4 Future Work

Our research provided us with answers to the original questions on the feasibility and performance of an interpretative approach to BM execution. It also raises a number of questions that we would like to investigate in the future.

Capturing system behaviour The formalism, as well as the tool side of BM interpretation, was explored. However, we did not investigate the process of actually capturing system behaviour within such a model. It would be helpful to have a methodology for such a process and to research how interpretation would fit to such a methodology. As the use of BMs for specification of management tasks has only been studied in recent years, there are no established guidelines. It seems to be beneficial to identify common patterns for management tasks as *best practices*, which could then be collected as BMs and subsequently used by means of model interpretation.

Employing model transformation While the transformation of BMs is well established — there is a sound body of research and a whole range of available tools — the application of this technique for runtime use and the application in a management context are ongoing research topics. It would be beneficial to further study the application of model transformations, such as refinement or partitioning of behaviour, in the context of network and systems management. The Investigation of the consistency issues that can arise when transforming a running model would also be very interesting. Such inconsistencies might appear in the execution specification,

e. g. in the history state configuration, but also between the execution specification and the BM itself, for example when missing pre-compiled expression statements for a newly added action.

Host-level concurrency We investigated concurrent interpretation in the context of parallel regions within a single model, but only superficially explored the implications of an underlying execution platform's parallelism in regard to the interpretation performance. Studying the effects that concurrently executing BMs have on each other would be a fitting complementary research topic to this thesis. This topic is also interesting because of the potential increase in execution speed due to the parallelism offered by modern multi-core processors or the facilitation of Graphics Processing Units (GPU). We suppose that by finding an efficient mapping of the interpreter's stepwise event processing routines to an underlying platform's parallel execution features one could increase the speed of a BM interpreter beyond the performance provided by conventional compiled languages.

Collective models Figure 2.15 introduces a Mapping step for assigning models to CUs. The idea behind this is to specify the behaviour of a collective of cooperating CUs and to automatically transform such an *overall* BM to a number of *local* ones, fitting to the network topology. The local models would then execute on the individual CUs, cooperating to achieve a common goal. A working system that follows this approach would be an important contribution to the autonomic systems engineering field. Our work on BM interpretation lays the foundation of such a system, but does not investigate methods and criteria for adaptation of a model to a given network topology or a collective of CUs.

Impact of the Implementation Language and Runtime System All of the interpreter implementations were created using the Java platform. The baseline implementation uses C++, but this is only an execution engine with code generated by Rhapsody, not a BM interpreter. The use case study with the resource-constrained interpreter also uses C++, but this is just an experiment for determining the smallest resource usage possible. It would be interesting to compare the performance of these implementations with interpreters that use programming languages with a different runtime system, especially with a full-grown BM interpreter using C++. Furthermore, it would be interesting to generate the performance benchmark using Java classes to assess the difference between interpretation and compilation approaches for this particular technology.

Performance indicators The selection of the performance indicators used for the benchmark definition is subjective — it contains what we believe to be the most meaningful indicators. Besides our experience and the data sets collected by us, there is currently no independent data that could support their significance. Although we are sure that the benchmark is both valid and the currently best possible tool for assessing the performance of BM execution mechanisms, it would be beneficial to re-visit the benchmark definition at a later time, to judge upon the practical relevance of the proposed indicators.

Further Applications Currently, we consider two application ideas for a closer investigation. The first one concerns the use of BM interpretation as a customisation mechanism for light-weight composition of telecommunication services. Telecommunication operators are providing APIs to access core network functions (e. g. the sending of text messages). Composition of services that use these APIs could be specified and executed using suitable BMs, while core network functions would be safely hidden by FCs. This approach is more lightweight, as similar technology that is already available from the business process engineering community uses heavyweight *programming in the large* components like BPEL engines (see Section 3.3.1). The second application idea is about constructing a mechanism for supervision of the dynamic aspects of service interfaces. This follows the idea of *interface automata* as proposed by L. Alfaro and T. Henzinger [5] to specify the temporal dependencies of method invocations on an interface. Using BMs one can constrain and monitor the message exchanges between communicating entities and thus, provide a runtime checking system that goes far beyond the capability of current type checkers. We now know that BM interpretation is a feasible mechanism, and these two ideas already show that it can be useful in a variety of other applications.

Appendices

A UML State Machines

UML 2 Behavioral State Machines are defined as consisting of the classes and relationships depicted in Figure A.1, which is taken from [255, p. 527] and the following text explains each of the classes in detail.

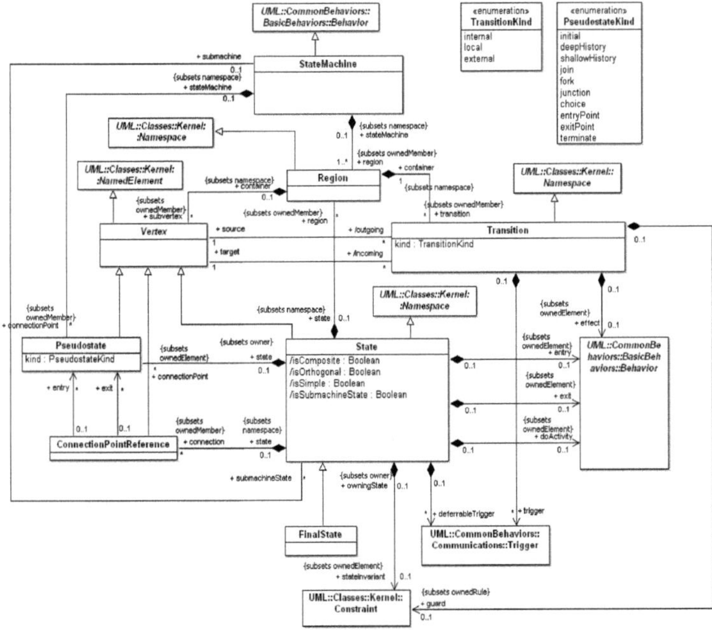

Figure A.1: Definition of state machines in UML 2.2

StateMachine This class serves as the root entity, containing the complete structure of the behaviour specification. It inherits from the generic *Behavior class*, which effectively enables the nesting of state machines. A *StateMachine* owns one or more parallel regions defined by the *Region* class, and these regions contain the actual vertices (see description below) and transitions that make up the behaviour. As UML is object-oriented, it is possible to define operations and attributes on classes. The *StateMachine* class provides — among others — operations for determining the hierarchical order of two states: "The operation `LCA(s1,s2)` returns an orthogonal state or region that is the least common ancestor of states s1 and s2, based on the statemachine composition hierarchy." and "The query `ancestor(s1, s2)` checks whether s2 is an ancestor state of state s1." [255, 15.3.12, "Additional Operations"]. These two methods can be utilised when determining the entry and exit actions associated with a transition as described in Section 2.2.2.

Region The *Region* class is used to implement parallelism in UML State Machines. According to [255, p. 550], regions are notationally defined by dividing a state using one or more dashed lines, as shown in Figure A.2.

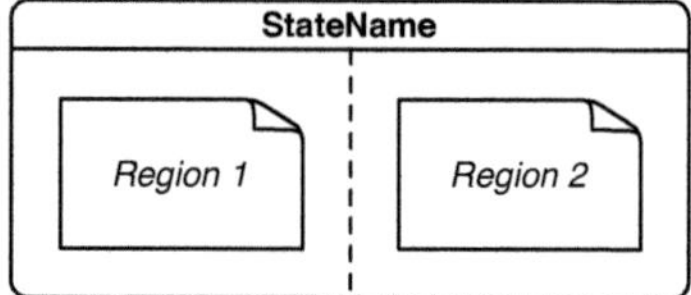

Figure A.2: Notation for a state with two regions in UML 2.2

Regions contain vertices and transitions. They also create a navigable composition hierarchy through associations with the containing *State* or *StateMachine* as well as the owned vertices. A *Region* is constrained to contain at most one initial and one history vertex.

Vertex Vertices are contained in a region and are connected by transitions. They define a graph structure through the associated incoming and outgoing transitions. A *Vertex* class is an abstract type and can occur in three forms: either as a *State*, as a *Pseudostate* or as a *ConnectionPointReference*. References to connection points are used when composing partial models by means of exit and entry points (see 2.1.4); the *State* and *Pseudostate* classes are each explained below. Vertices have no additional attributes.

Transition The *Transition* class defines a directed relationship between a source and a target vertex. Transitions support multiple triggers, can have an optional guard condition and an optional action statement (referred to as an *effect*). A *Transition* has a single additional attribute, *kind*, which defines the processing of entry and exit behaviours in regard to the source and target state. The *kind* attribute can take three different values: 'internal', 'local' and 'external'. This characterisation of transitions is particular to UML and defined in the standard [255, 15.3.15, "Semantics"] in the following manner ([...] denotes an omission in the cited text).

internal "[...] implies that the transition, if triggered, occurs without exiting or entering the source state. Thus, it does not cause a state change. This means that the entry or exit condition of the source state will not be invoked. An internal transition can be taken even if the state machine is in one or more regions nested within this state."

local "[...] implies that the transition, if triggered, will not exit the composite (source) state but it will apply to any state within the composite state and these will be exited and entered."

external "[...] implies that the transition, if triggered, will exit the composite (source) state."

Generally speaking, the semantics for the external transition kind are closest to the conventional behaviour for automata supporting entry and exit actions. Internal transitions have also been used in automata theory for some time (see 3.1.1), but the semantics for local transitions are novel.

The notation for a transition is an arrow, leading from a source to a target state. The arrow can be decorated with a label, which specifies optional event triggers, a guard condition and an effect. The transition label needs to adhere to the following format, given in EBNF.

label ::= (**trigger** (',' **trigger**)*)$^?$ ('[' **guard-constraint** ']')$^?$ ('/' **behavior-expression**)$^?$

All of the three components are optional. Should a transition not specify a trigger, then it is implicitly triggered on a state's completion event. UML dictates that completion events need to be sent once a state is completely entered (the *entry* and *do activities* have finished executing, see [255, 15.3.14, "Semantics", "Completion transitions and completion events"], and that completion events need to be processed before any other events (in particular any external event).

The specification [255, p. 581] also states that a transition arrow is drawn differently, depending on the transition kind. For internal transitions it is omitted completely. Figure A.3 A) shows the common[2] syntax for a *local* transition: the arrow starts at the border of the source state and ends at the border of the target state. An *external*

[2]Alternatively, a local transition can be marked with a '*' and drawn like an external one.

transition is depicted in Figure A.3 B). This one leaves the source state first and then re-enters it.

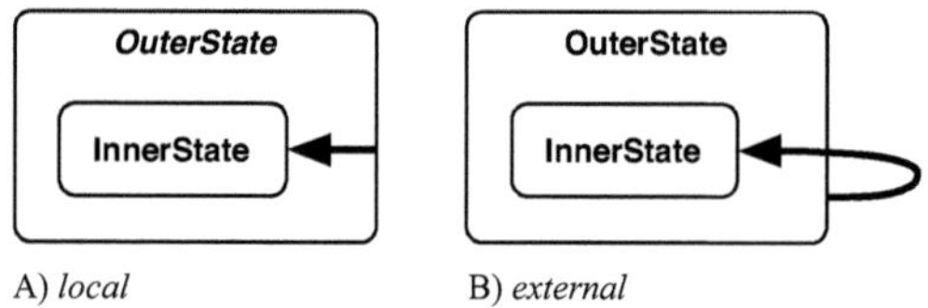

Figure A.3: Notation for *local* and *external* transitions in UML 2.2

State In UML, states are drawn as boxes. They might be compound, in which case they contain substates drawn as boxes within the *State* box. The opposite of a compound state is a simple state. A state is called orthogonal should it contain two or more regions. A state might also be a *submachine* state, meaning that it represents a complete state machine. UML allows the *State* class to represent a complete, external state machine, which is entered upon entering of the state and left upon completion of the external behaviour. Such a feature can help to structure complex BMs by enabling a separation into independently managed sub-models and supporting re-use of existing BMs.

A *State* can expose a number of behaviors: an **entry** behaviour, an **exit** behaviour and a **do-activity** (also called an in-state behaviour). Entry and exit behaviours are executed when entering or leaving a state. A do activity is an activity that executes while a system is in a certain state. Once it completes, a completion event is raised. In case that the state should be left before a do activity commences, the do activity would be implicitly aborted.

Each UML state relates to a set of deferrable trigger events. Should a system be supplied with an input event that occurs in one of the active state's deferred event sets, then the event is stored until a state is entered where the event can be consumed[3].

There is only one class that inherits from *State*: the class *FinalState*, which indicates a state where a BM has finished execution. In UML, a final state is depicted with the symbol shown in Figure A.4.

Pseudostate The *Pseudostates* class defines a number of types of transient vertices that a system can encounter, while in the process of changing states. The processing of a BM is not allowed to stop in a pseudostate and event processing needs to continue

[3]Exactly this feature forces one to implement a UML BM interpreter with a single message queue per control flow.

Figure A.4: The notation for final states in UML 2.2

until the BM has entered a state. *Pseudostate* is used to create compound transitions and to prescribe default routes for the control flow. A compound transition is defined as '[...] a "semantically complete" path made of one or more transitions, originating from a set of states (as opposed to pseudostate) and targeting a set of states.' [255, 15.3.14, "Semantics"]. Individual transition segments are connected by pseudostates and, as BM processing cannot conclude in a pseudostate, a compound transition needs to be processed as a single entity.

There are ten different kinds of pseudostates specified in [255, 15.3.8]. We introduce them in the following list, together with their common notation. There are a couple of notational variants and the reader is requested to refer to the standard document for a discussion of the alternative notations.

initial represents a *Vertex* with a single transition leading to a default start state. The transition is not allowed to have triggers or guard conditions, and only one initial vertex is allowed per region.

deepHistory represents the state configuration of the compound state containing this pseudostate and all of its substates when it was last exited. This state configuration is reestablished once the deep history pseudostate is entered. Similar to the initial pseudostate, a single transition can leave the vertex that defines the initial state entered, in case the deep history function has never been active before.

shallowHistory is similar to the deep history pseudostate, but remembers only the active state configuration of the containing state (and not of its substates).

fork enables the splitting of a single control flow into multiple ones that enter parallel regions. Outgoing transition segments for such a pseudostate cannot be annotated with conditions or triggers.

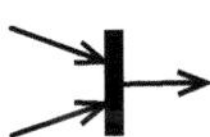

join has the opposite functionality of fork: the join pseudostate bundles a number of control flows, coming from different parallel regions, in a single one. Transition segments that enter a join pseudostate are not allowed to have triggers or guard conditions.

junction can be used to chain together multiple transition segments, including merging or splitting a transition (this does not fork the control flow). The path of transition segments that is taken depends on the guard conditions annotated on the outgoing transition segments for the pseudostate. The model designer needs to make sure that exactly one outgoing transition is valid in all cases — a specific *else* label is provided that might serve as a catch-all in case that no other guard condition is valid. Conditions on a junction pseudostate are evaluated before processing of the transition, meaning that actions encountered in previous transition segments are **not** able to influence the decision of the path to follow.

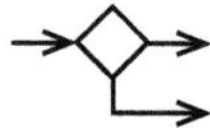

choice is similar to the junction pseudostate but evaluated dynamically at the time that the pseudostate is reached. This means that actions encountered in the previous transition segments can influence the decision taken at the choice pseudostate.

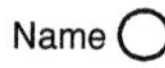

entryPoint is used with partial models for entering a state machine or composite state. It provides a single transition to a vertex within each of the regions of the entered state.

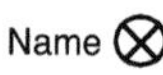

exitPoint is also used with partial models when exiting a composite or submachine state. On encountering this pseudostate, the complete state is left (including termination of orthogonal control flows) and the next system state is determined using the transition that has this pseudostate as source vertex.

terminate shuts down the execution of the state machine that this pseudostate belongs to. The termination does not call any other exit behaviours than the ones associated with the transition that enters this pseudostate.

Redefinition

UML 2 provides features for the redefinition of four elements related to state machines: the *StateMachine* itself as well as each *Region*, *State* and *Transition*. Figure A.5 shows the specification of redefinitions as defined in [255, p. 528].

Employing redefinition enables a model designer to extend existing BMs, while retaining a traceable relationship between the new features and the original ones. According to [28, page 192 ff.], the following kinds of redefinitions are defined in regard to UML 2 State Machines.

- Replacing a simple state through a composed or orthogonal one.

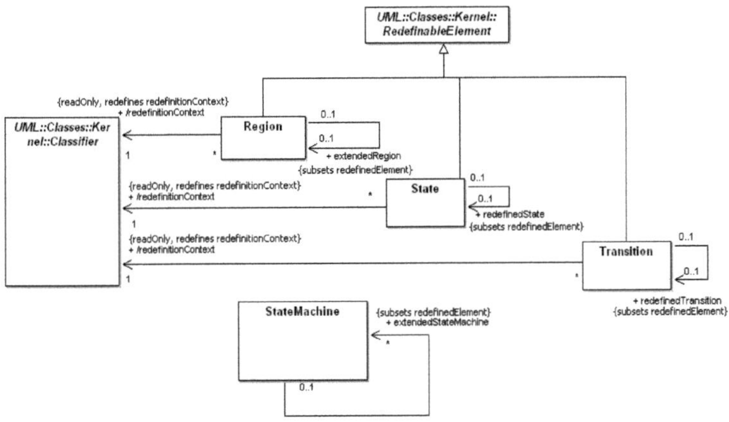

Figure A.5: Redefinition of state machines in UML 2.2

- Extending a composed or orthogonal state state with additional regions.
- Adding new transitions or substates to a composed or orthogonal state.
- Replacing a partial model with a conforming new one. The new partial model needs to offer all entry and exit points of the former one, but can also add new ones.
- Replacing an existing transition with a conforming new one. The new transition will need to leave the same source state and posses the same triggers as the replaced one, but needs to redefine the target state as well as the optional guard condition and action.

It is not possible to redefine states or transitions marked with {*final*}.

B State Chart XML

The language constructs of the SCXML are classified in modules (namely *Core*, *External Communications*, *Data*, *Script* and *Anchor*). Each of the SCXML modules groups a distinct set of features and is briefly described in the following text.

Core Module The core module defines the root element `<scxml>` along with the `<state>`, `<transition>`, `<initial>` and `<final>` elements for specification of the model structure. The `<parallel>` element allows to specify parallel regions. Explicit elements for fork and join have been excluded[4], as their functionality can be re-created using event triggers (a completion event is generated once all end states contained within a `<parallel>` are reached). State composition is created through the composition hierarchy of the XML elements, and control flow can be remembered using the `<history>` element.

Actions are specified using specific *executable content* elements. Executable content is attached to states using `<onentry>` or `<onexit>` elements, while direct child elements are used in case of an attachment to transitions. The core module defines five standard elements for executable content: `<raise>` for generating an (interpreter-local) event, `<log>` for writing logging entries as well as `<if>`, `<elseif>` and `<else>` for defining state- or transition internal choices. The set of executable content elements can be extended, either by other modules of the SCXML working draft or using proprietary extensions.

External Communications Module Defines executable content that enables sending messages and invoke services through the `<send>` and `<invoke>` elements. Contrary to `<raise>`, `<send>` is used to transmit events to **external** systems. The transport mechanism is not prescribed by the standard, but left open for the interpretation platform to define. It is possible to indicate the transport mechanism using a type attribute in the `<send>` element. Events can be delayed and cancelled in case that they have not already been sent.

Invocation of synchronous services is carried out using the `<invoke>` command, which can be used to emulate a Remote Procedure Call (RPC), including passing of parameters to the invoked service. The `<invoke>` command creates an instance of the external service and returns to the interpreter while the external service is running. The service might then generate several events, but needs to finish operation with a dedicated completion event, triggering execution of custom functionality specified using the `<finalize>` element. The `<finalize>` element can be used to aggregate the events sent by the service and stores the operation's result. If the model leaves a state with a running service invocation, the interpreter will cancel the invocation automatically. `<invoke>` is well suited for calling FCs from a BM specified in the SCXML.

Data Module Definition of the BM context and access to this data is provided by the data module through the `<datamodel>`, `<data>`, `<assign>`, `<validate>` and `<param>` elements. The `<datamodel>` element serves as the root for a tree of arbitrary but uniquely identified `<data>` XML nodes. Assignment to the data model is done

[4]`<join>` used to be part of the working draft until version 24 January 2006.

by specifying a data model location using the `<assign>` element. The expression language for describing a location is not prescribed by the SCXML working draft, but depends on the profile of the execution platform. All of the elements that contain conditional, location or value expressions have read access to the BM state. For example, this is the case for any guard condition, `<if>` conditions or `<param>` elements used in conjunction with `<invoke>` to pass data from a runtime BM state location directly to an external service. It is possible to validate state content from within the BM using the `<validate>` element. The usage of XML, as a format for runtime model state data, also permits using all existing technologies for describing state data (e. g. , name spacing, referencing of external data, transformation between representations, filtering of content). As useful as this might be, it also highlights one of the downsides of SCXML: the language is clearly geared towards a web infrastructure and integration with other platforms might be intricate and inelegant.

Script Module The script module enables the integration of a scripting language with SCXML by specifying a `<script>` element containing the functionality to execute. The scripting language is defined by the employed SCXML profile.

Anchor Module The anchor module defines a single element `<anchor>`, which is used to revert an executing model to a so-called snapshot. Such a functionality goes beyond the history construct, as snapshot data includes both the former active state configuration as well as the former context. During the work on this thesis, a new version of the working draft (13. May 2010) was published, which removed the anchor module.

The original goal for creation of SCXML was to specify a flow control language allowing for flexible interaction management in the context of the activities of the W3C Voice Browser Working Group and the W3C in general [221]. It soon became obvious that the language is general enough to meet the needs of other applications, e. g. Nokia Qt uses SCXML in their Qt animation framework [253], and we are employing it to specify BMs for network and systems management.

The extensibility of SCXML builds on a profile mechanism. There are profiles that define a concrete realisation of the language by specifying which modules are included, which data format is utilised and how certain expressions (conditional expressions, location expressions and value expressions) are to be evaluated. In the working draft dated October 2009, three profiles are defined:

Minimal Defines a state machine with no data model and no external communications, relying only on the *Core* module.

ECMAScript Defines state machines that facilitate the JavaScript Object Notation (JSON) for data models (see RFC 4627) and the ECMAScript Compact Profile

(ES-CP) [231] or ECMAScript for XML (E4X) [232] as expression languages. Requires the *Core*, *External Communications*, *Data* and *Script* modules.

XPath Defines state machines that use XML for the data model and XPath 2.0 [288] for specification of expressions. Relies on the *Core*, *External Communications* and *Data* modules.

The provided profiles are all geared towards usage in web environments. Although it is possible to utilise SCXML in a variety of contexts, its web heritage is obvious and it is most fruitfully applied in such an environment.

When using the ECMAScript profile, the combined syntax of the SCXML and ECMAScript can be confusing and hard to read. This problem also persists when defining proprietary profiles for integration of the SCXML with regular programming languages. For example, when integrating a platform based on Java technology via JEXL [217], most expressions will necessarily reflect concepts of the Java language (type system, data model access, etc.) and hence are visible in SCXML-based model format, making it necessary for a model designer to understand them.

As the data model format is left open, SCXML can include and work with any data format. Such a way of handling data has a clear downside: pure SCXML does only provide generic, non type-specific features for dealing with data (reading, assignment and validation of XML elements or sub-trees). This has practical implications when integrating executable content with a data model. For example, it is impossible to use simple data structures, like a list, within standard SCXML. We found two — implementation dependent — ways of dealing with this issue. One is to provide the necessary functions as executable content through appropriate features of the facilitated scripting language. The second is to extend SCXML through custom actions.

Custom Actions The Apache Software Foundation provides an implementation of SCMXL as part of the Apache Commons projects [215]. This software provides a mechanism to extend standard SCXML with additional executable content, by specification of new XML tags and their associated semantics using Java classes.

Technically, this is done by instantiating a user-created class that conforms to the *CustomAction* class provided by the Apache SCXML implementation. The instantiated object is then registered with the SCXML parser before reading the document. This enables the parser to bind user-provided functionality with the custom XML tags used in the document. A walk-through tutorial for this technique is given in the SCXML guide at `http://commons.apache.org/scxml/guide/custom-actions.html`.

A mechanism like this makes it quite easy to integrate new features seamlessly with the existing language, but also seems to undermine the standardisation efforts at the W3C. As such, we see it fitting for the exploration of new SCXML constructs, but not as a suitable solution employed for platform-independent BMs.

C ACElandic

To provide an overview of the language, we will first introduce an instructive example of an ACElandic program comprising the most important language features. The currently implemented language features are then discussed in detail using an Extended Backus-Naur Form (EBNF) [207] of the language syntax.

ACElandic by Example

The following lines show an introductory example of an ACElandic script. It describes the self-model of an ACE, which offers a multiplexing service. We are employing two supplementary services (data and location) for which we receive requests from a client and forward them to the appropriate service. Then the ACE receives replies from these services and returns them to the client. The example illustrates only the basic usage of the language. A number of features, such as timers, parallel execution of plans, inter-plan communication, etc. are not covered here.

```
XML "<!DOCTYPE selfModel SYSTEM \"../../dtd/selfmodel.dtd\">"

declare [
    request <- myapplication.events.MultiPlexerRequestEvent,
    reply <- myapplication.events.MultiPlexerReplyEvent,
    start <- myapplication.events.MultiPlexerStartEvent,
    stop <- myapplication.events.MultiPlexerStopEvent
];

selfmodel multiplexer {

  initial plan setup {
    reveal multiplex;
    accept -> multiplex.contract;
    discover service.date { select provider.date; }
    discover service.location { select provider.location; }
    contract server.contract [
      composer <- self/address,
      date <- local/provider.date,
      location <- local/provider.location];
    switch operate;
  }

  plan operate {
    receive start <= multiplex.contract;
    forever {
      choice {
      alternative {
        receive request <= multiplex.contract when message/type = date
        do {
          send request[type <- get] => server.contract : date;
```

```
          receive reply [now -> answer] <= server.contract;
          send reply[date <- local/answer] => multiplexer.contract : client;
        }
      }
      alternative {
        receive request <= multiplex.contract when message/type = location
        do {
          send request[type <- get] => server.contract : location;
          receive reply [here -> answer] <= server.contract;
          send reply[location <- local/answer] => multiplexer.contract : client;
        }
      }
      alternative {
        receive stop <= multiplex.contract do { exit; }
       }
     }
     switch finalize;
    }
  }

  plan finalize {
    cancel server.contract;
    cancel multiplex.contract;
    switch setup;
  }
}
```

The script starts with an XML header. The header is simply copied to the beginning of the XML output file. It specifies the document type using either a reference to a DTD (as in the example) or a XSD document. The next directive is a declare block that allows to choose aliases for otherwise very long identifiers. We assume that `myapplication.events` is a Java package and all the classes in this package are derived from the ACE toolkit type `ServiceUsageRequest` (thus, it is possible to set arbitrary fields within message of these types).

Then the actual self-model specification starts. It comprises three Plans, named `setup`, `operate` and `finalize`. The setup Plan starts with a service offer (`reveal`) with the associated goal `multiplex`. The `reveal` directive actually reacts to a GN message by sending an appropriate GA. The next line accepts an incoming contract and stores it under the name `multiplex.contract` into the global execution session, which is the context that an ACE maintains in its Executor organ. Then two subsequent `discover` directives are executed for each of the individual subservices, and respective GN messages are sent out. The inner `select` part is executed for incoming GAs. The addresses of the ACEs that sent the GAs are stored within the local execution session under the keys `provider.date` and `provider.location`, respectively. After committing a contract with identifier `server.contract` (stored in the global execution session), the execution switches to the Plan `operate`.

In the `operate` plan, a start message is first expected from the client sent over the `multiplex.contract`. After receiving it, a non-deterministic choice (controlled by the client) is entered. In the first alternative, the ACE reacts on requests sent over the `multiplex.contract` with the `type` field set to `date`. It forwards the request by sending a request message with its `type` set to `get` to the date provider (which has the `role` date in the `server.contract`). If no role expression is to be used in this statement, the request message will be send to all roles in the contract. After receiving a response, it stores the value of the field `now` in the local execution session under the key `answer`. Finally, the field `date` is set to `local/answer` in the final reply towards the client of the multiplexer service. The second alternative handles incoming requests to the location provider. Finally, a `stop` message is expected in the third alternative, which causes the enclosing loop to be terminated. The final statement in the `operate` Plan causes a switch to the `finalize` Plan. There, all contracts are cancelled and the setup Plan is re-invoked.

A compilation of the `multiplexer` self-model results in three self-models, one for each plan. Figure B.1 depicts a visualisation of the generated structure for the second plan `operate`, with transition labels omitted for brevity; compilation of the other plans yields only a number of consecutive states that are "chained" along a single path.

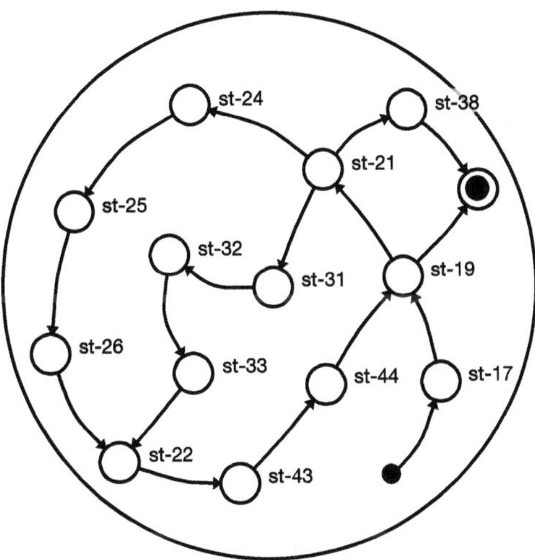

Figure B.1: Structural view of the compilation result for the `operate` Plan

The **choice** construct (st-21, entered from st-19) defined in line 27, is clearly visible in the structure, with each of the alternatives leaving via a different transition. The first alternative (receipt of a `date` type message) leads to st-24, the second alternative (receipt of a `location` type message) leads to st-31 and the final alternative (stopping of the operation) leads to st-38. The first two alternatives meet in state st-22, from which a switch to the `finalize` plan is triggered (see line 48). The `forever` loop could now theoretically continue by following the transition to st-21, but as the plan switch removes the old plan, this never occurs.

The ACElandic compiler is a first step into exploring the possibilities of BM generation using high-level languages. Therefore, it lacks properties common to mature tools, e. g. mechanisms for the optimisation of the final production artefact. An example is the transition from st-19 to the final state. This transition is purely an artefact resulting from the compilation mechanisms, it is never triggered (the transition is annotated with a condition that evaluates the expression $1 \neq 1$) and is therefore unnecessary for the model.

Extended Backus-Naur Forms

To describe the (context-free) syntax of ACElandic, a variant of EBNFs is used. EBNFs combine expressive means of context-free grammars and regular expressions (thus the language which can be defined by an EBNF is still strictly context-free). Non-terminal symbols are typeset in **boldfaced** letters, terminal symbols in `typewriter` font or in single quotes in the case of literal symbols such as '{' or '->'. EBNF rules are of the form

nonterminal $::= \alpha$,

where α is a regular expression comprising terminal and nonterminal symbols (see below). A string comprising terminal as well as non-terminal symbols is called a *sentence form*, a string comprising only terminal symbols is a *sentence*. We talk about a *derivation step* if we apply a rule of the above form to a sentence form. Repeated derivation steps starting from a distinguished non-terminal symbol — the so-called *start symbol* — form a *derivation*. A derivation is *terminal* if the resulting sentence form is a sentence.

On the right hand side of rules, we use the following types of expressions:

- $\alpha^?$ — α is an optional element
- $\alpha_1|\alpha_2|\dots|\alpha_k$ — one of the expressions α_i has to be selected
- α^* — α is repeated zero or more times
- α^+ — α is repeated zero or more times

Parenthesises are used if necessary. We sometimes use the syntax *q*:**nt**, where **nt** is a nonterminal symbol and *q* is an additional identifier that refers to the special usage of the nonterminal symbol in the context of a given syntactic rule. So for instance, we use goal:**identifier** to denote the nonterminal **identifier** and *goal* to express that a particular identifier refers to the name of a goal.

Moreover, for the sake of brevity, we confuse a nonterminal symbol with the set of sentences which can be derived from it. For instance, we might write "a plan comprises a sequence of **statements**" when we mean that "all the sentences which can be derived from the nonterminal **plan** comprise of sequences of sentences derivable from **statement**".

Syntax and Semantics

Vocabulary

ACElandic keywords are:
`selfmodel, declare, xml, plan, initial, global, local, message, failure, recover, self, receive, do, on, when, send, disseminate, reveal, call, wait, select, contract, if, elsif, else, default, discover, accept, from, while, forever, false, true, choice, cancel, alternative, exit, switch, run, halt, evaluate, no-ace-type, repository, visible, guard, cancellation, emitting, write, start-timer, stop-timer, timeout, repeat, try, minor, marginal, critical, catastrophic.`

Keywords may be written in uppercase letters, so plan is equivalent to PLAN but Plan is an identifier (see below).
Identifiers have to comprise of the letters 'a' ...'z', 'A' ...'Z', '0' ...'9', '_', '-', '.', but may not start with a digit or dot. Thus, examples of identifiers are 'my.contract', 'provider2-address', etc., but not 'contract' or '1.goal'. Numbers are usually given by non-empty sequences of digits (floats are not supported yet).

Headers, Self-Models and Plans

An ACElandic script can be headed by an XML header which is copied at the beginning of the output file. XML headers are of the form
`xml` "xml-code"
where xml-code is a string. Quotes occurring in xml-code have to be preceded by \.

Declares are specified by the following rule
declare ::= `declare` '[' *id*:**identifier** '<-' *def*:**identifier** (',' **identifier** '<-' **identifier**)* ']' ';'
A **declare** comprises a number of definitions of the form *id* <- *def*. In the subsequent **selfmodel** specification, the **identifier** *id* will be replaced by the **identifier** *def*.

Declares can be followed by an additional repository declaration section.

repository: `repository` '{' **function**$^+$ '}'
function : `emitting`$^?$ *f*:**identifier** ('[' '*' | **fparam** (',' **fparam**)* (',' '*')$^?$) ']')$^?$
'|->' *c*:**identifier** ':' *m*:**identifier** ('=>' *o*:**identifier**)$^?$';'
fparam : *v*:**identifier** ':' *t*:**identifier**

In the ACE toolkit, FCs are Java classes contained in a specific repository, and consequently ACElandic provides features for specifying dependencies on these FC. As all communication inside an ACE is based on events, also the execution of an FC is triggered using specific events, and the FC may dispatch result events when concluding execution. Notationally, FC bindings are specified with a **repository** declaration, consisting of a sequence of function signatures. A signature is given by a name *f*, an optional formal parameter specification and a mapping to its Java implementation. A formal parameter specification consists of a parameter name *v* and a (Java) type identifier *t*. The star symbol '*' is used to indicate that the function has a variable parameter list (*varargs*). The Java implementation is assumed to be the method *m* of the class *c* (a fully qualified class name is required). If the keyword `emitting` is used, the function is assumed to issue output events. In connection with emitting, an output mapper class *o* can be identified. If *o* is missing, then the `SimpleOutputMapper` class will be used.

A **selfmodel** is defined as

selfmodel ::= `selfmodel` *id*:**identifier** '{' **plan**$^+$ '}'

where *id* is the name of the **selfmodel**. A plan is given by a sequence of statements:

plan ::= `initial`$^?$ `plan` *id*:**identifier** '{' **statement**$^+$ '}'

where *id* is the name of the plan. The optional keyword `initial` marks a **plan** as *default plan* which is executed right after the start-up of an ACE.

ACElandic **statements** are of the following syntactic categories:

statement ::= **assignment** | **receive** | **cancel** | **cancellation** | **send** | **disseminate** | **wait** | **discover** | **reveal** | **contract** | **accept** | **conditional** | **loop** | **switch** | **run** | **halt** | **exit** | **choice** | **write** | **start_timer** | **stop_timer** | **timeout** | **failure** | **recovery** | **guard** | **visible**

Discovery and Contracting

To discover an ACE providing a service achieving a certain goal, the **discover** directive is available:

discover ::= `discover` *goal*:**identifier** ('{'
`select` *provider*:**identifier** '{' (**statement**)$^+$ '}'
'}')$^+$

A **discover** directive sends out a GN message with the specified *goal* and listens for incoming GA messages in the subsequent `select` clauses. The statement sequence performed within the `select` clauses is for each incoming GA with the specified *goal*; the sender address of the GA is stored in the local execution session under the key *provider*. The intention is that the select code can be used to determine an appropriate service provider.
On provider side, a reveal statement is available which responds to an incoming GN message with a specified *goal*:

reveal ::= `reveal` *goal*:**identifier**

To contract a set of service providers, use the following directive:

contract ::= `contract` *name*:**identifier** ('[' **role** (',' **role**)+ ']')?

role ::= *role*:**identifier** '<-' *address*:**expression**

Here, *name* is the key under which the contract is stored in the global execution session. An optional **role** specification comprises a sequence of pairs of the form *role* <- *address*, where *role* is the role of an ACE in the specified contract and *address* is an expression evaluating to the address of an ACE which assumes that role.
To accept a contract, an accept directive can be used:

accept ::= `accept` (`from` *contractor*:**expression**)? ('->' *name*:**identifier**)?';'

If the optional *contractor* **expression** is given, it is evaluated to the address of an ACE and the contract is accepted only if it is initiated by a contract directive on the *contractor's* side. If the optional *name* **identifier** is given, the contract is stored under the key name in the global execution session.
A contract can be cancelled using the chancel directive:

cancel ::= `cancel` *name*:**expression**';'

This cancels a contract with name *name*. The corresponding cancellation event can be caught using the **cancellation** directive:

cancellation : `cancellation` **expression** `do` '{' **statement**+ '}'

This directive can be used as an **alternative** in a **choice** directive.

Communication

ACElandic supports two communication modes: Sending and receiving messages within a contract (i. e. inter-ACE communication) and communication between plans executed in parallel. For sending a message over a given contract, the send directive has to be used:

send ::= `send` *msg*:**identifier** ('[' **param** (',' **param**)+ ']')?
  '=>' *name*:**expression** (':' *role*:**expression**)?';'

param ::= *key*:**identifier** '<-' *value*:**expression**

This directive results in sending a message of Java type *msg* (fully qualified) over the contract *name* to the ACE assuming the role *role*. If the last **expression** is omitted, the message is send to all ACEs within the contract *name*. Additionally, a number of *key/value* pairs can be set within the outgoing message.

Note: *msg* has to be derived from the ACE Toolkit class *ServiceUsageEvent*.
Internal communication is achieved by the **disseminate** directive.

disseminate ::= `disseminate` *msg*:**identifier** ('[' **param** (',' **param**)+ ']')$^?$ ';'

As before, *msg* is the fully qualified name of a Java class.
To receive an (intra- or inter-ACE) message, the **receive** directive has to be used:

receive ::= (`on`)$^?$`receive` *msg*:**identifier** ('[' **store** (',' **store**)+ ']')$^?$
  '<=' *name*:**expression** (':' *role*:**expression**)$^?$
  `when` *guard*:**condition**
  `within` *time*:**expression**
  (';' | **do-part expire-part** | **expire-part**)
do-part ::= `do` '{' **statement**+ '}'
expire-part ::= `on expire` '{' **statement**+ '}'
store ::= *key1*:**identifier** '->' *key2*:**identifier**

The receive directive receives a message of type *msg*.

- If the optional keyword `on` is used, the statement does not block the execution of a plan, but checks only if an appropriate message is available. If the `on` keyword is not used, the **do-part** has to be omitted.
- If a **store** sequence of element of the form *key1 -> key2* is used, the contents of the message stored under the key *key1* in the incoming message are stored in the local execution session under the key *key2*.
- An optional *guard* **condition** can be used to control the processing of the incoming message beyond the pure message type *msg*. To access the contents of the message stored under a *key*, use the qualified expression `message/`*key* (see below).
- If the keyword `within` is used, an additional *time* **expression** (evaluating to an integer value) and an additional timer is initialised to *time* ms. If the timeout occurs before a message is received, the **expire-part** is executed. An **expire-part** cannot be used without a `within` clause. The keyword `on` cannot be used in connection with a `within` clause.
- Finally, if a message is received, the optional **do-part** is executed.

Plan Execution

For plan execution, the following directives are available:

run ::= `run` *plan*:**identifier** ';'
switch ::= `switch` *plan*:**identifier** ';'
halt ::= `halt` ';'

A start directive starts a plan with name *plan*. A switch directive stops the current plan execution and initiates the execution of a given plan. A stop directive stops the execution of the current plan. Thus

`switch` my.plan ;

is equivalent to

`run` my.plan; `stop`;

Simple Statements

An **assignment** is of the form

assignment ::= (`global` | `local`) *key*:**identifier** '<-' *value*:**expression** ';'

It stores the value *value* under the key *key* in the global or local execution session, depending whether the keyword `global` or `local` is used.

A **call** statement is specified by

call ::= `call` *fun*:**identifier** ('[' **param** (',' **param**)+ ']')$^?$ ';'

It calls the specific functionality *fun* from the ACE internal repository passing the parameters specified in the **param** list.

To **wait** for *time* ms, use

wait ::= `wait` *time*:**expression** ';'

Finally, a write statement has been supported:

write ::= `write` '[' **channel** '<-'*string* ']'

channel::= `severe` | `warning` | `info` | `debug` | `fine` | `finer` | `finest` | `stdout` | `stderr`

This directive writes out a string to a given channel. The first seven channels (`severe` to `finest`) relate to the ACE logging mechanisms. The other two channels `stdout` and `stderr` write to the console (buffered and un-buffered, respectively).

Compound Statements

Conditionals are of the form

conditional ::= `if` **condition** '{' **statement**+ '}'
(`elsif` **condition** '{' **statement**+ '}')*
(`else` '{' **statement**+ '}')$^?$

with the usual semantics. There are two loop constructs, namely:

loop ::= `while` **condition** '{' **statement**+ '}' | `forever` '{' **statement**+ '}'

To terminate a `forever` statement, an **exit** statement is available:

exit ::= `exit` ';'

Note: To terminate a `while` loop, use an appropriate **condition**.

The choice statement introduces non-determinism into ACElandic:

choice :: = `choice` (`within` *time*:**expression**)$^?$ '{'
(`alternative` '{' **statement**+ '}')$^+$
(`default` '{' **statement**+ '}')$^?$
(`on expire` '{' **statement**+ '}')$^?$

An alternative is *enabled* if the first statement in the included statement sequence does not wait for an incoming message (i. e. it is not a blocking **receive** directive for which no incoming matching message is queued). The **choice** statement selects one of those enabled alternatives and executes the included statement sequence. If no enabled alternative exists, the `default` part is executed. If used with the **within** clause, an additional timer is initialised to time. If a timeout occurs, the `expired` clause is executed. A `expire` clause can only be used if a `within` clause is given.

Sometimes, a condition needs to be tested in order to proceed with the execution of a plan. For this purpose, a **guard** statement is available.

guard ::= `guard` *c*:**condition** (';' | `do` '{' **statement**$^+$ '}')

If the condition c evaluates to false, the execution of the next statement (or the optional statement block in the body of the directive) is not done. The condition is tested only once. The **guard** statement can (and should) be used as an alternative for a **choice** statement.

Conditions and Expression

ACElandic is not a fully fledged programming language, thus expressions and conditions are somewhat restricted:

expression ::= **integer** | **identifier** | **qualified** | **string**
qualified ::= (`global` | `local` | `self` | `message`) '/' *id*:**identifier**

Qualified expressions of the form `global`/*id* refer to the global execution session, those of the form `local`/*id* to the local execution session, `self`/*id* relates to the executing ACE itself (currently, only its `address` is supported and can be accessed by `self/address`). Finally, `message`/*id* is only allowed in the **guard** condition of a **receive** statement and related to its input message. Strings are given as usual by a sequence of characters enclosed in quotes.

Conditions are:

condition ::= **condition** ('&' | '|') **condition** | '!' **condition** | **relation**
relation ::= **expression** ('=' | '#' | '<' | '<=' | '>' | '>=') **expression**

Additional parenthesis are permitted. Logical and (&) binds stronger than logical or (|). The symbol ! is used to denote negation.

Timer Handling

For timer handling, the following constructs are available:

start_timer ::= `start_timer` *t*:**expression** '<-' *v*:**expression** ';'
stop_timer ::= `stop_timer` *t*:**expression** ';'
timeout ::= `timeout` *t*:**expression** (';' | `do` '{' **statement**$^+$ '}')

The **start_timer** directive initialises a timer with name t to expire after v milliseconds. The **stop_timer** directive stops the timer t. Finally, the **timeout** directive captures a timeout event for the timer t. It can be used as an alternative in a **choice** statement.

Failure Management and Supervision

To communicate with an external supervisor or an internal failure handling routine, a mechanism similar to the exception handling of modern programming language has been implemented. ACElandic defines four failure classes, namely `minor`, `marginal`, `critical` and `catastrophic`. A recovery block is described by the following syntax:

recovery ::= `try` '{' **statement**+ '}'
(`minor` '{' **statement**+ '}')?
(`marginal` '{' **statement**+ '}')?
(`critical` '{' **statement**+ '}')?
(`catastrophic` '{' **statement**+ '}')?

The **statement** sequence in the `try` block has to contain a **failure** directive:

failure ::= `failure` (`minor` | `marginal` | `critical` | `catastrophic`) ';'

If a failure is raised by this directive, the corresponding recovery block in the surrounding **recovery** directive is executed. Semantically, all states which belong to one of the recovery block receive a desirability value specific to the failure mode according to the following convention:

Failure Mode	Desirability Value
minor	2
marginal	3
critical	4
catastrophic	5

Minor and marginal failures are interpreted as local errors (i. e. those problems which can be resolved by the very ACE), while critical and catastrophic errors require the involvement of an external supervisor.

An external supervisor may contain a planner component which produces a coordinated course of actions concerning a number of ACEs to lead them back into a desirable state (value = 1 for all local states of all plans executed by these ACEs). Planning is done by means of a simulated execution of self-model plans. Since this simulation gets unfeasible if all execution details are considered, only the state/transition structure with trigger events of plans is used (i. e. no values from execution and global sessions). Sometimes, however it is necessary to take values into account in order to get a finer control over the evaluation of guard conditions of transitions. For this purpose, a **visibility** directive has been implemented:

visible ::= `visible` '{' *id*:**identifier**+ '}' ';'

This directive declares a set of identifiers referring to key values in the global session. If used, a planner is able to obtain this list and the global session and take the corresponding values into account while evaluating guard conditions, set parameter values for messages, etc. Note that this directive has no impact to the actual plan execution, but that such annotation of states enables recovery functionality that goes far beyond conventional exception handling strategies.

D Values from Benchmark Measurements

The following table contains the measured performance indicators for the benchmark using the three platform mappings. The name **Rhapsody** stands for the reference benchmark implementation using generated C++with the Rational Rhapsody tool. **UML Interp.** is the BM interpreter implementation using UML State Machines and Ecore (see Section 4.4) and **MPU** refers to the MPU implementation in Java and OSGi (see Section 4.5). If a value is below the specific measurement accuracy of a platform, the entry is shown as $< \delta$. The order of entries corresponds to the order in which the scenarios have been introduced in Section 6.1.

Indicator	Rhapsody	UML Interp.	MPU
SIZE.MEMORY.INIT	454.40 KB	28660.00 KB	35366.00 KB
SIZE.MEMORY.L0	465.52 KB	28715.00 KB	35368.00 KB
SIZE.MEMORY.L1	461.76 KB	29034.00 KB	35385.00 KB
SIZE.MEMORY.L2	457.28 KB	29183.00 KB	36795.00 KB
SIZE.MEMORY.L3	460.80 KB	30436.00 KB	38237.00 KB
SIZE.MEMORY.L4	465.76 KB	40192.00 KB	55509.00 KB
SIZE.MEMORY.GROW	—	1.04 KB/State	1.81 KB/State
SIZE.EXECUTABLE.INIT	315.82 KB	—	—
SIZE.EXECUTABLE.L0	317.86 KB	—	—
SIZE.EXECUTABLE.L1	318.03 KB	—	—
SIZE.EXECUTABLE.L2	327.90 KB	—	—
SIZE.EXECUTABLE.L3	429.37 KB	—	—
SIZE.EXECUTABLE.L4	1423.20 KB	—	—
SIZE.EXECUTABLE	—	100.67 KB	100.67 KB
SIZE.EXECUTABLE.GROW	0.10 KB/State	—	—
ALTERNATIVE.MIN	11.00 µs	37.00 µs	51.00 µs
ALTERNATIVE.AVG	12.20 µs	39.84 µs	53.20 µs
ALTERNATIVE.MAX	15.00 µs	65.00 µs	86.00 µs
EPSILON.MIN	0.33 µs	19.67 µs	13.33 µs
EPSILON.AVG	2.25 µs	25.33 µs	14.24 µs
EPSILON.MAX	4.67 µs	55.33 µs	26.67 µs
EVENT.MIN	1.00 µs	165.00 µs	64.00 µs
EVENT.AVG	23.38 µs	186.45 µs	70.06 µs
EVENT.MAX	128.00 µs	492.00 µs	233.00 µs
GUARD.MIN	2.00 µs	180.00 µs	183.00 µs
GUARD.AVG	24.16 µs	200.52 µs	191.96 µs
GUARD.MAX	198.00 µs	1140.00 µs	458.00 µs
COMPOUND.E02.MIN	$< \delta$	82.00 µs	52.00 µs

Indicator	Rhapsody	UML Interp.	MPU
COMPOUND.E02.AVG	8.91 µs	95.06 µs	57.50 µs
COMPOUND.E02.MAX	858.00 µs	302.00 µs	157.00 µs
COMPOUND.E03.MIN	$< \delta$	92.00 µs	54.00 µs
COMPOUND.E03.AVG	8.90 µs	105.52 µs	59.74 µs
COMPOUND.E03.MAX	672.00 µs	279.00 µs	197.00 µs
COMPOUND.E04.MIN	$< \delta$	102.00 µs	58.00 µs
COMPOUND.E04.AVG	8.76 µs	115.38 µs	63.08 µs
COMPOUND.E04.MAX	148.00 µs	317.00 µs	166.00 µs
COMPOUND.E05.MIN	$< \delta$	95.00 µs	54.00 µs
COMPOUND.E05.AVG	8.78 µs	108.63 µs	59.52 µs
COMPOUND.E05.MAX	118.00 µs	327.00 µs	155.00 µs
COMPOUND.E06.MIN	$< \delta$	104.00 µs	57.00 µs
COMPOUND.E06.AVG	9.32 µs	118.23 µs	62.77 µs
COMPOUND.E06.MAX	2172.00 µs	284.00 µs	158.00 µs
COMPOUND.E07.MIN	$< \delta$	108.00 µs	56.00 µs
COMPOUND.E07.AVG	8.93 µs	121.45 µs	62.50 µs
COMPOUND.E07.MAX	107.00 µs	327.00 µs	143.00 µs
COMPOUND.E08.MIN	$< \delta$	91.00 µs	55.00 µs
COMPOUND.E08.AVG	8.88 µs	104.66 µs	59.57 µs
COMPOUND.E08.MAX	206.00 µs	260.00 µs	149.00 µs
COMPOUND.E09.MIN	$< \delta$	100.00 µs	57.00 µs
COMPOUND.E09.AVG	8.86 µs	113.29 µs	62.62 µs
COMPOUND.E09.MAX	122.00 µs	313.00 µs	171.00 µs
COMPOUND.MIN	$< \delta$	82.00 µs	52.00 µs
COMPOUND.AVG	8.92 µs	110.28 µs	60.91 µs
COMPOUND.MAX	2172.00 µs	327.00 µs	197.00 µs
EXPRESSION.COUNT.MIN	34.00 µs	2581.00 µs	6657.00 µs
EXPRESSION.COUNT.AVG	64.78 µs	3216.29 µs	6918.77 µs
EXPRESSION.COUNT.MAX	5924.00 µs	7804.00 µs	8603.00 µs
EXPRESSION.EVENT.MIN	2.00 µs	60.00 µs	62.00 µs
EXPRESSION.EVENT.AVG	3.01 µs	69.94 µs	68.99 µs
EXPRESSION.EVENT.MAX	7.00 µs	209.00 µs	97.00 µs
EXPRESSION.CALL.MIN	$< \delta$	48.00 µs	413.00 µs
EXPRESSION.CALL.AVG	1.04 µs	66.37 µs	479.21 µs
EXPRESSION.CALL.MAX	2.00 µs	1259.00 µs	821.00 µs
EXPRESSION.GUARD1.MIN	$< \delta$	25.00 µs	40.00 µs
EXPRESSION.GUARD1.AVG	1.03 µs	30.67 µs	44.92 µs
EXPRESSION.GUARD1.MAX	2.00 µs	69.00 µs	74.00 µs
EXPRESSION.GUARD2.MIN	$< \delta$	28.00 µs	57.00 µs
EXPRESSION.GUARD2.AVG	1.01 µs	34.20 µs	64.08 µs
EXPRESSION.GUARD2.MAX	2.00 µs	150.00 µs	110.00 µs
EXPRESSION.GUARD3.MIN	$< \delta$	29.00 µs	77.00 µs
EXPRESSION.GUARD3.AVG	1.03 µs	36.51 µs	93.23 µs
EXPRESSION.GUARD3.MAX	2.00 µs	251.00 µs	479.00 µs
EXPRESSION.GUARD.MIN	$< \delta$	25.00 µs	40.00 µs
EXPRESSION.GUARD.AVG	1.02 µs	33.79 µs	67.41 µs
EXPRESSION.GUARD.MAX	2.00 µs	251.00 µs	479.00 µs

Indicator	**Rhapsody**	**UML Interp.**	**MPU**
CONCURRENT.MIN	3.00 µs	704.00 µs	338.00 µs
CONCURRENT.AVG	3.92 µs	785.96 µs	358.76 µs
CONCURRENT.MAX	8.00 µs	1036.00 µs	471.00 µs
HISTORY.MIN	5.00 µs	973.00 µs	468.00 µs
HISTORY.AVG	6.20 µs	1094.72 µs	480.12 µs
HISTORY.MAX	10.00 µs	1448.00 µs	587.00 µs
CONFIGURATION.MIN	4.00 µs	14.00 µs	12.00 µs
CONFIGURATION.AVG	7.68 µs	44.38 µs	16.04 µs
CONFIGURATION.MAX	14.00 µs	139.00 µs	31.00 µs
LIFECYCLE.MEMORY.BEGIN	393.00 KB	7903.00 KB	35832.00 KB
LIFECYCLE.MEMORY.INIT	471.00 KB	27203.00 KB	35834.00 KB
LIFECYCLE.MEMORY.START	507.00 KB	27167.00 KB	35837.00 KB
LIFECYCLE.MEMORY.MIN	552.00 KB	26991.00 KB	35791.00 KB
LIFECYCLE.MEMORY.AVG	561.62 KB	28023.26 KB	35862.14 KB
LIFECYCLE.MEMORY.MAX	565.00 KB	38519.00 KB	35973.00 KB
LIFECYCLE.MEMORY.END	569.00 KB	27274.00 KB	35964.00 KB
LIFECYCLE.ENTER.MIN	4.00 µs	972.00 µs	12982.00 µs
LIFECYCLE.ENTER.AVG	6.04 µs	1073.52 µs	13697.42 µs
LIFECYCLE.ENTER.MAX	10.00 µs	1275.00 µs	16318.00 µs
LIFECYCLE.OVERALL.MIN	17.00 µs	1108.00 µs	13177.00 µs
LIFECYCLE.OVERALL.AVG	19.06 µs	1226.40 µs	13898.46 µs
LIFECYCLE.OVERALL.MAX	24.00 µs	1435.00 µs	16524.00 µs
TIMESTAMP.MIN	$< \delta$	3.00 µs	$< \delta$
TIMESTAMP.AVG	2.13 µs	3.64 µs	0.22 µs
TIMESTAMP.MAX	5.00 µs	9.00 µs	1.00 µs
SPEED	1	22.30	20.33
MEMORY	1	64.09	81.07

E Self-Models for the Dynamic Reconfiguration Scenario

This section contains self-models used in the dynamic reconfiguration scenario (see Section 5.1.1). The self-models are described for the following five ACE types: Supervisor, Corellator, Assesor, Sensor and Effector. The Client and Provider self-models are not of interest, as the supervision functionality only relies on the heartbeat messages transmitted between the GCO objects.

Supervisor Self-Model

```
XML "<!DOCTYPE selfModel SYSTEM \"../../dtd/selfmodel.dtd\">"

declare [
        Config <- cascadas.supervision.interaction.protocol.SupervisionConfigEvent,
        Notification <-
                cascadas.supervision.interaction.protocol.SupervisionNotification
];

selfmodel supervisor {

  initial plan control {
    forever {

      reveal supervision;
      accept -> supervision-contract;
      receive Config[seller -> client,
        auction-center -> server,
        service-contract -> service-contract] <= supervision-contract;

      discover sensor {
        select sensor.client;
        select sensor.server;
      }
      discover effector {
        select effector.client;
        select effector.server;
      }
      discover correlator {
        select correlator.server;
        select correlator.receiver;
      }
      discover assessor {
        select assessor;
      }

      contract internal.supervision-contract[
              controller <- self/address,
```

```
                 sensor.client <- local/sensor.client,
        effector.client <- local/effector.client,
                 sensor.server <- local/sensor.server,
        effector.server <- local/effector.server,
        correlator.server <- local/correlator.server,
        correlator.client <- local/correlator.receiver,
        assessor <- local/assessor];

      write[info <- "sending.config.message.to.sensor.client"];
      send Config[effector <- local/effector.client,
            supervisable <- local/client,
        receiver <- local/server,
        service-contract <- local/service-contract,
        correlator.sender <- correlator.client,
        correlator.receiver <- correlator.server]
        => internal.supervision-contract : sensor.client;

      write[info <- "sending.config.message.to.sensor.server"];
      send Config[effector <- local/effector.server,
        supervisable <- local/server,
        receiver <- local/client,
        service-contract <- local/service-contract,
        correlator.sender <- correlator.server,
         correlator.receiver <- correlator.client]
        => internal.supervision-contract : sensor.server;

      write[info <- "sending.config.message.to.effector.client"];
      send Config[sender <- sensor.server, receiver <- sensor.client]
              => internal.supervision-contract : correlator.server;
      send Config[sender <- sensor.client, receiver <- sensor.server]
              => internal.supervision-contract : correlator.client;

      cancellation supervision-contract do {
        cancel internal.supervision-contract;
      }
    }
  }
}
```

Corellator Self-Model

```
XML "<!DOCTYPE selfModel SYSTEM \"../../dtd/selfmodel.dtd\">"

declare [
        Config <- cascadas.supervision.interaction.protocol.SupervisionConfigEvent,
        Notification <-
                cascadas.supervision.interaction.protocol.SupervisionNotification
];

repository {
```

```
        correlate[result : java.lang.String, last-sender : java.lang.String,
                last-receiver : java.lang.String]
            |-> heartbeat_validation.components.HeartbeatCorrelator:correlate;
    start |-> heartbeat_validation.components.HeartbeatCorrelator:start;
}

selfmodel correlator {

  initial plan correlate {
    forever {
            reveal correlator;
            accept -> internal.supervision-contract;
            write[info <- "internal.supervision.contract.accepted"];
            receive Config[sender -> sensor.sender, receiver -> sensor.receiver]
                  <= internal.supervision-contract : controller;
            write[info <- "got.config.message"];
            global sensor.sender <- local/sensor.sender;
       global sensor.receiver <- local/sensor.receiver;
       call start;
       forever {
          choice {
            alternative {
               receive Notification[data -> last.sender]
               <= internal.supervision-contract : global/sensor.sender;
                         write[info <- "got.notification.from.sender"];
            }
            alternative {
               receive Notification[data -> last.receiver]
               <= internal.supervision-contract : global/sensor.receiver;
                         write[info <- "got.notification.from.receiver"];
            }
            alternative {
               cancellation internal.supervision-contract do {
                      exit;
                    }
            }
          } // choice
          call correlate[result <- current-delay, last-sender <- last.sender,
                 last-receiver <- last.receiver];
          send Notification[result <- local/current-delay]
                 => internal.supervision-contract : assessor;
       } // forever
    } // forever
  } // plan
} // selfmodel
```

Assessor Self-Model

```
XML "<!DOCTYPE selfModel SYSTEM \"../../dtd/selfmodel.dtd\">"

```

```
declare [
        Config <- cascadas.supervision.interaction.protocol.SupervisionConfigEvent,
        Notification <-
                cascadas.supervision.interaction.protocol.SupervisionNotification
];

selfmodel assessor {

  initial plan setup {
     forever {
              reveal assessor;
              accept -> internal.supervision-contract;
              global THRESHOLD <- 4;
              global UPPER <- 1000;
              global current-delay.client <- 0;
              global current-delay.server <- 0;
        forever {
           choice {
              alternative {
                 receive Notification[result -> current-delay.client]
                 <= internal.supervision-contract : correlator.client;
                 global current-delay.client <- local/current-delay.client;
                 write[info <- "got.notification.from.client"];
              }
              alternative {
                 receive Notification[result -> current-delay.server]
                 <= internal.supervision-contract : correlator.server;
                 global current-delay.server <- local/current-delay.server;
                 write[info <- "got.notification.from.server"];
              }
              alternative {
                 cancellation internal.supervision-contract do {
                          exit;
                 }
              }
           } // choice
           if global/current-delay.client > global/THRESHOLD &
                   global/current-delay.client < global/UPPER {
                    write[warning <- "threshold.exceeded.for.client"];
                    send Notification[type <- act]
                      => internal.supervision-contract : effector.client;
           } elsif global/current-delay.server > global/THRESHOLD &
                   global/current-delay.client < global/UPPER {
              write[warning <- "threshold.exceeded.for.server"];
                    send Notification[type <- act]
                      => internal.supervision-contract : effector.server;
           } else {
              write[warning <- "no.problem.detected"];
           }
        } // forever
```

```
      } // forever
   } // plan
} // selfmodel
```

Effector Self-Model

```
XML "<!DOCTYPE selfModel SYSTEM \"../../dtd/selfmodel.dtd\">"

declare [
        Config <- cascadas.supervision.interaction.protocol.SupervisionConfigEvent,
        Notification <-
                cascadas.supervision.interaction.protocol.SupervisionNotification,
        GatewayMessage <- cascadas.ace.supervision.GatewaySupervisionEvent,
        SupervisionMessage <- cascadas.ace.supervision.SupervisionEvent
];

repository {
        emitting connect[
          supervision-contract : cascadas.ace.session.Contract] |->
                  heartbeat_validation.components.HeartbeatEffector:connect;
}

selfmodel effector {
   initial plan setup {
      forever {
        reveal effector;
        accept -> internal.supervision-contract;
        accept -> external.supervision-contract;
        call connect[supervision-contract
                <- global/external.supervision-contract];
         receive SupervisionMessage when message/type = ack;
            forever {
                choice {
                    alternative {
                        receive Notification <= internal.supervision-contract :
                                assessor when message/type = act do {
                                     disseminate GatewayMessage[type <- act];
                                }
                    }
                    alternative {
                        cancellation internal.supervision-contract do {
                                exit;
                        }
                    }
                }
            }
        }
    }
}
```

Sensor Self-Model

```
XML "<!DOCTYPE selfModel SYSTEM \"../../dtd/selfmodel.dtd\">"

declare [
        Config <- cascadas.supervision.interaction.protocol.SupervisionConfigEvent,
        Notification <-
                cascadas.supervision.interaction.protocol.SupervisionNotification,
        GatewayMessage <- cascadas.ace.supervision.GatewaySupervisionEvent,
        Stop <- cascadas.ace.supervision.StopSupervisionEvent,
        SupervisionMessage <- cascadas.ace.supervision.SupervisionEvent
];

repository {
      emitting deploy-supervision-hook[
      supervision.contract : cascadas.ace.session.Contract,
      sender : cascadas.ace.AceAddress,
      receiver : cascadas.ace.AceAddress,
      service-contract : cascadas.ace.session.Contract,
      heartbeat-delay : java.lang.String]
              |-> heartbeat_validation.components.HeartbeatSensor:deploySupervisionHookExt;
      process[in : java.lang.String, out : java.lang.String]
        |-> heartbeat_validation.components.HeartbeatSensor:process;
      start |-> heartbeat_validation.components.HeartbeatSensor:start;
}

selfmodel sensor {

   initial plan config {
      forever {
         reveal sensor;
             write[info <- "sensing.revealed"];
         accept -> internal.supervision-contract;
             write[info <- "contracting.done.switching.to.setup"];
         receive Config[effector -> effector,
                supervisable -> supervisable, receiver -> receiver,
                service-contract -> service-contract,
                correlator.sender -> correlator.sender,
                correlator.receiver -> correlator.receiver]
                                <= internal.supervision-contract : controller;
         global correlator.sender <- local/correlator.sender;
         global correlator.receiver <- local/correlator.receiver;
         write[info <- "contracting.externally"];
         contract external.supervision-contract [
                supervisable <- local/supervisable,
                sensor <- self/address, effector <- local/effector];
         write[info <- "deploying.supervision.hook"];
         call deploy-supervision-hook[
                supervision.contract <- global/external.supervision-contract,
                sensor <- self/address, effector <- local/effector,
```

```
                sender <- local/supervisable, receiver <- local/receiver,
                supervisable <- local/supervisable,
                service-contract <- local/service-contract,
                heartbeat-delay <- 500];
         receive SupervisionMessage when message/type = ack;
         global running <- yes;
         run monitor;
         cancellation internal.supervision-contract do {
            forever {
                write[warning <- "wait.until.completion.of.monitor.plan"];
                if global/waiting = yes {
                   global running <- no;
                   write[warning <- "monitoring.complete.-.stop"];
                   send Stop => external.supervision-contract;
                   cancel external.supervision-contract;
                   exit;
                }
            }
         }
      }
   }

   plan monitor {
      global waiting <- no;
      call start;
      forever {
         if global/running = yes {
            disseminate GatewayMessage[type <- data-request.incoming];
            receive SupervisionMessage[data -> raw-data.incoming]
                    when message/type = data-reply.incoming;
            call process[in <- raw-data.incoming, out <- processed-data.incoming];
            send Notification[data <- local/processed-data.incoming]
                    => internal.supervision-contract : global/correlator.sender;
            disseminate GatewayMessage[type <- data-request.outgoing];
            receive SupervisionMessage[data -> raw-data.outgoing]
                    when message/type = data-reply.outgoing;
            call process[in <- raw-data.outgoing, out <- processed-data.outgoing];
            send Notification[data <- local/processed-data.outgoing]
                    => internal.supervision-contract : global/correlator.receiver;
         } else {
            halt;
         }
         global waiting <- yes;
         wait 1000;
         global waiting <- no;
      }
   }
}
```

F Behaviour Models for the Management in the Network Scenario

In this section, we depict the BMs used in the *management in the network* use case study (see Section 5.2) for both the troubleshooting as well as the router-load monitoring scenarios.

Troubleshooting Models

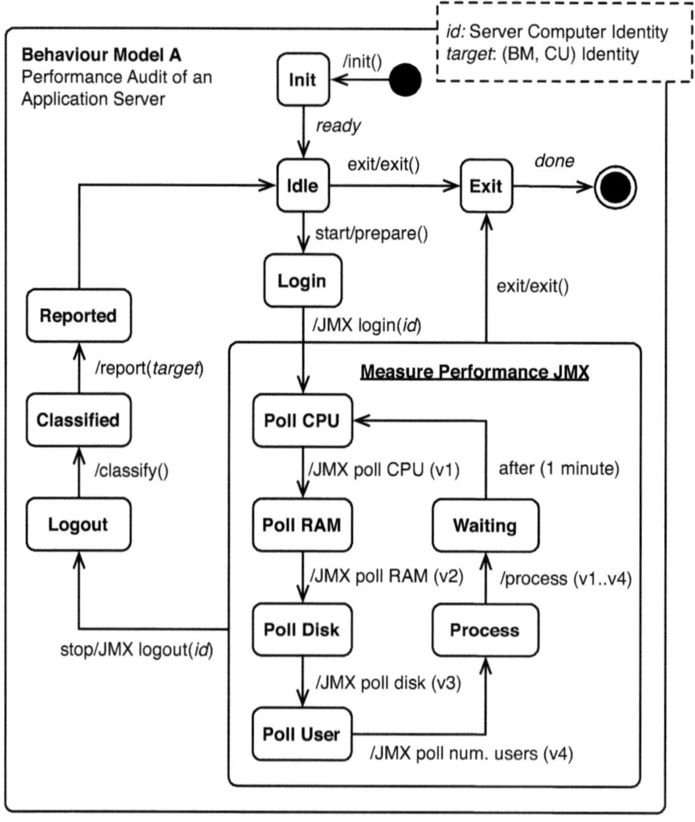

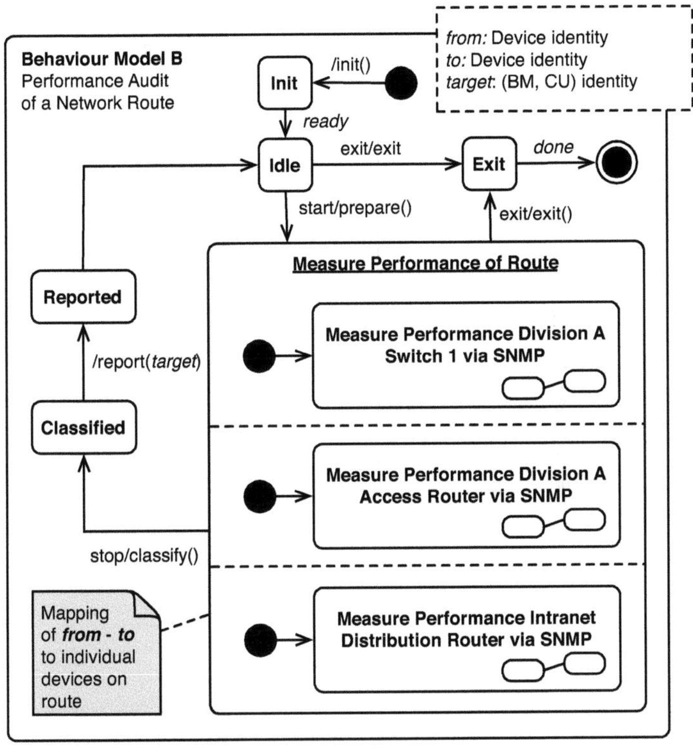
from: Device identity
to: Device identity
target: (BM, CU) identity
Behaviour Model B
Performance Audit
of a Network Route
Init
/init()
ready
Idle
exit/exit
Exit
done
start/prepare()
exit/exit()
Measure Performance of Route
Reported
Measure Performance Division A
Switch 1 via SNMP
/report(target)
Classified
Measure Performance Division A
Access Router via SNMP
stop/classify()
Mapping
of from - to
to individual
devices on
route
Measure Performance Intranet
Distribution Router via SNMP

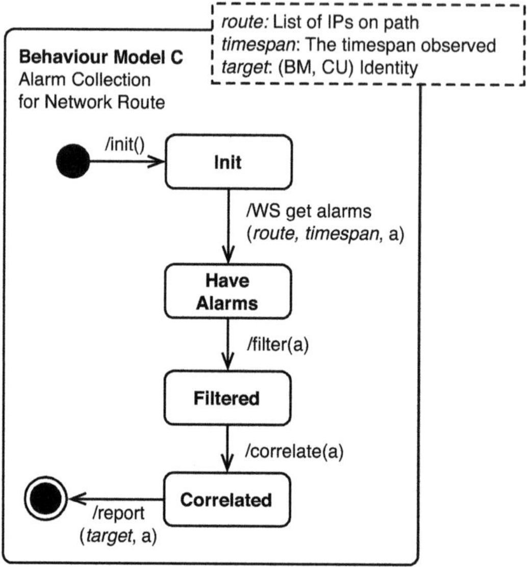
route: List of IPs on path
timespan: The timespan observed
target: (BM, CU) Identity
Behaviour Model C
Alarm Collection
for Network Route
/init()
Init
/WS get alarms
(route, timespan, a)
Have
Alarms
/filter(a)
Filtered
/correlate(a)
Correlated
/report
(target, a)

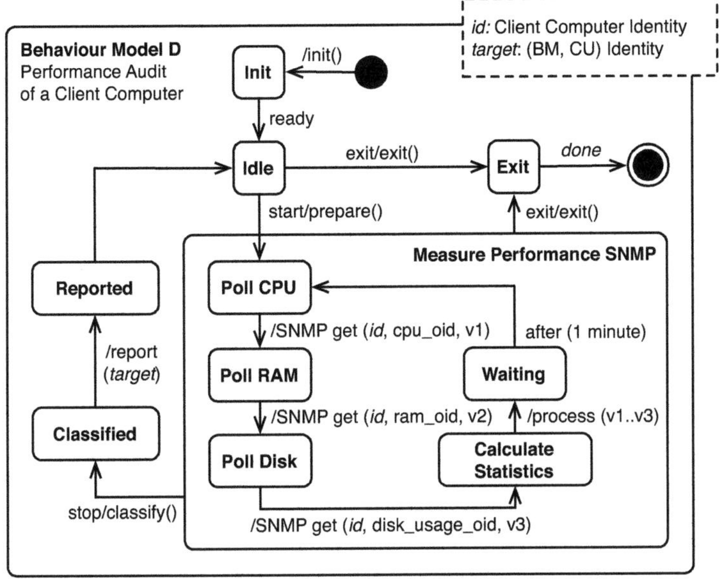

id: Client Computer Identity
target: (BM, CU) Identity
Behaviour Model D
Performance Audit
of a Client Computer
Init
/init()
ready
Idle
exit/exit()
Exit
done
start/prepare()
exit/exit()
Measure Performance SNMP
Reported
Poll CPU
/SNMP get (id, cpu_oid, v1)
after (1 minute)
/report
(target)
Poll RAM
Waiting
Classified
/SNMP get (id, ram_oid, v2)
/process (v1..v3)
Poll Disk
Calculate
Statistics
stop/classify()
/SNMP get (id, disk_usage_oid, v3)

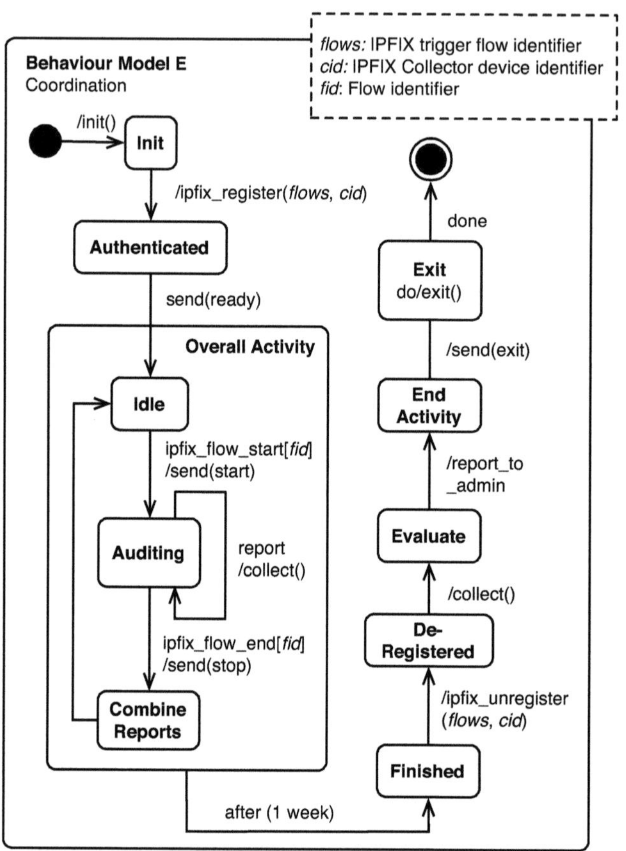
Behaviour Model E
Coordination
flows: IPFIX trigger flow identifier
cid: IPFIX Collector device identifier
fid: Flow identifier
/init()
Init
/ipfix_register(flows, cid)
Authenticated
send(ready)
Overall Activity
Idle
ipfix_flow_start[fid]
/send(start)
Auditing
report
/collect()
ipfix_flow_end[fid]
/send(stop)
Combine
Reports
after (1 week)
done
Exit
do/exit()
/send(exit)
End
Activity
/report_to
_admin
Evaluate
/collect()
De-
Registered
/ipfix_unregister
(flows, cid)
Finished

Behaviour Model for Router-Load Monitoring

This BM monitors router load for the scenario described in Section 5.2.2. It is specified in the plan format used by the MPU (see Section 4.5) and corresponds loosely to BM D, which is shown on page 251.

```
<?xml version="1.0"?>
<Plan id="MonitorRouterLoad" xmlns="http://fokus.fraunhofer.de/mbim/plan">

     <Provides/>

     <Requires>
          <Capability targettype="x-mbim-invocation">
               <FunctionalComponent id="Snmp" version="1.0"/>
          </Capability>
          <Capability targettype="x-mbim-invocation">
               <FunctionalComponent id="StatisticsCalculator" version="1.0"/>
          </Capability>
          <Capability targettype="x-mbim-invocation">
               <FunctionalComponent id="Classificator" version="1.0"/>
          </Capability>
          <ExternalPlan targettype="x-mbim-event" id="Collector"
               location="jms://10.0.2.1/CoordinationPlan" />
     </Requires>

     <Behaviour>
        <scxml xmlns="http://www.w3.org/2005/07/scxml" version="1.0"
             xmlns:cs="http://commons.apache.org/scxml"
             initial="Init" profile="xpath">

        <datamodel>
                <data id="Context">
                        <Values xmlns="">
                                <CPU>0</CPU>
                                <RAM>0</RAM>
                        </Values>
                        <Averages xmlns="">
                                <CPU>0</CPU>
                                <RAM>0</RAM>
                        </Averages>
                        <Classification xmlns="">Green</Classification>
                </data>
        </datamodel>

        <state id="Init">
            <transition event="ready" target="Idle"/>
        </state>

        <state id="Idle">
            <transition event="start" target="MeasurePerformanceSNMP"/>
```

```
            <transition event="exit" target="Exit"/>
        </state>

        <state id="MeasurePerformanceSNMP" initial="PollCPU">

              <transition event="stop" target="Classify"/>
              <transition event="exit" target="Exit"/>

              <state id="PollCPU">
               <invoke targettype="x-mbim-invocation" src="FC://Snmp"
                       id="pollcpu">
                       <param name="address" expr="'udp:10.0.0.1/161'"/>
                       <param name="community" expr="'public'"/>
                       <param name="oid" expr="'1.3.6.1.2.1.25.3.3.1.2.768'"/>
               </invoke>
               <transition target="PollRAM" event="'done.invoke.pollcpu'">
                       <assign location="Data(Context, 'Values/CPU')"
                            expr="_eventdatamap['done.invoke.pollcpu'].Value"/>
               </transition>
              </state>

              <state id="PollRAM">
               <invoke targettype="x-mbim-invocation" src="FC://Snmp"
                     id="pollram">
                       <param name="address" expr="'udp:10.0.0.1/161'"/>
                       <param name="community" expr="'public'"/>
                       <param name="oid" expr="'1.3.6.1.2.1.25.2.3.1.6.1'"/>
               </invoke>
               <transition target="CalcStatistics" event="'done.invoke.pollram'">
                       <assign location="Data(Context, 'Values/RAM')"
                            expr="_eventdatamap['done.invoke.pollram'].Value"/>
               </transition>
              </state>

              <state id="CalcStatistics">
               <invoke targettype="x-mbim-invocation" src="FC://StatisticsCalculator"
                     id="calcstats" namelist="Context"/>
               <transition target="Waiting" event="'done.invoke.calcstats'"/>
              </state>

              <state id="Waiting">
               <onentry>
                       <send target="'#_internal'" event="'timeout'" delay="60s"/>
               </onentry>
              <transition target="PollCPU" event="'timeout'"/>
              </state>

        </state>

        <state id="Classify">
```

```
            <invoke targettype="x-mbim-invocation" src="FC://Classificator"
                id="classification" namelist="Context"/>
            <transition target="Report" event="'done.invoke.classification'"/>
        </state>

        <state id="Report">
            <onentry>
                <send targettype="'x-mbim-event'" target="'plan://Collector'"
                        event="'report'">
                    <param name="classification"
                            expr="'Data(Context, 'Classification')'"/>
                </send>
            </onentry>
            <transition target="Idle"/>
        </state>

        <state id="Exit">
            <transition event="done" target="End"/>
        </state>

        <final id="End"/>

        </scxml>
    </Behaviour>
</Plan>
```

G Behaviour Models for the Intrinsic Monitoring Scenario

This part of the appendix contains the BMs used for the intrinsic monitoring use case study (see Section 5.3).

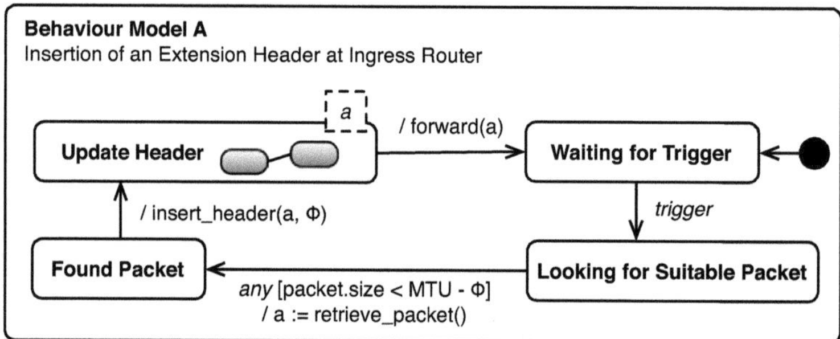

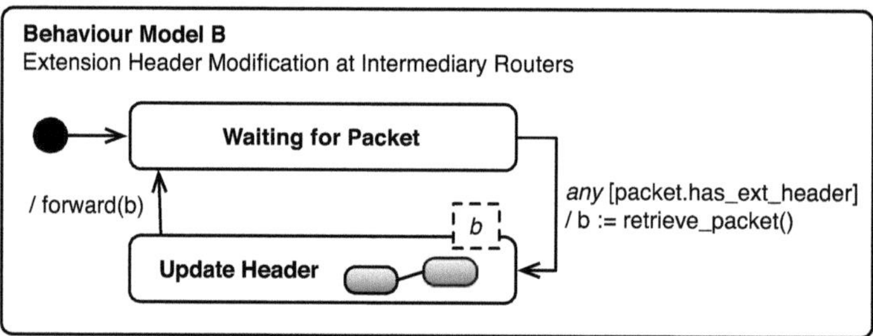

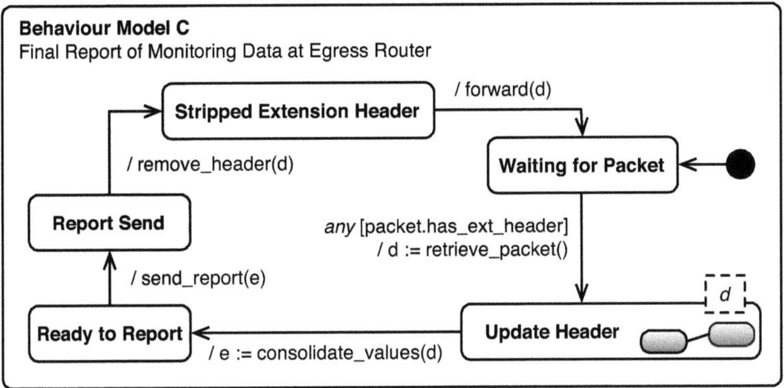
Behaviour Model C
Final Report of Monitoring Data at Egress Router
Stripped Extension Header
/ forward(d)
Waiting for Packet
/ remove_header(d)
Report Send
any [packet.has_ext_header]
/ d := retrieve_packet()
/ send_report(e)
d
Ready to Report
Update Header
/ e := consolidate_values(d)

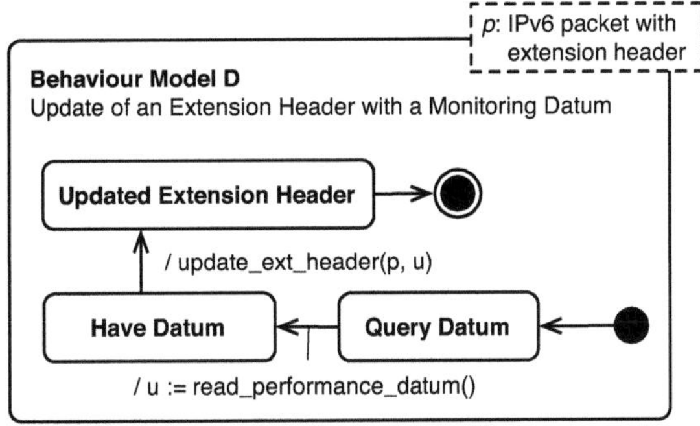
p: IPv6 packet with
extension header
Behaviour Model D
Update of an Extension Header with a Monitoring Datum
Updated Extension Header
/ update_ext_header(p, u)
Have Datum
Query Datum
/ u := read_performance_datum()

Glossary

Behaviour Model A formalised description of system runtime behaviour, based on statecharts. To interpret a BM, it needs to be associated with execution information – this process is referred to as *instantiation*. A BM can have many instances, this distinction is usually omitted in cases where it is not relevant for the discussion.

Behaviour Model Interpreter A program that executes a BM by processing the elements of a model instance at runtime. The BM Interpreter creates the system behaviour at runtime. It supports the modification of an associated BM during the runtime execution of instances of the model.

Behaviour Model Repository A management component responsible for persistently storing BMs and providing access to them as part of the BM activation process (see Section 2.3).

Collective A group of BMs that cooperate towards a common goal. The term is also used to designate a group of interpreters or computational units, which are executing the individual BM instances that form the collective.

Computational Unit A platform that is able to execute one, or more, interpreter programs.

Context A collection of data, which is associated with a BM instance. It is also referred to as *session data* or *state data*. Access to the context is done using expressions.

Control Flow A single path through the state-transition structure in a BM. During execution, an interpreter might process concurrent control flows within a BM instance.

Control Interface A subsystem of the generic interpreter architecture that enables access for the MA to the BM Interpreter (see Section 4.1.2).

Environment Everything that a BM instance interacts with, except the BM instance itself. Interaction is conducted through the sending and receiving of messages, which are referred to as events.

Expression A statement used in a condition or action label. An expression needs to be evaluable to a boolean result, when used in condition labels. For use in action labels, the evaluation result is ignored.

Event Interface A subsystem found in the generic interpreter architecture for transmitting messages that originate in an interpreted BM instance between the BM Interpreter and it's environment (see Section 4.1.2).

Event Queue A subsystem found in the generic interpreter architecture that stores incoming event messages for later retrieval by the step-processing logic of the Interpreter Engine (see Section 4.1.2).

Evolvability The ability of a system to not only scale in regard to resource utilisation, but also in regard to functionality.

Functional Component A software component that enables or encapsulates the execution of a function. FCs are invoked by a BM instance during its execution.

Functional Component Repository A management component that is responsible for persistently storing FCs and providing access to them as part of the BM activation process (see Section 2.3).

Homeostasis The ability of a system to continue to operate correctly in the face of changes in the operational environmental and without human intervention (also see Ashby's definition [8, chapter 5/3]).

Interpreter Engine A subsystem of the generic interpreter architecture that contains the logic for a stepwise interpretation of the BM instances (see Section 4.1.2).

Management Authority A management component responsible for deploying the BMs used in a CU Collective and for maintaining the Collective itself (see Section 2.3).

Run-To-Completion Semantics The strategy for stepwise processing of external events dispatched to an Interpreter engine. RTC semantics makes sure that a single event is processed completely before other events are taken from the Event Queue. A general algorithm with RTC semantics is provided on page 32.

State Configuration During execution of a BM instance, each control flow is always in a distinct state. A state configuration is a complete specification of the state of each control flow in a BM. The *active state configuration* at a given time is the current state configuration of an executing BM instance at that time.

List of Abbreviations

[...]	Omission of text (used with citations)
~	Approximately
µs	Microseconds
ACE	Autonomic Communication Element
ACM	Association for Computing Machinery
AI	Artificial Intelligence
AJAX	Asynchronous JavaScript and XML
API	Application Programming Interface
AS	Autonomic System
ASF	Apache Software Foundation
ASM	Abstract State Machine
ASP	Adaptive Systems Profile
AST	Abstract Syntax Tree
ASTL	Automaton Standard Template Library
ATL	ATLAS Transformation Language
AutoRM	Autonomic Reliable Multicast
AXP	Application eXtension Platform
B2B	Business-to-Business
BCO	Bus Checker Object
BM	Behaviour Model
BML	Behavioral Modeling Language
BPEL	Business Process Execution Language
BPMN	Business Process Modeling Notation
CASE	Computer-Aided Software Engineering
CBE	Common Base Event
CIL	Common Intermediate Language
CIM	Common Information Model
CMP	CU Management Protocol
CORBA	Common Object Request Broker Architecture
CSP	Communicating Sequential Processes
CU	Computational Unit
DEN-ng	Directory Enabled Networks – next generation
DFA	Deterministic Finite Automata
DHT	Distributed Hash Tables
DM	Data Model
DMTF	Distributed Management Task Force
DPI	Deep Packet Inspection
E4X	ECMAScript for XML
EBNF	Extended Backus-Naur Form
ECA	Event-Condition-Action
Ecore	EMF core
EEPROM	Electrically Erasable Programmable Read Only Memory
EFSM	Extended Finite State Machine
EHA	Extended Hierarchical Automaton
EMF	Eclipse Modelling Framework
ES-CP	ECMAScript Compact Profile
ESB	Enterprise Service Bus

f. and the following page (used with references)

FC Functional Component

ff. and the following pages (used with references)

FOCALE Foundation, Observation, Comparison, Action and Learning Environment

FPGA Field-Programmable Gate Array

FSM Finite State Machine

FXU Framework for Executable UML

GA Goal Achievable

GCC GNU Compiler Collection

GCO Gateway Checker Object

GEN Group Event Notification

GigE Gigabit Ethernet

GN Goal Needed

GPU Graphics Processing Unit

GUI Graphical User Interface

GXL Graph eXchange Language

HTTP Hypertext Transfer Protocol

I/O Input/Output

IEEE Institute of Electrical and Electronics Engineers

IETF Internet Engineering Task Force

IM Information Model

IOS Internetwork Operating System

IP Internet Protocol

IPC Inter-Process Communication

IPv6 Internet Protocol, version 6

ISR Integrated Services Router

IT Information Technology

J2EE Java 2 Enterprise Edition

JEXL Java Expression Language

JIT Just In Time

JMS Java Message Service

JMX Java Management Extensions

JSON JavaScript Object Notation

KB Kilobyte

LAN Local Area Network

MA Management Authority

MB Megabyte

MBIM Model Based Integrated Management

MCNC Microelectronics Center of North Carolina

MDA Model Driven Architecture

MDT Model Development Tools

MIB Management Information Base

MOM Message Oriented Middleware

MPI Message Passing Interface

MPU Model Processing Unit

ms Milliseconds

MTU Maximum Transmission Unit

Mutex Mutual Exclusion

MVC Model View Controller

MVEL MVFLEX Expression Language

NETCONF Network Configuration Protocol

NFA Non-deterministic Finite Automata

OBR OSGi Bundle Repository

OCL4X OCL for Execution

ODM On-Demand Monitoring

OO Object Orientation

OPS4J Open Participation Software for Java

OSGi A name (formerly known as "Open Services Gateway initiative")

PaaS Platform-as-a-Service

PBM Policy-Based Management

PDA Pushdown Automaton

PDU Protocol Data Unit

POSA Pattern-Oriented Software Architecture

POSIX Portable Operating System Interface

PREP Programmable Electronics Performance Corporation

PubSub Publish-Subscribe

QVT Query View Transformation

RAM Random-Access Memory

RFC Request For Comments

ROOM Real-Time Object Oriented Modeling

RPC Remote Procedure Call

RSA Rational Software Architect

RTC Run-To-Completion

SAX Simple API for XML

SCTL Statechart Transformation Language

SCXML State Chart XML

SDL Specification and Description Language

SID Shared Information and Data Model

SIGDA Special Interest Group on Design Automation

SMI Structure of Managed Information

SPEC Standard Performance Evaluation Corporation

SSH Secure Shell

STX Streaming Transformations for XML

SUS System Under Supervision

TM Forum TeleManagement Forum

TMPL Template Matching Processor Language

TT Trouble Ticket

UDP User Datagram Protocol

UML Unified Modeling Language

USB Universal Serial Bus

VHDL Very High Speed Integrated Circuit Hardware Description Language

VM Virtual Machine

Vol. Volume (used with references)

W3C World Wide Web Consortium

WBEM Web-Based Enterprise Management

WS Web Service

WS-CDL Web Services Choreography Description Language

XABSL Extensible Agent Behavior Specification Language

XDMS XML Document Management Server

XMI XML Metadata Interchange

XML eXtensible Markup Language

XPath XML Path Language

xUML Executable UML

Bibliography

[1] T. Abdellatif, E. Cecchet, and R. Lachaize. Evaluation of a Group Communication Middleware for Clustered J2EE Application Servers. In *Proc. of the 2004 International Symposium on Distributed Objects and Applications*, pages 1571–1589, 2004.

[2] M. Agarwal, V. Bhat, H. Liu, V. Matossian, V. Putty, C. Schmidt, G. Zhang, L. Zhen, and M. Parashar. Automate: Enabling Autonomic Grid Applications. In *Proc. 5th Annual Int. Active Middleware Services Workshop*, pages 48–57, June 2003.

[3] A. V. Aho, R. Sethi, and J. D. Ullmann. *Compilerbau Teil 1 & Teil 2*. Oldenbourg Verlag, 1999.

[4] I. Aib, N. Agoulmine, M. S. Fonseca, and G. Pujolle. Analysis of Policy Management Models and Specification Languages. In *Proc. 2nd Int. Conf. on Network Control and Engineering for QoS, Security, and Mobility*, pages 26–50, October 2003.

[5] L. Alfaro and T. Henzinger. Interface Automata. In *Proc. 8th European Software Engineering Conference*, pages 109–120, September 2001.

[6] Y. Amir, C. Nita-Rotaru, J. Stanton, and G. Tsudik. Secure Spread: An Integrated Architecture for Secure Group Communication. *IEEE Transactions on Dependable and Secure Computing*, 2(3):248–261, July 2005.

[7] M. Andreolini, S. Casolari, and M. Colajanni. Self-Inspection Mechanisms for the Support of Autonomic Decisions in Internet-Based Systems. In *Proc. 3rd Int. Conf. on Autonomic and Autonomous Systems*, June 2007.

[8] W. R. Ashby. *Design for a Brain.* Chapman and Hall, 1960. ISBN 0-412-20090-2.

[9] P. C. Attie and N. A. Lynch. Dynamic Input/Output Automata: a Formal Model for Dynamic Systems. In *Proc. 12th Int. Conference on Concurrency Theory*, pages 137–151, November 2001.

[10] Ö. Babaoğlu, G. Canright, A. Deutsch, G. D. Caro, F. Ducatelle, L. Gambardella, N. Ganguly, M. Jelasity, R. Montemanni, and A. Montresor. Design Patterns from Biology for Distributed Computing. *ACM Transactions on Autonomous and Adaptive Systems*, 1(1):26–66, 2006.

[11] Ö. Babaoğlu and M. Jelasity. Self-* Properties through Gossiping. *Philosophical Transactions of the Royal Society A: Mathematical, Physical and Engineering Sciences*, 366(1881):3747–3757, 2008.

[12] Ö. Babaoğlu, H. Meling, and A. Montresor. Anthill: A Framework for the Development of Agent-Based Peer-to-Peer Systems. In *Proc. 22nd int. Conf. on Distributed Computing Systems*, pages 15–22, July 2002.

[13] R. M. Bahati, M. A. Bauer, E. M. Vieira, O. K. Baek, and C.-W. Ahn. Mapping Policies into Autonomic Management Actions. In *Proc. Int. Conf. on Autonomic and Autonomous Systems*, pages 38–44, July 2006.

[14] A. Bailly, M. Clerbout, and I. Simplot-Ryl. Component Composition Preserving Behavioural Contracts Based on Communication Traces. In *Proc. 10th Int. Conference on Implementation and Application of Automata*, pages 54—65, November 2005.

[15] H. Balakrishnan, M. F. Kaashoek, D. Karger, R. Morris, and I. Stoica. Looking Up Data in P2P Systems. *Communications of the ACM*, 46(2):48, February 2003.

[16] C. Ballagny. *MOCAS: Un Modèle de Composants Basé États pour L'auto-Adaptation.* PhD thesis, University of Pau, France, 2010.

[17] C. Ballagny, N. Hameurlain, and F. Barbier. Dynamic Adaptive Software Components: the MOCAS Approach. In *Proc. 5th Int. Conf. on Soft Computing as Transdisciplinary Science and Technology*, pages 517–524, 2008.

[18] C. Ballagny, N. Hameurlain, and F. Barbier. MOCAS: A Model-Based Approach for Building Self-Adaptive Software Components. In *Proc. 5th th European Conf. on Model-Driven Architecture*, pages 5–11, June 2009.

[19] B. Ban. JavaGroups – Group Communication Patterns in Java. Technical report, Department of Computer Science, Cornell University, December 1998.

[20] S. Banerjee and B. Bhattacharjee. Scalable Secure Group Communication over IP Multicast. *IEEE Journal on Selected Areas in Communications*, 20(8):1511–1527, 2002.

[21] S. Baron-Cohen, A. M. Leslie, and U. Frith. Does the Autistic Child have a "Theory of Mind"? *Cognition*, 21:37–46, 1985.

[22] B. Baumgarten. *Petri-Netze – Grundlagen und Anwendungen.* Spektrum Akademischer Verlag, 2nd edition, 1996.

[23] C. Becker, M. Handte, G. Schiele, and K. Rothermel. PCOM – A Component System for Pervasive Computing. In *Proc. 2nd Int. Conf. on Pervasive Computing and Communications*, pages 67–76, March 2004.

[24] O. Becker. *Serielle Transformationen von XML – Probleme, Methoden, Lösungen.* PhD thesis, Humboldt Universität zu Berlin, 2004.

[25] S. Beer. *Brain of the Firm.* J. Wiley, 2nd edition, 1972. ISBN 978-0-471-94839-1.

[26] B. K. Benkő, N. Brgulja, E. Höfig, and R. Kusber. Adaptive Services in a Distributed Environment. In *Proc. 8th Int. Workshop on Applications and Services in Wireless Networks*, pages 66–75, May 2008.

[27] B. K. Benkő, A. D. Ferdinando, E. Höfig, M. Mamei, N. Brgulja, M. Giacometto, R. Kusber, and C. Moiso. Autonomic Communication Elements: Design, Evaluation and Application. *ACM Transactions on Autonomous and Adaptive Systems*, **under submission**.

[28] M. Born, E. Holz, and O. Kath. *Softwareentwicklung mit UML 2.* Addison-Wesley Verlag, 2004.

[29] A. Bottaro, J. Bourcier, C. Escoffier, and P. Lalanda. Autonomic Context-Aware Service Composition. *Proc. 2nd IEEE Int. Conf. on Pervasive Services*, July 2007.

[30] S. Bouchenak, N. de Palma, D. Hagimont, and C. Taton. Autonomic Management of Clustered Applications. In *Proc. IEEE Int. Conf. on Cluster Computing*, pages 1–11, September 2006.

[31] Z. Boudjemil, S. Davy, D. Muldowney, and C. Fahy. Deliverable 3.1 - Information Model. Technical report, Autonomic Internet (AutoI) Project, January 2009.

[32] R. Boutaba and I. Aib. Policy-Based Management: A Historical Perspective. *Journal of Network and Systems Management*, 15(4):447–480, November 2007.

[33] D. Brand and P. Zafiropulo. On Communicating Finite-State Machines. *Journal of the ACM*, 30(2):323–342, 1983.

[34] N. Brgulja, R. Kusber, B. K. Benkő, E. Höfig, P. H. Deussen, M. Giacometto, and M. Mamei. Deliverable 1.5 - Integrated Prototype (Final Release). Technical report, EU IST Project CASCADAS, December 2008.

[35] L. Broto, D. Hagimont, P. Stolf, N. Depalma, and S. Temate. Autonomic Management Policy Specification in Tune. *Proc. ACM Symposium on Applied Computing*, pages 1658–1663, 2008.

[36] K. L. Calvert, J. Griffioen, and S. Wen. Scalable Network Management Using Lightweight Programmable Network Services. *Journal of Network and Systems Management*, 14(1):15–47, 2006.

[37] R. Chaparadza. A Composition Language for Programmable Traffic Flow Monitoring in Multi-Service Self-Managing Networks. *Proc. 6th Int. Workshop on the Design of Reliable Communication Networks*, pages 1–8, Ocotber 2007.

[38] H. Chen, S. Hariri, and F. Rasul. An Innovative Self-Configuration Approach for Networked Systems and Applications. In *IEEE Int. Workshop on Computer Systems and Applications*, pages 537–544, March 2006.

[39] K.-T. Cheng and A. S. Krishnakumar. Automatic Functional Test Generation Using the Extended Finite State Machine Model. In *Proc. of the 30th Int. Conference on Design Automation*, December 1993.

[40] A. Clemm. *Network Management Fundamentals.* Cisco Press, May 2006. ISBN 978-1-58720-137-0.

[41] D. Coleman, F. Hayes, and S. Bear. Introducing Objectcharts or How to Use Statecharts in Object-Oriented Design. *IEEE Transactions on Software Engineering*, 18(1):9–18, January 1992.

[42] R. Colvin and I. J. Hayes. A Semantics for Behavior Trees. Technical Report ACCS-TR-07-01, ARC Centre for Complex Systems, School of ITEE, The University of Queensland, Australia, 2007.

[43] D. E. Comer. *Computer Networks and Internets.* Pearson Prentice Hall, 4th edition, 2004. ISBN 0-13-123-637-X.

[44] R. C. Conant and W. R. Ashby. Every Good Regulator of a System Must be a Model of that System. *International Journal of System Science*, 1(2):89–97, 1970.

[45] M. L. Crane and J. Dingel. On the Semantics of UML State Machines: Categorization and Comparison. Technical Report 2005-501, School of Computing, Queen's University, Kingston, Ontario, Canada, 2005.

[46] R. N. Cronk, P. H. Callahan, and L. Bernstein. Rule-Based Expert Systems For Network Management and Operations: An Introduction. *IEEE Network*, 2(5):7–21, 1988.

[47] N. Damianou, N. Dulay, E. Lupu, and M. Sloman. The Ponder Policy Specification Language. In *Proc. Workshop on Policies for Distributed Systems and Networks*, pages 18–38, January 2001.

[48] S. Davy, B. Jennings, and J. Strassner. The Policy Continuum – A Formal Model. In *Proc. 2nd IEEE Int. Workshop on Modelling Autonomic Communications Environments*, volume 6 of *Lecture Notes*, pages 65–78. Multicon, September 2007.

[49] J. E. L. de Vergara, V. A. Villagrá, J. I. Asensio, and J. Berrocal. Ontologies: Giving Semantics to Network Management Models. *IEEE Network*, 17(3):15– 21, 2003.

[50] J. den Haan. Model driven development: Code generation or model interpretation? "Birds of a Feather" session at the Code Generation 2010 conference, June 2010. `http://www.theenterprisearchitect.eu/archive/2010/06/28/model-driven-development-code-generation-or-model-interpretation`.

[51] G. Denaro, L. Mariani, M. Pezzè, and D. Tosi. Adaptive Runtime Verification for Autonomic Communication Infrastructures. In *Proc. 1st Int. IEEE WoWMoM Workshop on Autonomic Communications and Computing*, pages 553–557, June 2005.

[52] A. Derezińska and R. Pilitowski. Interpretation of History Pseudostates in Orthogonal States of UML State Machines. In *Proc. 7th Conf. on Next Generation Information Technologies and Systems*, pages 26—37, 2009.

[53] P. H. Deussen. Model Based Reactive Planning and Prediction for Autonomic Systems. In *Proc. Workshop on Innovative Service Technologies*, pages 1–10, October 2007.

[54] P. H. Deussen, M. Baumgarten, M. Mulvenna, A. Manzalini, and C. Moiso. Autonomic Re-configuration of Pervasive Supervision Services. In *Proc. 1st Int. Conference on Emerging Network Intelligence*, pages 33–38, 2009.

[55] P. H. Deussen, C. Fahy, E. Höfig, and S. van der Meer. A Discussion on Fundamental Approaches for the Engineering of Autonomic Systems. In *Proc. 2nd Int. Conference on Bio-Inspired Models of Network, Information, and Computing Systems*, October 2007.

[56] P. H. Deussen and E. Höfig. Self-Organizing Service Supervision: Concept Demonstration. In *Proc. 2nd Int. Conference on Bio-Inspired Models of Network, Information, and Computing Systems*, pages 245–246, December 2007.

[57] P. H. Deussen, E. Höfig, M. Baumgarten, M. Mulvenna, C. Moiso, and A. Manzalini. Component-ware for Autonomic Supervision Services - The CASCADAS Approach. *Int. Journal On Advances in Intelligent Systems*, 3(1 & 2):87–105, 2010. Invited article.

[58] Y. Diao, J. L. Hellerstein, S. Parekh, R. Griffith, G. Kaiser, and D. Phung. Self-Managing Systems: A Control Theory Foundation. In *Proc. 12th IEEE Int. Conf. and Workshops on the Engineering of Computer-Based Systems*, pages 441–448, April 2005.

[59] Distributed Management Task Force. CIM System Virtualization Model White Paper. Document Number DSP2013, Version 1.0.0, November 2007.

[60] K. R. Dittrich, S. Gatziu, and A. Geppert. *Rules in Database Systems*, volume 985, pages 1–17. Springer, 1995.

[61] W. Dong, J. Wang, X. Qi, and Z.-C. Qi. Model Checking UML Statecharts. In *Proc. 8th Asia-Pacific Software Engineering Conf.*, pages 363– 370, 2001.

[62] X. Dong, S. Hariri, L. Xue, H. Chen, M. Zhang, S. Pavuluri, and S. Rao. Autonomia: An Autonomic Computing Environment. *Proc IEEE Int. Conf. on Performance, Computing, and Communications Conference*, pages 61– 68, April 2003.

[63] S. Donikian. HPTS: A Behaviour Modelling Language for Autonomous Agents. In *Proc. 5th Int. Conf. on Autonomous Agents*, pages 401–408, May 2001.

[64] G. Dromey. From Requirements to Design: Formalizing the Key Steps. In *Proc. 1st Int. Conf. Software Engineering and Formal Methods*, pages 2–11, September 2003.

[65] J. Ebert. Efficient Interpretation of State Charts. In *Proc. 9th Int. Symposium on Fundamentals of Computation Theory*, pages 212–221, December 1993.

[66] X. Elkorobarrutia, M. Muxika, G. Sagardui, F. Barbier, and X. Aretxandieta. A Framework for Statechart Based Component Reconfiguration. In *Proc 5th IEEE Workshop on Engineering of Autonomic and Autonomous Systems*, pages 37–45, March 2008.

[67] W. Emmerich. *Engineering Distributed Objects.* John Wiley & Sons, Ltd, 2000.

[68] P. T. Eugster, P. A. Felber, R. Guerraoui, and A.-M. Kermarrec. The Many Faces of Publish/Subscribe. *ACM Computing Surveys*, 35(2):114–131, June 2003.

[69] H. Fecher, M. Kyas, and J. Schönborn. Semantic Issues in UML 2.0 State Machines. Technical Report 0507, Christians-Albrecht-Universität Kiel, Institut für Informatik und Praktische Mathematik, June 2005.

[70] I. Ferdelja. Component Behavior Modeling. Master's thesis, Faculty of Electrical Engineering and Computing, University of Zagreb, Croatia, May 2009.

[71] A. G. F. Filho and H. Liesenberg. Transforming Statecharts into Reactive Systems. In *Proc. 19th Conferencia Latinoamericana de Informática*, pages 501–509, February 1993.

[72] S. Floyd, V. Jacobson, C.-G. Liu, S. McCanne, and L. Zhang. A Reliable Multicast Framework for Light-Weight Sessions and Application Level Framing. *IEEE/ACM Transactions on Networking*, 5(6):784–803, 1997.

[73] I. Foster and C. Kesselman, editors. *The GRID - Blueprint for a New Computing Infrastructure.* Morgan Kaufmann Publishers, 2nd edition, 2004. ISBN 1-55860-933-4.

[74] H. Frank and J. Eder. Equivalence Transformations on Statecharts. In *Proc. 12th Int. Conf. on Software Engineering and Knowledge Engineering*, pages 150–158, July 2000.

[75] E. Gamma, R. Helm, R. Johnson, and J. Vlissides. *Entwurfsmuster – Elemente Wiederverwendbarer Objektorientierter Software.* Addison Wesley, 1996.

[76] D. Garlan, S.-W. Chengand, A.-C. Huang, B. Schmerl, and P. Steenkiste. Rainbow: Architecture-Based Self-Adaptation with Reusable Infrastructure. *IEEE Computer*, 37(10):46–54, 2004.

[77] J. J. Garrett. Ajax: A New Approach to Web Applications. `http://www.adaptivepath.com/ideas/essays/archives/000385.php`.

[78] B. Gaudin and P. H. Deussen. Supervisory Control on Concurrent Discrete Event Systems with Variables. In *Proc. American Control Conference*, pages 4274–4279, July 2007.

[79] S. Gnesi, D. Latella, and M. Massink. Model Checking UML Statechart Diagrams Using JACK. In *Proc. 4th IEEE Int. Symposium on High-Assurance Systems Engineering*, pages 46–55, March 1999.

[80] S. Gnesi and F. Mazzanti. On the Fly Model Checking of Communicating UML State Machines. In *Proc. 2nd ACIS Int. Conf. on Software Engineering Research, Management and Applications*, pages 331–338, May 2004.

[81] C. Gonzalez-Perez, B. Henderson-Sellers, and G. Dromey. A Metamodel for the Behavior Trees Modelling Technique. In *Proc. 3rd Int. Conf. on Information Technology and Applications*, volume 1, pages 35–39, July 2005.

[82] P. Graham. The Hundred-Year Language. Keynote at PyCon DC, March 2003.

[83] T. J. Green, G. Miklau, M. Onizuka, and D. Suciu. Processing XML Streams with Deterministic Automata. In *Proc. 9th Int. Conf. on Database Theory*, pages 173–189, 2002.

[84] O. Grossman and D. Harel. On the Algorithmics of Higraphs. Technical Report CS97-15, The Weizmann Institute of Science, December 1997.

[85] N. Guelfi and B. Ries. SCTL: A StateChart Transformation Language for Test Sets Reduction. In *Proc. ERCIM Workshop on Dependable Software Intensive Embedded Systems*, August 2005.

[86] A. Gupta. Network Management: Current Trends and Future Perspectives. *Journal of Network and Systems Management*, 14(4):483–491, 2006.

[87] F. Harary. *Graph Theory.* Westview Press, 1994. ISBN 978-0-201-41033-4.

[88] D. Harel. Statecharts: A Visual Formalism for Complex Systems. *Science of Computer Programming*, 8(3):231–274, December 1987.

[89] D. Harel. On Visual Formalisms. *Communications of the ACM*, 31(5), May 1988.

[90] D. Harel and E. Gery. Executable Object Modeling with Statecharts. *IEEE Computer*, 30(7):31–42, 1996.

[91] D. Harel and H. Kugler. The Rhapsody Semantics of Statecharts (or, on the Executable Core of the UML). *Integration of Software Specification Techniques for Applications in Engineering, Lecture Notes in Computer Science*, 3147:325–354, 2004.

[92] D. Harel, H. Lachover, A. Naamad, A. Pnueli, M. Politi, R. Sherman, A. Shtull-Trauring, and M. Trakhtenbrot. STATEMATE: A Working Environment for the Development of Complex Reactive Systems. *IEEE Transactions on Software Engineering*, 16(4):403–414, 1990.

[93] H.-G. Hegering, S. Abeck, and B. Neumair. *Integrated Management of Networked Systems: Concepts, Architectures and their Operational Application.* Morgan Kaufmann Publishers, August 1999. ISBN 978-1-55860-571-8.

[94] C. L. Heitmeyer, R. D. Jeffords, and B. G. Labaw. A Benchmark for Comparing Different Approaches for Specifying and Verifying Real-time Systems. In *Proc. 10th Int. Workshop on Real-Time Operating Systems and Software*, page n.p., May 1993.

[95] J. L. Hellerstein, Y. Diao, S. Parekh, and D. M. Tilbury. *Feedback Control of Computing Systems.* Wiley-IEEE Press, 2004. ISBN: 978-0-471-26637-2.

[96] R. Helm, I. M. Holland, and D. Gangopadhyay. Contracts: Specifying Behavioral Compositions in Object-Oriented Systems. In *Proc. Conference on Object-Oriented Programming: Systems, Languages, and Applications*, pages 169–180, October 1990.

[97] C. Herring and S. Kaplan. Cybernetic Components: a Theoretical Basis for Component Software Systems. In *Proc. Component Oriented Software Engineering Workshop*, November 1998.

[98] A. Hinnerichs and E. Höfig. An Efficient Mechanism for Matching Multiple Patterns on XML Streams. In *Proc. of the IASTED Int. Conference on Software Engineering 2007*, pages 164–170, February 2007.

[99] C. A. R. Hoare. Communicating Sequential Processes. *Communications of the ACM*, 21(8):666–667, January 1978.

[100] E. Höfig. Dezentrale Verteilung von Daten in Heterogener Umgebung: Konzeption und Realisierung einer Komponentenbasierten Infrastruktur. Master's thesis, Technical University of Berlin, December 2003.

[101] E. Höfig. Template Matching on XML Streams. In *Proc. of the IASTED Int. Conference on Software Engineering*, pages 113–118, February 2006.

[102] E. Höfig. Autonomic Reliable Multicast: Application-Level Group Communication Using Self-Organization Principles. In *Proc. 2nd Int. Conference on Bio-Inspired Models of Network, Information, and Computing Systems*, December 2007.

[103] E. Höfig and H. Coşkun. Using Pattern Bound Policies to Construct Regulatory Mechanisms for Autonomic Systems. In *Proc. 10th Int. Conference on Quality Engineering in Software Technology*, pages 373–393, September 2007.

[104] E. Höfig and H. Coşkun. Intrinsic Monitoring Using Behaviour Models in IPv6 Networks. In *Proc. 4th Int. Workshop on Modelling Autonomic Communication Environments*, pages 86–99, October 2009.

[105] E. Höfig and P. H. Deussen. Document-Based Network and System Management: Utilizing Autonomic Capabilities for Enterprise Management Integration. In *Proc. 2nd Int. Conference on Autonomic Computing and Communication Systems*, September 2008.

[106] E. Höfig and P. H. Deussen. Model-based Integrated Management: Applying Autonomic Systems Engineering to Network and Systems Management. *Int. Journal of Autonomous and Adaptive Communiations Systems*, 4(1):100–118, 2011. Invited article.

[107] E. Höfig, P. H. Deussen, and H. Coşkun. Statechart Interpretation on Resource Constrained Platforms: a Performance Analysis. In *Proc. 4th Int. Workshop models@run.time*, October 2009.

[108] J. E. Hopcroft. Automata Theory: Its Past and Future. In *A Half-Century of Automata Theory: Celebration and Inspiration.* World Scientific Publishing, 2001.

[109] J. E. Hopcroft and J. D. Ullman. *Introduction to Automata Theory, Languages, and Computation.* Addison-Wesley Publishing Company, 1979. ISBN 0-201-02988-X.

[110] M. Hosseini, D. T. Ahmed, S. Shirmohammadi, and N. D. Georganas. A Survey of Application-Layer Multicast Protocols. *IEEE Communications Surveys & Tutorials*, 9(3):58–74, 2007.

[111] D. Huffman. The Synthesis of Sequential Switching Circuits. *J. Franklin Inst*, 257(3):161–190, 1953.

[112] IBM Corporation. An Architectural Blueprint for Autonomic Computing. White Paper, 4th edition, June 2006. `http://www.ibm.com/software/tivoli/autonomic/pdfs/AC_Blueprint_White_Paper_4th.pdf`.

[113] B. Jacob, R. Lanyon-Hogg, D. N. Nadgir, and A. F. Yassin. *A Practical Guide to the IBM Autonomic Computing Toolkit.* IBM, April 2004. `http://ibm.com/redbooks`.

[114] B. Jennings, S. van der Meer, S. Balasubramaniam, D. Botvich, M. Ó. Foghlú, W. Donnelly, and J. Strassner. Towards Autonomic Management of Communications Networks. *IEEE Communications Magazine*, 45(10):112–121, 2007.

[115] Y. Jin, R. Esser, and J. W. Janneck. Describing the Syntax and Semantics of UML Statecharts in a Heterogeneous Modelling Environment. In *Proc. 2nd Int. Conf. on Diagrammatic Representation and Inference*, pages 320–334, April 2002.

[116] F. Jouault and I. Kurtev. On the Architectural Alignment of ATL and QVT. In *Proceedings of the 2006 ACM symposium on Applied computing*, page 1195, April 2006.

[117] L. Jóźwiak, D. Gawłowski, and A. Ślusarczyk. An Effective Solution of Benchmarking Problem - FSM Benchmark Generator and Its Application to Analysis of State Assignment Methods. In *Proc. 7th EUROMICRO Systems on Digital System Design*, pages 160–167, August 2004.

[118] S. Kliman. PREP Benchmarks Reveal Performance and Capacity Tradeoffs of Programmable Logic Devices. In *Proc. 7th Annual IEEE Int. ASIC Conf. and Exhibit*, pages 376–382, 1994.

[119] A. Knapp and S. Merz. Model Checking and Code Generation for UML State Machines and Collaborations. In *Proc. 5th Workshop on Tools for System Design and Verification, Technical Report*, pages 59–64, 2002.

[120] A. Knapp and H. Störrle. Unified Modeling Language 2.0: Syntax, Semantics, Pragmatics. Tutorial Session at the IASTED International Conference on Software Engineering, Innsbruck, Austria, February 2007.

[121] M. M. Kokar, K. Baclawski, and Y. A. Eracar. Control Theory-Based Foundations of Self-Controlling Software. *IEEE Intelligent Systems*, 14(3):37–45, 1999.

[122] A. V. Konstantinou, D. Florissi, and Y. Yemini. Towards Self-Configuring Networks. In *Proc. DARPA Active Networks Conference and Exposition*, pages 143–156, May 2002.

[123] G. P. Kumar and P. Venkataram. AI Approaches to Network Management: Recent Advances and A Survey. *Computer Communications*, 20(1):1313–1322, 1997.

[124] D. Latella, I. Majzik, and M. Massink. Automatic Verification of a Behavioural Subset of UML Statechart Diagrams Using the SPIN Model-Checker. *Formal Aspects of Computing*, 11(6):637–664, 1999.

[125] S. Lee and S. Sluizer. An Executable Language for Modeling Simple Behavior. *IEEE Transactions on Software Engineering*, 17(6):527–543, 1991.

[126] L. H. Lehman, S. J. Garland, and D. L. Tennenhouse. Active Reliable Multicast. In *Proc. 17th Annual Joint Conf. of the IEEE Computer and Communications Societies*, volume 2, pages 581 – 589, March 1998.

[127] H. Liu, M. Parashar, and S. Hariri. A Component Based Programming Framework for Autonomic Applications. In *Proc. Int. Conf. on Autonomic Computing*, pages 10–17, May 2004.

[128] M. Lötzsch, M. Risler, and M. Jüngel. XABSL - A Pragmatic Approach to Behavior Engineering. In *Proc. of IEEE/RSJ Int. Conf. on Intelligent Robots and Systems*, pages 5124–5129, October 2006.

[129] N. A. Lynch, R. Segala, and F. Vaandrager. Hybrid I/O Automata. Technical report, MIT Laboratory for Computer Science, January 2003. MIT-LCS-TR-827d.

[130] N. A. Lynch and M. R. Tuttle. Hierarchical Correctness Proofs for Distributed Algorithms. In *Proc. 6th Annual ACM Symposium on Principles of Distributed Computing*, pages 137–151, August 1987.

[131] A. Maggiolo-Schettini and A. Peron. A Graph Rewriting Framework for Statecharts Semantics. In *Proc. 5th Int. Workshop on Graph Grammars and Their Application to Computer Science*, pages 107–121, November 1994.

[132] S. S. Manvi and P. Venkataram. A Method of Network Monitoring by Mobile Agents. In *Proc. Int. Conf. on Communications, Control, and Signal Processing*, pages 214–218, July 2000.

[133] V. L. Maout. Tools to Implement Automata, a First Step: ASTL. In *Proc. 2nd Int. Workshop on Implementing Automata*, pages 104—108, December 1997.

[134] V. L. Maout. Cursors. In *Proc. 5th Int. Conference on Implementation and Application of Automata*, pages 195–207, May 2000.

[135] P. Marrow and M. Koubarakis. Self-Organising Applications Using Lightweight Agents. In *Proc. 3rd Int. Workshop on Engineering Self-Organising Systems*, pages 120–129, July 2005.

[136] P. K. McKinley, S. M. Sadjadi, E. P. Kasten, and B. H. Cheng. Composing Adaptive Software. *IEEE Computer*, 37(7):56–64, 2004.

[137] G. H. Mealy. A Method for Synthesizing Sequential Circuits. *Bell System Technical Journal*, 34(5):1045–1079, 1955.

[138] S. J. Mellor and M. J. Balcer. *Executable UML: A Foundation for Model-Driven Architecture.* Addison-Wesley, 2002. ISBN 0-201-74804-5.

[139] B. Meyer. Applying "Design by Contract". *IEEE Computer*, 25(10):40–51, 1992.

[140] P. Michiardi, P. Marrow, R. Tateson, and F. Saffre. Aggregation Dynamics in Service Overlay Networks. In *Proc. 1st Int. Conf. on Self-Adaptive and Self-Organizing Systems*, pages 129–140, July 2007.

[141] Z. Milosevic and G. Dromey. On Expressing and Monitoring Behaviour in Contracts. In *Proc. 6th Int. Enterprise Distributed Object Computing Conf.*, pages 3– 14, September 2002.

[142] K. Mochalski and H. Schulze. Deep Packet Inspection – Technology, Applications & Net Neutrality. Whitepaper from ipoque GmbH, 2009. `http://www.ipoque.com/userfiles/file/DPI-Whitepaper.pdf`.

[143] T. Modica. Eine Attributierte Getypte Graphgrammatik zum Syntaxgesteuerten Editieren von UML State Machines. Master's thesis, Technical University of Berlin, January 2006.

[144] E. F. Moore. Gedanken-Experiments on Sequential Machines. *Automata studies*, 34:129–153, 1956.

[145] R. Mortier and E. Kiciman. Autonomic Network Management: Some Pragmatic Considerations. *Proc. Workshop on Internet Network Management*, pages 89–93, September 2006.

[146] L. E. Moser, P. M. M. Smith, D. A. Agarwal, R. K. Budhia, and C. A. Lingley-Papadopoulos. Totem: a Fault-Tolerant Multicast Group Communication System. *Communications of the ACM*, 39(4):54–63, April 1996.

[147] I. A. Niaz and J. Tanaka. Code Generation from UML Statecharts. In *Proc. 7th IASTED Int. Conf. on Software Engineering and Application*, pages 315–321, 2003.

[148] S. Nordstrom, S. Shetty, D. Yao, S. Ahuja, S. Neema, and T. Bapty. The Action Language: Refining a Behavioral Modeling Language. In *Proc. 12th IEEE Int. Conf. and Workshops on the Engineering of Computer-Based Systems*, pages 315– 320, April 2005.

[149] O. Ozkasap, Z. Xiao, and K. P. Birman. Scalability of Two Reliable Multicast Protocols. Technical Report TR99-1748, Cornell University, Dept. of Computer Science, 2001.

[150] B. Paech and B. Rumpe. A New Concept of Refinement used for Behaviour Modelling with Automata. In *Proc. 2nd Int. Symposium of Formal Methods*, pages 154–174, October 1994.

[151] S. Paul, K. K. Sabnani, J. C. Lin, and S. Bhattacharyya. Reliable Multicast Transport Protocol (RMTP). *IEEE Journal on Selected Areas in Communications*, 15(3):407–421, 1997.

[152] G. Pavlou. On the Evolution of Management Approaches, Frameworks and Protocols: A Historical Perspective. *Journal of Network and Systems Management*, 15(4):425–445, 2007.

[153] C. A. Petri. *Kommunikation mit Automaten.* PhD thesis, University of Bonn, 1962.

[154] D. Pezaros, D. Hutchison, R. Gardner, F. Garcia, and J. Sventek. Inline Measurements: A Native Measurement Technique for IPv6 Networks. In *Proc. Int. Networking and Communications Conf.*, pages 105 – 110, June 2004.

[155] R. Pilitowski and A. Derezińska. Code Generation and Execution Framework for UML 2.0 Classes and State Machines. In *Innovations and Advanced Techniques in Computer and Information Sciences and Engineering*, pages 421–427. Springer Netherlands, 2007. ISBN 978-1-4020-6267-4.

[156] M. Pistore, A. Marconi, P. Traverso, and P. G. Bertoli. Automated Composition of Web Services by Planning at the Knowledge Level. In *Proc. 19th Int. Joint Conf. on Artificial Intelligence*, pages 1252–1259, July 2005.

[157] A. Pras, J. Schönwälder, M. Burgess, O. Festor, G. M. Pérez, R. Stadler, and B. Stiller. Key Research Challenges in Network Management. *IEEE Communications Magazine*, 45(10):104–110, 2007.

[158] C. M. Prashanth and K. C. Shet. Efficient Algorithms for Verification of UML Statechart Models. *Journal of Software*, 4(3):175, 2009.

[159] R. Quitadamo and F. Zambonelli. Autonomic Communication Services: a New Challenge for Software Agents. *Autonomous Agents and Multi-Agent Systems*, 17(3):457–475, December 2008.

[160] S. Ramesh. Efficient translation of statecharts to hardware circuits. In *Proc. 12th Int. Conf. on VLSI Design*, pages 384–389, January 1999.

[161] C. Reichert and D. Witaszek. An Implementation of the Group Event Notification Protocol. Technical Report TR-2002-0301, Fraunhofer FOKUS, 2002.

[162] R. Renesse, K. Birman, and S. Maffeis. Horus: a Flexible Group Communication System. *Communications of the ACM*, 39(4):76–83, April 1996.

[163] T. H. Romer, D. Lee, G. M. Voelker, A. Wolman, W. A. Wong, J.-L. Baer, B. N. Bershad, and H. M. Levy. The Structure and Performance of Interpreters. *Proc. 7th Int. Conf. on Architectural Support for Programming Languages and Operating Systems*, pages 150–159, October 1996.

[164] B. Rumpe, M. Schoenmakers, A. Radermacher, and A. Schürr. UML+ROOM as a Standard ADL? In *Proc. 5th Int. Conference on Engineering of Complex Computer Systems*, pages 43–53, 1999.

[165] F. Saffre and H. R. Blok. "SelfService": A Theoretical Protocol for Autonomic Distribution of Services in P2P Communities. In *Proc. 12th IEEE Int. Conf. and Workshops on the Engineering of Computer-Based Systems*, pages 528–534, April 2005.

[166] M. Samek. *Practical Statecharts in C/C++.* Newnes, 2nd edition, 2008. ISBN 0-75068-706-1.

[167] M. Sánchez, I. Barrero, J. Villalobos, and D. Deridder. An Execution Platform for Extensible Runtime Models. In *Proc. 3rd Int. Workshop on models@run.time*, pages 107–116, September 2008.

[168] I. Satoh. Building and Selecting Mobile Agents for Network Management. *Journal of Network and Systems Management*, 14(1):147–169, May 2006.

[169] D. Schmidt, M. Stal, H. Rohnert, and F. Buschmann. *Pattern-Oriented Software Architecture: Patterns for Concurrent and Networked Objects.* John Wiley & Sons, Ltd, 2000.

[170] M. Schrefl, G. Kappel, and P. Lang. Modeling Collaborative Behavior Using Cooperation Contracts. *Data & Knowledge Engineering*, 26(2):191–224, 1998.

[171] A. Schumann and Y. Pencolé. Scalable Diagnosability Checking of Event-Driven Systems. In *Proc. 20th Int. Joint Conf. on Artificial Intelligence*, pages 575–580, January 2007.

[172] B. Selic. An Efficient Object-Oriented Variation of the Statecharts Formalism for Distributed Real-Time Systems. In *Proc. 11th IFIP Conference on Hardware Description Languages and Their Applications*, pages 335–344, January 1993.

[173] G. D. M. Serugendo, N. Foukia, S. Hassas, A. Karageorgos, S. K. Mostéfaoui, O. F. Rana, M. Ulieru, P. Valckenaers, and C. V. Aart. Self-Organisation: Paradigms and Applications. In *Proc. 2nd Int. Joint Conf. on Autonomous Agents & Multiagent Systems*, pages 1–19, July 2003.

[174] A. Sharpanskykh and J. Treur. Modeling of Agent Behavior Using Behavioral Specifications. Technical Report 06-02ASRAI, Vrije Universiteit Amsterdam, Department of Artificial Intelligence, 2006.

[175] L. Shi and A. Davy. Security Considerations for Intrinsic Monitoring within IPv6 Networks. In *Proc. 9th Int. Workshop on IP Operations and Management*, pages 167–172, September 2009.

[176] L. Shi and A. Davy. Intrinsic Monitoring within an IPv6 Network: Relating Traffic Flows to Network Paths. In *Proc. IEEE Int. Conf. on Communications*, May 2010.

[177] L. Shi, A. Davy, D. Muldowney, E. Höfig, and X. Fu. Intrinsic Monitoring within an IPv6 Network: Mapping Node Information to Network Paths. In *Proc. 6th Int. Conf. on Network and Service Management*, pages 370–373, October 2010.

[178] S. Shlaer and S. J. Mellor. *Object Lifecycles: Modeling the World in States.* Yourdon Press, 1991. ISBN 0-13-629940-7.

[179] M. Sloman. Policy Driven Management for Distributed Systems. *Journal of Network and Systems Management*, 2(4):333–360, 1994.

[180] M. Smirnow. Autonomic Communication: Research Agenda for a New Communication Paradigm. White Paper from Fraunhofer Fokus, October 2004. `http://www.autonomic-communication.org/publications/doc/WP_v02.pdf`.

[181] W. R. Stevens and S. A. Rago. *Advanced Programming in the UNIX Environment.* Addison Wesley, 2nd edition, 2005.

[182] E. Stoyanov, M. Wischy, and D. Roller. Using Managed Communication Channels in Software Components. *Proc. 3rd Conf. on Computing Frontiers*, pages 177–186, May 2006.

[183] J. Strassner. DEN-ng: Achieving Business-Driven Network Management. In *Proc. IEEE/IFIP Int. Network Operations and Management Symposium*, pages 753–766, August 2002.

[184] J. Strassner. *Policy-Based Network Management: Solutions for the Next Generation.* Morgan Kaufman Publishers, 2003. ISBN 1-55860-859-1.

[185] J. Strassner. Using Lifecycles and Contracts to Build Better Telecommunications Systems. In *Proc. 3rd European Conference on Universal Multiservice Networks*, pages 483–497, October 2004.

[186] J. Strassner. Knowledge Management Issues for Autonomic Systems. In *Proc. 16th Int. Workshop on Database and Expert Systems Applications*, pages 398–402, August 2005.

[187] J. Strassner, J. W.-K. Hong, and S. van der Meer. The Design of an Autonomic Element for Managing Emerging Networks and Services. In *Proc. 1st IEEE Int. Conf. on Ultra Modern Telecommunications & Workshops*, pages 1–8, October 2009.

[188] J. Strassner, D. O'Sullivan, and D. Lewis. Ontologies in the Engineering of Management and Autonomic Systems: A Reality Check. *Journal of Network and Systems Management*, 15(1):5–11, March 2007.

[189] J. Strassner, J. N. Souza, S. van der Meer, S. Davy, K. Barrett, D. Raymer, and S. Samudrala. The Design of a New Policy Model to Support Ontology-Driven Reasoning for Autonomic Networking. *Journal of Network and Systems Management*, 17(1-2):5–32, 2009.

[190] J. Strassner, S. van der Meer, D. O'Sullivan, and S. Dobson. The Use of Context-Aware Policies and Ontologies to Facilitate Business-Aware Network Management. *Journal of Network and Systems Management*, pages 255–284, 2009.

[191] G. Sunyé, A. L. Guennec, and J.-M. Jézéquel. Using UML Action Semantics for Model Execution and Transformation. *Information Systems*, 27(6):445–457, 2002.

[192] D. Sykes, W. Heaven, J. Magee, and J. Kramer. From Goals to Components: A Combined Approach to Self-Management. *Proc. Int. Workshop on Software Engineering for Adaptive and Self-Managing Systems*, pages 1–8, May 2008.

[193] C. Szyperski. *Component Software – Beyond Object-Oriented Programming.* Addison Wesley, 1999.

[194] G. Taentzer, K. Ehrig, E. Guerra, J. de Lara, L. Lengyel, T. Levendovszky, U. Prange, D. Varro, and S. Varro-Gyapay. Model Transformation by Graph Transformation: A Comparative Study. In *Proc. Workshop Model Transformation in Practice*, pages 120–127, October 2005.

[195] A. S. Tanenbaum and M. van Steen. *Distributed Systems – Principles and Paradigms.* Prentice Hall, 2002. ISBN 0-13-088893-1.

[196] D. L. Tennenhouse and D. J. Wetherall. Towards an Active Network Architecture. In *Proc. DARPA Active NEtworks Conference and Exposition*, pages 2–15, May 2002.

[197] X. Than, H. Miao, and L. Liu. Formalizing the Semantics of UML Statecharts with Z. In *Proc. 4th Int. Conf. on Computer and Information Technology*, pages 1116– 1121, September 2004.

[198] H. H. To, S. Krishnaswamy, and B. Srinivasan. Mobile Agents for Network Management: When and When Not! *Proc. of the 2005 ACM Symposium on Applied Computing*, pages 47–53, March 2005.

[199] S. Uchitel, J. Kramer, and J. Magee. Behaviour Model Elaboration using Partial Labelled Transition Systems. In *Proc. 9th European Software Engineering Conference*, pages 19–27, September 2003.

[200] G. Valetto and G. Kaiser. Using Process Technology to Control and Coordinate Software Adaptation. In *Proc. 25th Int. Conf. on Software Engineering*, pages 262–272, May 2003.

[201] S. van der Meer, A. Davy, S. Davy, R. Carroll, B. Jennings, and J. Strassner. Autonomic Networking: Prototype Implementation of the Policy Continuum. *Proc. 1st Int. Workshop on Broadband Convergence Networks*, pages 163–172, April 2006.

[202] S. van der Meer, W. Donnelly, J. Strassner, B. Jennings, and M. Ó. Foghlu. Emerging Principles of Autonomic Network Management. In *Proc. 1st IEEE Workshop on Modelling Autonomic Communicaiton Environments*, pages 29–48, October 2006.

[203] M. Völter, A. Schmid, and E. Wolff. *Server Component Patterns: Component Infrastructures Illustrated with EJB.* John Wiley & Sons, Ltd, 2002.

[204] R. P. Weicker. Dhrystone: A Synthetic Systems Programming Benchmark. *Communications of the ACM*, 27(10):1013–1030, October 1984.

[205] A. Winter, B. Kullbach, and V. Riediger. An Overview of the GXL Graph Exchange Language. In S. Diehl, editor, *Software Visualization*, volume 2269 of *Lecture Notes in Computer Science*, pages 324–336. Springer, 2001.

[206] K. Winter. Formalising Behaviour Trees with CSP. In *Proc. 4th Int. Conf. on Integrated Formal Methods*, pages 148–167, April 2004.

[207] N. Wirth. What can we do about the unnecessary diversity of notation for syntactic definitions? *Communications of the ACM*, 20(11):822 – 823, November 1977.

[208] S. M. Yacoub and H. H. Ammar. A Pattern Language of Statecharts. In *Proc. Conference on Pattern Languages of Programs*, August 1998.

[209] S. Yang. Logic Synthesis and Optimization Benchmarks User Guide Version 3.0. In *Proc. 1st Int. Workshop on Logic Synthesis*, May 1991.

[210] B. D. Zakaria, N. Simoni, M. Chevanne, and S. Betge-Brezetz. An Information Model for Service and Network Management Integration: from Needs Towards Solutions. In *Proc. IEEE / IFIP Network Operations and Management Symposium*, pages 527–540, April 2004.

[211] C. Zhang, M. Li, and Q. Pan. An ECA Rules Based Middleware Architecture for Wireless Sensor Networks. In *Proc. 6th Int. Conference on Parallel and Distributed Computing, Applications and Technologies*, pages 586–588, December 2005.

[212] P. Ziemann, K. Hölscher, and M. Gogolla. Coherently Explaining UML Statechart and Collaboration Diagrams by Graph Transformations. *Electronic Notes in Theoretical Computer Science*, 130:263–280, 2005.

Technical References

[213] T. Allweyer. *BPMN 2.0*. BoD, February 2010. ISBN 3-8391-4985-1.

[214] amazon.com. Amazon Simple Notification Service. http://aws.amazon.com/de/sns.

[215] Apache Software Foundation. Commons SCXML v0.9, December 2008. http://commons.apache.org/scxml.

[216] Apache Software Foundation. Apache Felix 2.0.1, October 2009. http://felix.apache.org.

[217] Apache Software Foundation. Java Expression Language v1.1, November 2009. http://commons.apache.org/jexl.

[218] Apache Software Foundation. ActiveMQ 5.3.2, May 2010. http://activemq.apache.org.

[219] Apple, Inc. Xcode Developer Tools. http://developer.apple.com/technologies/xcode.html.

[220] M. Banzi, D. Cuartielles, T. Igoe, G. Martino, and D. Mellis. Arduino Electronics Prototyping Platform, 2010. http://www.arduino.cc.

[221] M. Bodell. SCXML. Presentation at the W3C Voice Browser Working Group, October 2006. http://www.w3.org/Voice/2006/scxml-bodell.pdf.

[222] CASCADAS Consortium. ACE Toolkit, 2008. http://sourceforge.net/projects/acetoolkit.

[223] D. A. Chappell. *Enterprise Service Bus*. O'Reilly Media, 2004. ISBN 978-0-596-00675-4.

[224] Cisco Systems. Cisco 2800 Series Integrated Services Routers, 2010. http://www.cisco.com/en/US/products/ps5854.

[225] Cisco Systems. Cisco Application eXtension Platform, 2010. http://www.cisco.com/web/go/axp.

[226] G. Cugola and G. P. Picco. REDS: A Reconfigurable Dispatching System. In *Proc. 6th IEEE Int. Workshop on Software Engineering and Middleware*, pages 9–16, November 2006.

[227] C. v. B. Daniel Balasubramanian, Anantha Narayanan and G. Karsai. The Graph Rewriting and Transformation Language: GReAT. In *Proc. 3rd Int. Workshop on Graph Based Tools*, September 2006.

[228] Distributed Management Task Force. Representation of CIM in XML, Version 2.3.1. DSP0201, August 2009.

[229] Distributed Management Task Force. Web-Based Enterprise Management. DMTF Standards, 2010. http://www.dmtf.org/standards/wbem.

[230] J. Dubrovin. Jumbala — an Action Language for UML State Machines. Research Report A101, Helsinki University of Technology, Laboratory for Theoretical Computer Science, 2006.

[231] ECMA International. ECMAScript 3rd Edition Compact Profile. ECMA-327 Standard, June 2001. http://www.ecma-international.org/publications/standards/Ecma-327.htm.

[232] ECMA International. ECMAScript for XML (E4X) Specification. ECMA-357 Standard, December 2005. http://www.ecma-international.org/publications/standards/Ecma-357.htm.

[233] ECMA International. Common Language Infrastructure (CLI), 4th edition. ECMA-335 Standard, June 2006. http://www.ecma-international.org/publications/standards/Ecma-335.htm.

[234] R. Enns, ed. NETCONF Configuration Protocol. IETF Network Working Group, RFC 4741, December 2006.

[235] R. Fielding, J. Gettys, J. Mogul, H. Frystyk, L. Masinter, P. Leach, and T. Berners-Lee. Hypertext Transfer Protocol – HTTP/1.1. IETF Network Working Group, RFC 2616, June 1999.

[236] Fraunhofer FOKUS. FOKUS XML Document Management Server. http://www.open-ims.org/xdms.

[237] Google. Google Web Toolkit, 2010. http://code.google.com/webtoolkit.

[238] E. Höfig and A. Hinnerichs. Template Matching Specification Language, 2007. http://sourceforge.net/projects/tmpl.

[239] IBM Corporation. Rational Rhapsody. Product Web Page. http://www.ibm.com/software/awdtools/rhapsody.

[240] Institute of Electrical and Electronics Engineers. Very High Speed Integrated Circuit Hardware Description Language. IEEE Standard 1076-1993, 1993.

[241] Institute of Electrical and Electronics Engineers. Gigabit Ethernet over Twisted Pair. IEEE Standard 802.3ab-1999, June 1999.

[242] K. Jiang, L. Zhang, and S. Miyake. OCL4X: An Action Semantics Language for UML Model Execution. In *Proc. 31st Int. Computer Software and Applications Conf.*, pages 633–636, 2007.

[243] F. Jouault and I. Kurtev. Transforming Models with ATL. In *Proc. Satellite Events at the MoDELS 2005 Conference*, pages 128–138, January 2006.

[244] M. B. Jurič, B. Mathew, and P. Sarang. *Business Process Execution Language for Web Services BPEL and BPEL4WS*. Packt Publishing, 2nd edition, January 2006. ISBN 1-904811-81-7.

[245] A. Kalnins, J. Barzdins, and E. Celms. Basics of Model Transformation Language MOLA. In *Proc. Workshop on Model Transformation and Execution in the Context of MDA*, pages 62–76, June 2004.

[246] I. Kurtev. State of the Art of QVT: A Model Transformation Language Standard. In *Proc. Applications of Graph Transformations with Industrial Relevance*, pages 377–393, October 2007.

[247] T. Lindholm and F. Yellin. *The Java Virtual Machine Specification.* Prentice Hall, 2nd edition, April 1999. ISBN 978-0-201-43294-7.

[248] P. Marrow. The DIET Project: Building a Lightweight, Decentralized and Adaptable Agent Platform. *AgentLink News*, (12):3–6, 2003. Network of Excellence for Agent Based Computing.

[249] Y. Matsumoto. The Ruby Programming Language. `http://www.ruby-lang.org`.

[250] K. McCloghrie, D. Perkins, and J. Schoenwaelder. Structure of Management Information Version 2 (SMIv2). IETF Network Working Group, RFC 2578, April 1999.

[251] D. Megginson. Simple API for XML. `http://www.saxproject.org`.

[252] Message Passing Interface Forum. MPI: A Message-Passing Interface Standard Version 2.2. MPI Forum Standard, September 2009. `http://www.mpi-forum.org/docs/docs.html`.

[253] Nokia Qt Labs. SCXML Importer for the Qt State-Machine Framework, January 2010. `http://qt.gitorious.org/qt-labs/scxml`.

[254] North Carolina State University. The Benchmark Archives at CBL. `http://www.cbl.ncsu.edu:16080/benchmarks`.

[255] Object Management Group. OMG Unified Modeling Language (OMG UML), Superstructure, Version 2.2. OMG Specification, February 2002. `http://www.omg.org/spec/UML/2.2/Superstructure`.

[256] Object Management Group. *MDA Guide Version 1.0.1*, June 2003. `http://www.omg.org/cgi-bin/doc?omg/03-06-01.pdf`.

[257] Object Management Group. CORBA Notification Service, version 1.1. OMG Specification, October 2004. `http://www.omg.org/technology/documents/formal/notification_service.htm`.

[258] D. Ogle, H. Kreger, A. Salahshour, J. Cornpropst, E. Labadie, M. Chessell, B. Horn, J. Gerken, J. Schoech, and M. Wamboldt. Canonical Situation Data Format: The Common Base Event V1.0.1. IBM Specification, April 2003. `http://www.ibm.com/developerworks/library/specification/ws-cbe/`.

[259] Open Participation Software for Java Project. Pax Web, 2010. `http://wiki.ops4j.org/display/paxweb/Pax+Web`.

[260] Oracle. Java HotSpot Virtual Machine, 2010. `http://java.sun.com/javase/technologies/hotspot`.

[261] OSGi Alliance. OSGi Bundle Repository. OSGI RFC-0112, February 2006. `http://www.osgi.org`.

[262] OSGi Alliance. OSGi Service Platform Release 4.1, May 2007. `http://www.osgi.org`.

[263] POSTECH Software Engineering Laboratory. ASADAL CASE Tool. `http://http://selab.postech.ac.kr/asadal/index.html`.

[264] A. Pras and J. Schoenwaelder. On the Difference between Information Models and Data Models. IETF Network Working Group, RFC 3444, January 2003.

[265] C. Raistrick, P. Francis, J. Wright, C. Carter, and I. Wilkie. *Model Driven Architecture with Executable UML*. Cambridge University Press, 2004. ISBN 0-521-53771-1.

[266] W. C. Richardson, D. Avondolio, S. Schrager, M. W. Mitchell, and J. Scanlon. *Professional Java JDK 6 Edition*. Wiley Publishing, 2007. ISBN 978-0-471-77710-6.

[267] D. Saff, E. Gamma, E. G. H. Meade, and K. Beck. JUnit – Java Unit Testing Framework. `http://sourceforge.net/projects/junit`.

[268] H. Schildt. *C – the Complete Reference*. Osborne, 3rd edition, 1995. ISBN 0-07-882101-0.

[269] Standard Performance Evaluation Corporation. SPEC CPU2006 Benchmark Suite. `http://www.spec.org/cpu2006`.

[270] F. Strauss and J. Schoenwaelder. SMIng - Next Generation Structure of Management Information. IETF Network Working Group, RFC 3780, May 2004.

[271] B. Stroustrup. *Die C++ Programmiersprache*. Addison-Wesley, 3rd edition, 1998. ISBN 0-201-88954-4.

[272] S. T. Taft, R. A. Duff, R. L. Brukardt, E. Ploedereder, and P. Leroy. *Ada 2005 Reference Manual*, volume 4348 of *Lecture Notes in Computer Science*. Springer, May 2007.

[273] TeleManagement Forum. Shared Information/Data (SID) Model - Business View Concepts, Principles, and Domains. NGOSS Release 6.1, November 2005.

[274] TGI group, University of Hamburg. Petri Nets World. `http://www.informatik.uni-hamburg.de/TGI/PetriNets`.

[275] The Codehaus. MVFLEX Expression Language, October 2009. `http://mvel.codehaus.org`.

[276] The Codehaus. Performance of MVEL 2.0, June 2010. `http://mvel.codehaus.org/Performance+of+MVEL+2.0`.

[277] The DaCapo Project. DaCapo Benchmark Suite. `http://www.dacapobench.org`.

[278] The Eclipse Foundation. Eclipse Modeling Framework v2.5.0, Juni 2009. `http://www.eclipse.org/modeling/emf/`.

[279] The Eclipse Foundation. Equinox, Version 3.5, June 2009. `http://www.eclipse.org/equinox`.

[280] The Eclipse Foundation. UML2 Implementation v3.0.1 from the Model Development Tools Project, August 2009. `http://www.eclipse.org/modeling/mdt`.

[281] The Knopflerfish Project. Knopflerfish, Version 2, June 2010. `http://www.knopflerfish.org`.

[282] Topcased Consortium. The Topcased Project. http://www.topcased.org.

[283] USB Implementers Forum, Inc. Universal Serial Bus Revision 2.0 Specification. http://www.usb.org.

[284] G. van Rossum. The Python Programming Language. http://www.python.org.

[285] E. D. Willink. UMLX: A Graphical Transformation Language for MDA. In *Proc. 2nd OOPSLA Workshop on Generative Techniques in the context of Model Driven Architecture*, pages 13–24, October 2003.

[286] World Wide Web Consortium. Web Services Architecture. W3C Working Group Note, February 2004. http://www.w3.org/TR/ws-arch.

[287] World Wide Web Consortium. Web Services Choreography Description Language Version 1.0. W3C Candidate Recommendation, November 2005. http://www.w3.org/TR/ws-cdl-10.

[288] World Wide Web Consortium. XML Path Language v2.0. W3C Recommendation, January 2007. http://www.w3.org/TR/xpath20.

[289] World Wide Web Consortium. State Chart XML (SCXML): State Machine Notation for Control Abstraction. W3C Working Draft, October 2009. http://www.w3.org/TR/2009/WD-scxml-20091029.

[290] T. Ylonen and C. Lonvick, ed. The Secure Shell (SSH) Protocol Architecture. IETF Network Working Group, RFC 4251, January 2006.

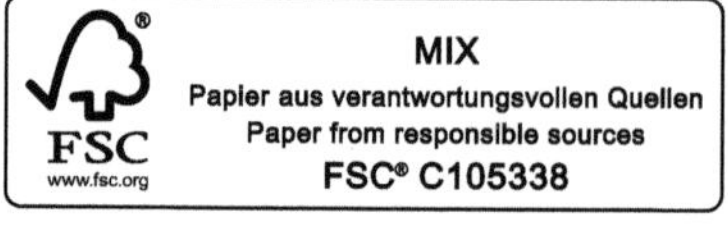

Printed by Books on Demand GmbH, Norderstedt / Germany